HOPE

for the future

ABOUT THIS PUBLICATION

This publication is not designed to be read front to back! As a quick glance will tell you, it's packed with loads of information covering a wide range of topics and the idea is that you dip in and out of them as they interest and concern you.

Thinking you've seen all of this before? Think again! This book is full of brand new case studies and information, taking what we've learned from the first year of HOPE so we can keep going and make it even better in the future!

HOPE is not prescriptive – it's all about you finding what works for you and your community, but we thought you might find these stories, tips and ideas helpful as you plan and prepare future activities.

A bit of background

HOPE was launched as HOPE 08 – the idea being to encourage the church to get involved in spreading the good news through words and actions for a year. But the aim was always that it would continue long into the future and, to our delight, that is exactly what is happening. Many churches have used HOPE as a springboard to think more about mission and are showing no signs of slowing down. Many we hope will use this new publication to help them get involved for the first time or to increase their current activity.

You can still use the HOPE logo (available from www.hope08.com) if you would like to and you'll also find more resources and ideas on the website which will be available for some time to come.

This book is designed to give you everything you need to get out into your community, from the biblical understanding of why we should bother, through to ideas for activities and on to resources and places to go to get started. It's all here so get stuck in and see where it takes you!

INSIDE HOPE

Setting the scene

HOPE for the future

Big ideas

High Points:

We can't stress enough that HOPE is not over, but it's over to you! We know that loads of you have no intention of stopping because you've loved seeing what God has done as you've stepped out.

Editor/writer: Liza Hoeksma
Managing Editors: Steve Clifford and Laurence Singlehurst

CHAPTER 1
THE STORY SO FAR

Roy Crowne, Youth for Christ
Andy Hawthorne, Message Trust
Mike Pilavachi, Soul Survivor

A few years ago, when we had this crazy idea to encourage the whole church to get involved in a year of mission, we had no idea where it would go. To be honest, if you guys hadn't got on board it would have gone exactly nowhere! Instead it's been more than we dared hope; thousands upon thousands of Christians have been taking Jesus' commission even more seriously – living out his love, proclaiming the gospel in words and deeds and doing it all in unity with other Christians. Amazing! Our original hope was to get around 500 UK locations signed up – in fact it ended up being just under 1500!

So we want to say a huge thank you to all the individuals, churches and organisations that got on board with the HOPE vision and worked tirelessly to see it come alive. You have blown us away! We're absolutely delighted to be able to include so many of your stories here as we know they will inspire so many more people.

This book is not just a reflection on an amazing year where churches were moved to reach out into their communities in all manner of creative ways – far from it. The very last thing we want is for this book to be a memorial to an event gone by! HOPE was always about finding long-term strategies for serving our communities and being good news; 2008 was just the start. The stories in this book give you loads more fresh

> One of the really encouraging things that has come out of HOPE is so many churches proving that you don't have to have a huge budget, loads of spare time on your hands or an army of willing church members to get things going.

ideas so whether you're new to HOPE and are wondering where to start or whether you did loads in 2008 and are wondering what else you could get involved in – this book is packed full of stuff for you. These ideas have been put into practice so we know they work – and not just in one village, town or city – we believe they can be replicated around the country with fantastic results. Plus we asked people to share what they've learned along the way so that we can all keep getting better and better at this stuff.

We can't stress enough that HOPE is not over, but it's over to you! We know that loads of you have no intention of stopping because you've loved seeing what God has done as you've stepped out. For others, this may be new to you and we'd encourage you to read through some of these stories, be inspired and ask God what you can be doing in your community. One of the really encouraging things that has come out of HOPE is so many churches proving that you don't have to have a huge budget, loads of spare time on your hands or an army of willing church members to get things going. Some of the best ideas are the most simple ones that can be done with very little time and money. Whatever you think might hold you back, don't be put off – every one of us can play our part in advancing God's kingdom as long as we're willing to get involved.

'Doing more, doing it together, doing it in word and deed'

Our strapline for HOPE was 'Doing more, doing it together, doing it in word and deed' and that's certainly been the case!

DOING MORE: We knew there was absolutely loads of amazing stuff going on in churches around the country, but that didn't stop you thinking about what else you could do and how you could step things up a gear.

DOING IT TOGETHER: One of the things we've loved seeing is what HOPE has meant for Christian unity. The way you guys have teamed up and worked together has been awe inspiring. We know that there's a huge blessing that comes with unity and we've seen some of the fruit of it already with more people being reached for the gospel as well as many of us finding out we have more in common with each other than perhaps we first thought!

DOING IT IN WORD AND DEED: One of the key messages with HOPE is that it's time to make sure our words and our actions match up. We speak of a loving God and we need to make sure people who don't know Jesus hear the good news in a way that they understand, demonstrated in our actions as well as spoken from our mouths. Our lives have to live up to the love that we speak of. While we're here on this earth we're to do what Jesus did and love our neighbours, help those in need and love everyone regardless of their beliefs. (If you'd like to read a bit more about the theology behind HOPE go to Chapter 2.)

The HOPE framework

We've suggested that churches plan their activities around the usual 'high points' in the church calendar, namely Easter, Pentecost (over the May Bank Holiday weekend), autumn (which is a great time for new Alpha-style courses to start up) and Christmas. In addition to that there are loads of other ideas that can be put into practice at any point during the year and what you choose will be

Let's keep God right at the centre of everything, offering all of our outreach as an expression of our love for him and continually asking him to fill us with his love for his world.

totally dependent on the needs of your community and the resources available to you. There's no set way to do this as you'll see from all the stories in this book!

Fresh ideas

We felt there were a couple of key areas we didn't do justice to last time round, so you'll find a few new chapters in this book on using sport, ministering in the workplace, working with children, developing the use of the arts and reaching groups that are on the edge of our society.

So there's loads for you to sink your teeth into and we hope this book serves to inspire and resource you as you look to live out your life for Jesus and bring his good news to your community. And as we go out, as we love and serve our neighbours, let's not forget that we do all of this out of our love for Jesus. If we lose sight of him, we'll soon give up when the going gets tough or start thinking we're the best evangelists the world has ever seen if things go well! Let's keep God right at the centre of everything, offering all of our outreach as an expression of our love for him and continually asking him to fill us with his love for his world.

Let's keep going for it – if the HOPE activity so far is anything to go by, we can only imagine what amazing things God will do in the UK in the coming years!

God bless,
Andy, Mike & Roy

CHAPTER 2
WHY BOTHER?
THE THEOLOGY BEHIND HOPE

Laurence Singlehurst, Cell UK
Paul Bayes, Archbishop's Council

GOD'S MISSION AND HOPE

'In today's world there is great need both at home and abroad. There is a great challenge to the church, to demonstrate God's love. Through HOPE 08 many people were impacted by the love of God. As the church sought to do more, to do it together and to do it in words and action, and as they sought to demonstrate the love of God in Christ Jesus, there was a fantastic response and so the challenge is to continue with HOPE . . .'

WHAT

We seek to do more because God is always calling his people to press on, to move forward, and to share in his mission. He's not calling us to be frantically busy for its own sake – our mission has to be rooted in the peace and grace of God. But Paul was not ashamed to tell the Philippians 'there is *one thing I always do. Forgetting the past and straining towards what is ahead, I keep trying to reach the goal and get the prize for which God called me through Christ to the life above*' (Philippians 3:13,14, NCV, my italics).

We pray that the Lord will give his church that hunger to press forward, and joyfully to use our creativity and our energy to do more where we are, so that his kingdom may come more fully.

> We seek to do more because God is always calling his people to press on, to move forward, and to share in his mission.

As we respond to the call of God to do more, the HOPE vision calls us to act as Christians *together*. Again, this is not something we do for the sake of it. Jesus' prayer in John 17 is 'I pray that they can be one. As you are in me and I am in you, I pray that they can also be one in us. *Then the world will believe that you sent me*' (v. 21, NCV, my italics). Christian unity flows from obedience to God's mission, not out of our own guilt or from the decisions of our committees. The expressions of unity around the country as people have got on board with HOPE have been incredible. Differences have been put aside in order to achieve more in Jesus' name, producing strong and lasting relationships between churches and achieving far more to bless many communities. As we join together to discern the work God wants us to do, we will see that other Christians are God's gift to us for the furtherance of his mission. We will need the love God has given them, if God's purpose in our village, town or city is to be fulfilled.

As well as doing things together we're called to do mission in *word and deed*. Indeed, this is one way the Lord will draw his people together. Some Christians give their main energies to the preaching of the gospel, and others to social action and involvement. But for Jesus Christ there was no distinction. When Luke wants to remind Theophilus what Jesus was, at the beginning of Acts, he says 'I wrote ... about everything Jesus began to *do and teach* until the day he was taken up into heaven ...' (Acts 1:1,2, NCV, my italics).

This book is full of ideas for the proclamation of the gospel, and for serving people where they are with the practical love of Jesus. Unless we hold these things together – unless we do and teach – then we'll fall short of the mission model of our Lord.

WHY?

Well, OK. Do more, do it together, do it in word and deed. That explains what we are doing in HOPE. But *why* are we doing it? What's our deepest motivation?

There is no better place for us to draw inspiration than John 3:16: 'For God so loved the world that he gave his one and only Son, that whoever believes in him shall not perish but have eternal life' (NIV).

From this well known and powerful verse we have three simple principles to inspire us in mission. Firstly, 'God so loved the world'. Mission and evangelism is so often seen as an action and we get caught up, sometimes reluctantly, in all sorts of methodology. But real mission begins out of love. God's mission to redeem the world came out of his all-encompassing love so we could say that mission begins with a question: how big are our hearts? When I (Laurence) was a young man I had an experience that changed my life. I was asked to look after a group of children in the slums of Melbourne, Australia, and I was told that one of them would be very dirty and hard to love. Well, how difficult can that be? I thought to myself. Until this little boy ran towards me to be picked up and then I realised his underwear was soaked in urine, full of human excrement and he smelt so bad I wanted to be ill. Sadly, I could not pick the boy up and I turned my back. That night, as I was feeling very depressed, the leader of our Christian

We need to be involved with people in friendship, in deeds and action, in words and, above all, in lifestyle just like Jesus was.

community said to me, 'Loving people is difficult, isn't it?' 'Not difficult,' I replied. 'Impossible.' She took me to a passage of Scripture in 2 Corinthians 5, from verse 14, and showed me three principles. Christ died for all which means that every human has great value, the value of Christ himself, whether we are rich or poor, clean or dirty, we all have the same value. Secondly, 2 Corinthians goes on to say, do not look at people from the outside – instead we need to catch a glimpse of that inner value. Thirdly, Christ dying is sacrificial which tells us the nature of real love; it is not a feeling, but a choice.

A few days later I met the little boy again but this time, by the grace of God, armed with many prayers for a bigger heart, I saw the little boy in a whole new way and was able to pick him up. As we reach out let us ask God for a big heart.

The second principle that we see in John 3 is love is incarnational. God sent his Son and the second aspect of our mission is we have to go in the same way. We have to go out of love, not scalp hunting, not out of a motivation to make our churches bigger but just because we love people. We need to be involved with people in friendship, in deeds and action, in words and, above all, in lifestyle just like Jesus was. These days people are very suspicious of words, sadly. We've grown to distrust people who say, 'I have the truth.' We are looking for reality. So, as we go, as best we can, we need to be real, authentic and make sure we're doing what we're saying. It is this that will make a difference. The people that we go to may have a very negative picture of God and Christians and we want to help them on a journey to change their perception of what God is really like, through changing their perceptions of Christians and the church.

Thirdly, we see that mission is a message. God so loved the world that he sent his Son that we would 'not perish but have eternal life'. So we need to think about what we are going to say and how we are going to say it. In evangelism our responsibility is to help people understand and this is a journey for them. It is not just about telling people the words but if they can't understand God's message because of the language we use or the way we say it or because at this point they are not really ready to receive all these words, we are not being helpful. We'll go into the language of sharing our faith in more detail later.

The journey to faith

Some years ago, James Engel devised a scale of one to ten to picture a person on a journey to faith. This is a scale from negative to positive. The negative is how they originally may see God and church and the positive is how they can see God and the church in a new way. So if we meet somebody who is at point minus one on the scale with a negative picture of God and the church and, through our love and words, they go from point one to point

> Through Christ, God reaches out to us to bring us back into friendship and intimacy.

three, we have been involved in mission; this is successful mission. I once met a very clever female journalist on a train who had had very bad experiences of Christianity and she was appalled to think that she was sitting next to a card-carrying preacher/missionary. During our two-hour train journey I listened a lot and said a little and at the end she said to me, 'Laurence, you are the first nice Christian I have ever met.' She did not give her heart to God but she did begin the journey. And, if we find somebody at point eight on the scale who has met many other Christians, and been prayed for many times, we may have the privilege of seeing them give their life to Jesus. The point is not where we meet them, it's that however we help them along the scale, we're engaging in mission.

So what we're doing in HOPE flows from the

love of God and the example of Jesus. And so does our motivation. It begins with a big *heart*, as God himself has. It is *incarnational*, living out our reality as Jesus did, and it is communicating the *message* in a way that people understand.

The message has always been the same. That God loves us and is longing for friendship; that our selfishness and sin has separated us from him. Through Christ, God reaches out to us to bring us back into friendship and intimacy as we seek his help to deal with our selfishness, our principle of self-rule and our desire to live for ourselves.

So there you go. That's the 'what' and the 'why' of sharing in God's mission. Now check out the tried and tested ideas in this book, which will hopefully point you to some more of the 'how's – how to be God's mission people where you are.

HOPE-FILLED PRAYER

Let's keep prayer at the heart of all we do, to discover God's heart and to allow him to grow ours. For ideas on how to pray throughout the year, see Chapter 18.

RESOURCES

· **Church on the Edge** by Chris Stoddard and Nick Cuthbert. Exploring foundational principles of culturally relevant mission, looking at how twenty-two diverse congregations are making a difference in their own community. A book designed to envision, inspire and encourage anyone who is committed to reaching this generation with the gospel. Authentic, £7.99.

· **Freestyle** by Jo Wells and Andy Frost. A book about radical discipleship, mission and social justice. Authentic, £5.99.

· **Intelligent Church: A Journey Towards Christ-centered Community** by Steve Chalke and Anthony Watkis. This book seeks to reclaim the true heartbeat of the church; the passion to save not itself but the world. Rooted in deep theology but highly practical this book gives you vision of a church that equips its members for frontline work. Zondervan, £7.99.

> Let's keep prayer at the heart of all we do, to discover God's heart and to allow him to grow ours.

For ideas on how to pray throughout the year, see Chapter 18.

· **RUN – (Reaching the Unchurched Network)** is a growing network of churches passionate about mission in contemporary culture. Members of RUN have access to leading edge outreach thinking and up-to-date ideas, high quality resources and links with churches and ministries across the UK and beyond to benefit from a wide range of experience. Find out more and join RUN (annual subscription £44 for churches or individuals) at www.run.org.uk.

· **Sowing, Reaping, Keeping** by Laurence Singlehurst. This book helps the reader explore what it means to love people, to sow seeds of faith, to reap the harvest at the right time and to nurture growing faith. IVP, £6.99.

· **Worship Evangelism Justice** by Mike Pilavachi with Liza Hoeksma. This book explores the meaning of loving God with all our hearts and loving our neighbours as ourselves, providing practical tips for evangelism and social justice. Survivor, £5.99.

CHAPTER 3

THE WORDS OF THE GOSPEL

When we think of mission and evangelism the thought that has traditionally jumped to our mind is the picture of someone preaching – in a meeting, on the streets or conversationally – and this declaration of the gospel through words has historically been one of our primary tools for evangelism. More recently, however, there has been a more 'incarnational' approach – like that which HOPE has adopted – meaning we seek to demonstrate God's love, be a part of the people's lives who we want to reach and serve those around us. This aspect of outreach has grown in the last 20 years which is fantastic but in all that we're doing practically we don't want to forget the actual words of the gospel! Jesus of course demonstrated God's love powerfully in an incarnational way but he also used words to help people understand the Christian message so we know the two things must go hand in hand. We want to live out God's love and passion for justice, but we must also be ready to explain to people just who our God is and what being a Christian is all about.

How has preaching the gospel changed?

If we think about people like Billy Graham who preached very successfully in the 1950s, we can quickly see the culture they were preaching into was very different from our own. They used very traditional Bible language, words such as repent, born again, forgiveness and lordship; and people understood what they meant. Many of the people he was speaking to would have gone to Sunday school and been aware of a Christian heritage. As such, when he spoke, people realised they perhaps had not followed God as they should, felt a measure of conviction and responded. But in our world today things have changed.

Many of these words have lost meaning, the general public no longer understands or relates to words like 'sin' and 'sinner', 'saved' and 'born again', 'repent' and 'lordship', and perhaps the challenge for our preaching today is: can we speak the gospel message without the use of these words? Can we find other words that convey the same thing in ways that people can understand? For all of us the language we use will be different. Much of it depends on who we are; the way we speak in normal life and the way we have understood the gospel ourselves. Much depends, too, on the age, background and experiences of the people we are talking to. But there are of course some common things for us all to be thinking about and that's what we want to think about here.

There needs to be some good news!

Years ago that might have been the avoidance of hell by going to heaven. The early church emphasised symbols such as the anchor and the shepherd's staff and their message is, 'God is with you'. The anchor also expresses hope, that life is more than just the now. So what might we say today? Well hope certainly is a good message for many people facing difficulties in their current situations. Friendship with a God who is constant and loving is great news for the many in our society plagued by loneliness. Other people might find it better news that not only can we have an eternal hope, but we can change the world we live in today. This isn't about twisting the gospel to fit – all these things are true – we just might place a different emphasis on different ones with different people.

The big issues

In a similar way we need to think about what the big issues are for the people we're talking to. Everyone is coming from a different place, so when we're in conversation with someone we need to be aware of what the big issues are for them. (Did they lose someone they loved or go through a painful experience and struggle to believe God is loving? Do they see Christianity as a sign of weakness? Is their faith in science?)

We also need to be able to explain some of the fundamental principles of our faith such as:

- God's love. Fundamentally God created us out of love and wants us to be in relationship with him.

- If we're not following Jesus then we're trying to live life our own way and this separates us from the God who designed us and knows the best way for us to live. In the Bible this is called sin but 'selfishness' may make more sense to people.

- We can't earn our way into heaven. We've all done things we're ashamed of whether they are big or small. We've all hurt other people whether we intended to or not. By trying to do things our own way, we – the human race – have messed the world up.

> Friendship with a God who is constant and loving is great news for the many in our society plagued by loneliness.

- God won't let this go on forever: at some point God will call us to account for all that we've done and we'll have no excuses. But because his desire is to be in relationship with us, he came up with a solution himself.

- Jesus' death and resurrection. Jesus died to take our punishment because there was nothing we could do. Through him we are offered grace, forgiveness and a new way of life.

Counting the cost

Jesus was very clear in his teaching that there is a cost to following him. He didn't water it down and play up the more palatable elements of Christianity to try and increase his numbers. Instead he laid out the truth and encouraged people to think through what they would be leaving behind if they wanted to follow him. If we try and paint a rosy picture just to win people over, we may find we have more new Christians but we're also likely to discover that they don't stay the distance.

Why are you doing this?

When you're serving people without asking for anything in return it raises eyebrows. Many of our HOPE activities will prompt people to ask 'why?'. Why are we sacrificing our own time, energy, money and resources to help someone we don't even necessarily know? What a great opportunity for us to share something of our faith!

Before you begin your tasks spend some time thinking about your answer. Is it that you feel so overwhelmed with what God has given you that you want to share it with others? Do you feel like God has shared some of his passion for justice and equality and you want to spend time doing what you can to address that? Do you want people to know that God loves them without them ever having to do a thing for him first? Think about your motivation and be ready to share as the opportunity arises.

Your story

Each of us has a unique story. Many of us make the mistake of discounting it as an effective way to

preach the gospel unless we were rescued from an extreme situation such as drug addiction or a life of severe crime. Whatever your story it can be a great tool and it's a good idea to think it through ahead of time so that when someone says 'how did you become a Christian?' or 'why do you believe?' you're ready with an answer. Think about: what made you believe in God? What was the process in your heart and mind for you? Why do you think being a Christian is a positive thing both for the here and now and for eternity? How do you know God is real?

Leave space for the Holy Spirit

When you get into conversation with someone, be praying silently for the Holy Spirit to be filling your speech. Ask him to fill your words with his power that your friend may hear the truth in them. Ask him to prompt you about directions to take the conversation in and the words to use. Simple words have a huge impact when they are filled with the Holy Spirit.

We don't have all the answers!

People have many questions and even if you've got a Masters in Theology you wouldn't be able to answer them all. God is huge. The universe is huge. How could we ever get our heads around it enough to explain it all to someone else?! That's not to say we give up or bluff it if someone asks us a difficult question; many people appreciate someone of faith who doesn't pretend to know everything. If someone shows an interest in a particular subject (like how we know the Bible is real or what evidence there is that Jesus lived) maybe you could lend them a talk on CD or a book to read on the subject. Think about the types of media they enjoy and use regularly and look for Christian resources that may help them on their journey.

We need to give people a choice

If we needed any evidence that we can't *make* anyone give their lives to God, let's remember that people walked away from Jesus. There are no magic words, no fail-safe formula, no guaranteed way of preaching the gospel. People walked away from Jesus because the cost was too

Simple words have a huge impact when they are filled with the Holy Spirit.

great and they may well do the same from us. As we discussed in the theology chapter we're not in this to win scalps – our motivation is to love people and, when we're given opportunity, to explain clearly why we believe and follow God. The rest is up to them. Our job is to love and respect people regardless. Walking away when people say no could cause great damage and cause people to wonder if we ever genuinely cared about them or just the numbers in our churches.

Evangelistic events

If you're feeling stuck for words then one great way to get the message across to someone who is showing an interest, is to take that person along to an evangelistic event. This may be a guest service at church, an Alpha-style course or a one-off event where you know the gospel will be preached – again it will depend on what stage in the journey your friend is at and what you think might suit them.

This is really very simple advice and all we're really encouraging you to do is to think through how you will choose to explain your faith. The focus of HOPE is 'do more, do it together and do it in word and action' and that's what we want to keep aiming for. Unity amongst Christians speaks volumes in itself and then, as opportunity arises we use our words and our actions to let people know in the clearest way we know how that God loves them and wants to be in relationship with them. Let's keep praying for opportunities to share these words of life with those who don't yet know Jesus.

Premier Love London

Premier CHRISTIAN RADIO

Have you got the Love?

What would happen if in every one of London's 33 boroughs there was a group of highly visible and well-coordinated churches working together to reach their communities for Christ?

What if Premier, the UK's largest Christian media organisation, decided to spend the next four years doing all that it can to make sure this happens and to help them succeed?

Find out how your church can get involved

visit www.love-london.info

Prayer
Evangelism
Fellowship
Social Action

Look out for Love GB... coming soon

Premier Love GB

CHAPTER 4

WHAT PEOPLE HAVE SAID ABOUT HOPE

'There is no doubt that HOPE has succeeded in offering hope to people . . . not the wishy-washy maybe everything will get better kind of hope but the roll up your sleeves and actually do something about it kind of hope.'
The Rt Hon Stephen Timms MP, the Vice President for Faith in the Labour Party

'Thank the Lord for HOPE – it has been the best thing that has happened across the country since I can't remember when!'
Marion Barker, Knutsford

'I believe that HOPE has given many churches a new confidence in the message of the gospel. Churches have been re-energised to believe that we have the greatest message and when we work together we can communicate this in many different ways to a needy generation.'
Mark Ritchie, 73rd Trust

'HOPE has broken down walls and made creative mission possible where before it seemed out of reach. I have heard testimony from around the country of new creative ecumenical co-operation which before was beyond even dreams. The legacy of HOPE will be a stronger church and transformed lives. Oh, and discovery that God works through churches that are different from the ones we think are the only way! God has truly blessed this venture, and people have found faith and hope in God. I will settle for that any day!'
Rev Ian Bunce, Head of Mission Department, Baptist Union of GB

'HOPE has broken down walls and made creative mission possible where before it seemed out of reach.'

'Friends of ours from the Wokingham and Vineyard Church and HOPE have really helped to bolster our numbers and our spirits by coming along to work alongside us. I know I speak for all of us when I say how much we appreciate their support.'
Bob Elsey, Headmaster of Edgbarrow School, Crowthorne

'We have been reliably informed that while we have been praying and working together, crime in the City has dropped by a significant amount. There is a good sense of "something is going on" in the area.'
Bob Duerden, Hull

'We have had many HOPE events and have seen much fruit – and hope there will be much more to come!'
Jan Kirkham, Isle of Man

'We have had an incredible year. We all needed something like HOPE to give us "passport" to do what many of us were longing to do, that is to reach out to one another and to the wider community. All of this has helped us as individuals to grow, but also, as a result, our working/worshipping/loving has been with the other church denominations. Wonderful!'
Ann Warboys, Thrapston

'I would like simply to say thank you from the whole of the city.'
Mayor of Bath Cllr Tim Ball at the launch of Street Pastors

'People of faith have been at the heart of just about every social movement that has transformed society in this country, from the abolition of slavery through to Make Poverty History. I applaud all those involved in HOPE.'
Rt Hon Gordon Brown MP, Prime Minister

'Being involved in HOPE Bradford has strengthened my conviction that when churches turn their attention outwards, focusing on the communities they are called to serve and on engaging together in mission, great things can be accomplished.'
Ruth Smith, Livability Community Mission (part of HOPE Bradford)

'We are rejoicing at the very positive fruit that is being produced through HOPE initiatives and I believe that the prime reason for this success is to do with the great volume of prayer that has under girded HOPE since day one. I believe that HOPE has served to reinforce the powerful link that exists between prayer and mission. When these two great disciplines engage, there is potential for personal, community, and national transformation. Our prayer must be that more doors will be opened for the proclamation and demonstration of the gospel.'
Alistair L. Cole, Chair, National Prayer Network of the Elim Churches UK

'HOPE lived up to its name, drawing people together, strengthening communities and lifting spirits across the UK.'
Rt Hon Stephen Timms MP, Labour Party Vice Chair for Faith Groups

'HOPE is to be applauded for it has contributed to the building of strong and safer communities the length and breadth of the UK.'
Caroline Spelman MP, Shadow Communities and Local Government Minister

'HOPE has achieved a tremendous amount in mobilising and resourcing churches in community mission, and the challenge now is for us to continue to build on those excellent foundations . . .'
Fran Beckett OBE, CEO of Church Urban Fund

'HOPE reached out in Jesus' name and brought real, vibrant and relevant hope into so many lives, which is tremendously needed at this time.'

His Royal Highness The Prince of Wales paid tribute to HOPE and those involved for their 'devotion and ability to motivate people'. He said, 'It's so encouraging to hear how it seems to have struck a chord. It's wonderful to witness the fact that so many denominations are working together and overcoming possible suspicion – you are helping to overcome all that, and display that kind of witness which is so incredibly valuable.'

'HOPE reached out in Jesus' name and brought real, vibrant and relevant hope into so many lives, which is tremendously needed at this time.'
Commissioner Elizabeth Matear, Moderator of Free Churches

'HOPE blessed our communities in such a powerful way that it left them with a clear message: hope has many hands and faces.'
Rev Joel Edwards, Micah Challenge International

'HOPE definitely delivered on its vision of stirring thousands and thousands of local churches to step up, do more and to serve people as Jesus would in their communities. Thank you!'
Rev David Coffey OBE, President of World Baptist Alliance

CHAPTER 5

PLANNING YOUR HOPE ACTIVITY

Laurence Singlehurst, CELL UK

HOPE has enabled churches to do mission through many new and creative ideas – some of these ideas came out of the best practice of the last few years, and others were well tried and tested favourites. One of the brilliant things is that HOPE probably won't look the same in any two communities, because every area and every church that serves it is different! But when it comes to planning our activities, there are some common things we can all be thinking about.

Researching your community

We can have the best plans in the world but if what we're offering is not what people want then we will have missed the mark. Before starting any big activities it's really worth finding out the needs of your community and that doesn't have to be a daunting task. There are lots of things you can do such as:

- **Talk to the council and police**. They will have loads of information about the area, its needs and ways you can be part of the solution. See Chapter 22 for more details.

- **You could drop a short paper questionnaire** to local homes then go back and collect the responses, or do one on the streets.

> HOPE has enabled churches to do mission through many new and creative ideas.

It's also a great way to meet new people and to discuss your desire to bless the community.

- **You could speak to local schools**, health visitors, shopkeepers – anyone involved in the community – to find out what they think the needs are.

- **Use a resource** such as Livability's *Getting to Know Your Neighbours* which is available to download for free from www.livability.org.uk. It tells you everything you need to know about planning and carrying out a community audit.

- **Try holding a Poverty Hearing** which allows people with direct experiences of poverty to speak out and encourages those with power, authority and different experiences to listen. See www.church-poverty.org.uk for more details.

Where are you now?

When you know the needs of your community the next thing to think about is where you, as a church, are at. Think about:

- **The number of resources** available to you such as people, time, skills and money.

- **The things you are currently doing**, how they are going and how they could potentially be added to or improved.

• **What links you have already** with other churches and organisations in the area that could help you address some of the issues in your community.

• **Using a resource like Faithworks Church Audit** to help you work out your church's potential to rise to the challenge of effective, sustainable community engagement. See Resources and www.faithworks.info for more details.

What can you do?

The best projects are ones that are sustainable over the long-haul. There may be times for increased and focused activities such as fun days or weekend social-action projects, but ideally think about ways you can serve your community on a week-in, week-out basis. That way we become integral to community life, build relationships and get to know people as well as helping to bring change that may not be possible in the short-term.

Working together

One of the key messages of HOPE has been unity amongst churches and it has had a wonderful impact across the UK as churches have joined together to serve their communities. We can all learn something from each other and can all bless one another if we're willing to work together; so whether you're a big church or a small one, think about who you work with and begin to build relationships with each other. It may take time and energy to work out the common ground between you but it will be more than worth it for you and your community.

Understanding God's love

As we discussed in the theology chapter, mission begins in our hearts. We take a journey in seeing how important lost people are and our hearts are moved by their value and God's love for them. But it is not just about loving people, it is about loving our area and the institutions in our area. We can love our streets and therefore pick the rubbish up that currently litters it; we can love our school

> Ideally think about ways you can serve your community on a week-in, week-out basis.

or workplace and see a great deal more of God's kingdom impact it. As a part of our strategy we need to intentionally think about how as churches we can have bigger hearts – what teaching we might need in the church that will encourage us to think about our hearts, and what opportunities we need to give for prayer in this area. A key to mission is that we all ask God for bigger hearts on a regular basis.

Training

It may be that members of the church staff would benefit from some training in the areas of mission and evangelism, or that you think the whole church would find it useful to go through something similar in their small groups. See the Resources section for some ideas of training courses that may help.

STRUCTURING THE YEAR

We have planned HOPE around the natural high points of our church calendar, which has already proved to be very useful and therefore something we can take forward and make a constant part of our church life. The basic structure is:

Easter has always been a very important festival for us as believers but now we have found creative ways, as you can see from Chapter 7, to make Easter a big celebration for the whole of our community.

Pentecost is a great opportunity for us to celebrate the coming of the Holy Spirit which gives us power to love people in words and actions. As you see in Chapter 8 there are all sorts of creative ways that we can go out and do good works, put on fun events and go out on the streets to let people see something of the wonder of God's love.

Autumn is the time of year that we can reap in the harvest; we see it in the fields and in the church. We can put on our Alpha-style courses, our guest services and pray that the love, prayer, good works and good words that we have sown into our communities come back to us and that people during this time will respond and will begin their own journey in knowing God.

Christmas is both the end and beginning of the cycle. It is the easiest event of the year to invite our non-Christian friends to so that they can experience just a little bit of the Christian message. Whether it is through a pantomime, a carol service or any of the other Christmas initiatives you see in Chapter 10 we take this opportunity to reclaim the real meaning of Christmas. This is a great way to end the year but it also begins the cycle of the New Year and it's a good idea to be planning your January/February activities in advance so you can invite anyone who comes to your Christmas services to your New Year events.

Other activities throughout the year

With these high points in the church calendar addressed, it's a great idea to be thinking about what else you can be doing to stand alongside these activities throughout the year. This book gives you loads of ideas and resources covering a whole variety of things such as using sport, celebrating the summer, reaching out to those on the edge and ways you can use the arts. What you choose to do will depend on lots of factors including the needs of your area and the resources available to you and your church.

Prayer

Of course it is vital to underpin all of our activity with prayer, calling out to God for big hearts

and commending our community and ourselves to his love and purpose. For more ideas on how prayer can be a part of all your mission activity see Chapter 18.

LESSONS LEARNED

As you begin to put your strategy into action and adopt some of the principles of HOPE, take it a step at a time; begin with changing people's values and hearts and build on your activities. Then, every church needs an enthusiast, someone who is part of the leadership team who takes responsibility for helping the church to become and stay missional, someone who can encourage people. Our hope is that in the end every member of every church is being missional, every small group and cell group is being challenged to empower one another to reach out, and the structures and events of church help us to do that so that, in the end, we do more, we do it together with other churches, and we do it in word and action.

> Our hope is that in the end every member of every church is being missional.

RESOURCES

Engage is an initiative from Care for the Family designed to encourage and support you as you take your next steps in engaging with your local community. See www.engagetoday.org.uk for lots of practical ideas, news of training events, loads of stories and tips to get you started.

Faithworks Church Audit helps you to work out your church's potential to rise to the challenge of effective, sustainable community engagement. Buy online for £4 (electronic copy) or £6 for a paper version at www.faithworks.info.

Livability's *Getting to Know Your Neighbours* is available to download for free from www.livability.org.uk and tells you everything you need to know about planning and carrying out a community audit.

The Social Action Journey is a free two-page download from Livability giving ideas, direction and focus to people wanting to engage with their community – www.livability.org.uk.

The Winning Ways Leaders Consultation is an online church health and outreach audit. Using a combination of presentation and guided discussion questions on the issues of Discipleship, Community and Outreach, the consultation provides leaders with a personalised and graphical picture of church health and strategy, with recommendations for development. Available at www.winningwaysweb.com.

Books

40 Days of Community by Rick Warren helps churches deepen authentic community within their church family and reach out to the local community outside the church. Resources available from www.purposedriven.co.uk

The Naked Church, produced by GWEINI (the council for the Christian voluntary sector in Wales), addresses the opportunities and challenges facing Christian welfare initiatives in Wales today, providing an invaluable introduction to community development principles for churches everywhere. £4.95 from www.gweini.org.uk.

Winning Ways – How to Create a Culture of Outreach in Your Church by Philip Jinadu and David Lawrence. Authentic, £8.99.

Training

Blowing Your Cover by Kevin Higham and Mike Sprenger. This six-part training course on lifestyle evangelism covers communicating the gospel, connecting with your culture and living a spirit-filled life. Many resources are available to help you run the course. For more information and a free sampler DVD see www.blowingyourcover.com.

CaFE

Catholic Faith Exploration (CaFE) run a series called *Pass It On* to help church groups consider their role as evangelists and learn how to run outreach programmes. The course consists of five talks (four x 20 mins and one x 40 mins) available on video or audio, a course manual which includes small group discussion questions and a *Pass It On* book taking a more comprehensive look at evangelism. For more details and to order see www.faithcafe.org.

DNA

Part of the Pioneer Trust, DNA is a full-time programme running yearly from October to August training you in culturally relevant evangelism and church based discipleship. You can find out more and apply online at www.dna-uk.org.

Evangelism Explosion run a number of courses for both church leaders and congregation members. See www.ee-gb.org.uk for more details.

Evangelism Training Database

To find details of hundreds of training courses relating to mission and evangelism take a look at the **Evangelical Training Database** at www.trainforChrist.org/english.

Faithworks offer a number of training courses that can be delivered as one- or half-day workshops in your area to help your church develop its role in the community. Find out more at www.faithworks.info or by emailing info@faithworks.info.

we do Summer Outreaches

short-term missions trips ... opportunities in the UK ... in Europe ... and the world.

Genetik – Message Trust

The Tribe Academy is based at the Message Trust and aims to train and equip 18- to 25-year-old evangelists in creative arts and urban mission. Sharing a common biblical studies foundation two distinct streams are offered: Creative Ministry and Urban Youthwork. Each stream offers a blend of workshops and practical opportunities working alongside local churches. For more information contact Genetik@message.org.uk, or see www.message.org.uk.

J.John and the Philo Trust

Breaking News (Authentic) is a six-week evangelistic training book that can be used by individuals, small groups and whole churches. The sessions provide you with a ready-made training programme to engage you and your church in evangelism. Individual copies are £4.99 but prices are reduced for bulk orders. Please see www.philotrust.com or call 01923 287777.

Lost for Words

Lost for Words is a resource to help people of every age share their faith naturally. It includes three separate courses (children, youth and adults) with leader's notes, a CD-ROM with PowerPoint presentations, handouts, activities and publicity material. Available from CPAS, telephone 01926 458458 for £39.95 – www.cpas.org.uk.

Urban Saints in conjunction with Church Pastoral Aid Society and London School of Theology offers *Christian Life and Children*, a

series of six teaching sessions on video to teach about evangelism with children. Each session has three sections to be followed by discussion, Bible study and prayer, and the course covers topics including how children grow spiritually, how to build healthier families inside and outside of the church and developing a strategy for effective children's work. Package including video, notes and CD-ROM costs £7. www.urbansaints.org.

YFC – *The Art of Connecting*

This Youth For Christ course looks at evangelism from the point of view of three stories: yours, your friend's and God's. Over the seven weeks it helps you to see the value of your own testimony and experiences, to listen better to others and to work out how to tell God's story. Leader's pack is £29 + £3 p&p. www.theartofconnecting.org and/or www.yfc.co.uk

YWAM

Youth With A Mission run a School of Evangelism course that includes looking at character, understanding the good news and how to effectively communicate it. The course consists of 13 weeks study followed by a 12-month outreach programme. See www.ywam-england.com for more details.

CHAPTER 6

EVALUATION OF HOPE

Theos, an independent public theology think tank

'In order to learn from the first year of HOPE and to understand the impact it had made we, the HOPE leadership board, commissioned Theos to undertake an independent evaluation of the mission. Here you will find an executive summary of their findings, based on activity that took place in 2008.'
Steve Clifford, Evangelical Alliance

HOPE sought to catalyse, encourage and support churches across the UK as, through words and actions, they worked together and with public bodies such as government, police and the media in service to their communities. HOPE was **grass roots** – supporting local churches in their commitment to neighbourhoods. HOPE was **collaborative** – always seeking ways to connect different groups, churches and agencies. HOPE aimed to **resource** participants through a range of materials and the expertise of associate groups. Overall, the vision of HOPE was to help Christians **raise their game** impacting individuals and communities in **word** and **action**. HOPE partners worked to meet the immediate needs in their

> HOPE enjoyed extraordinary success in achieving its aims and the country continues to experience the fruits of its vision.

neighbourhoods, but they also worked with an eye to the long-term legacy of living out the gospel in villages, towns and cities across the UK. HOPE enjoyed extraordinary success in achieving its aims and the country continues to experience the fruits of its vision.

This vision was summed up by HOPE's strap line ***Do More. Do It Together. Do it in Word and Action.***

1. FEATURES OF HOPE

HOPE aimed to:
- **Encourage** as much participation as possible while remaining non-prescriptive.
- **Give away its logo** and allow use of the HOPE brand free of charge.
- **Run with a small support staff** and on a modest budget.
- **Empower local churches** rather than control resources.
- **Limit itself to one year** so as to resist institutionalisation.

HOPE activities were registered in **1,474** locations throughout the UK. This number far exceeds the original 500 locations identified by HOPE as ideal places for a HOPE presence.

A network of over 150 volunteer **HOPE Champions** dedicated themselves to promoting HOPE in their areas. As well as overseeing events, liaising with workers and beneficiaries of HOPE projects and representing HOPE to their local churches and communities, the HOPE Champions were also valuable sources of information and feedback about HOPE activities on the ground.

- **82%** of those surveyed report that HOPE has inspired their congregations.
- **83%** thought HOPE has made a tangible difference.
- **94%** indicate that they are enthusiastic about the goals and visions of HOPE for the future.

2. THE YEAR OF HOPE

The planning team identified five High Points which roughly corresponded to the traditional Church calendar and which provided some structure to the year.

- **Fresh HOPE:** In the New Year season groups were encouraged to offer services for local people wanting to make a fresh start. Fresh HOPE events might also mark the launch of HOPE projects in individual churches for the coming year
  - **70%** of HOPE Champions polled participated in this
  - This high take-up is notable, since this was the first High Point of the year and for many congregations their first real exposure to HOPE.
- **The Big HOPE:** Churches working together were encouraged to express Easter in ways that were imaginative and inviting to the whole community.
  - **73%** participated in this
  - Amongst many creative ideas **Blood Donor Drives** constituted one Big HOPE activity. The National Blood Service calculates that HOPE-related contributions have resulted in '**360 lives saved** to date'.

HOPE sought to catalyse, encourage and support churches across the UK as, through words and actions, they worked together and with public bodies such as government, police and the media in service to their communities.

- **HOPE on the Streets:** During May HOPE partners were encouraged to reach a target of a million Hours of Kindness, by working together to deliver social action projects. Events for children and young people were a focus here, as were the hosting of family fun days.
  - The highest take up at **78%**
    - **325,602** Hours of Kindness logged, and an additional 137,288 pledged with many more Acts left unreported
  - Many groups running a **Fun Day** relate that this marked the high point of their HOPE year.
- **HOPE Explored:** In the autumn, churches could offer an explanation for their actions by inviting people to take part in courses providing an introduction to the Christian faith.
  - **67%** of those polled linked their church's seeker courses to HOPE in some way, many pooling their resources with other groups to make a bigger impression than ever before.
- **The Gift of HOPE:** Christmas was an excellent opportunity to make the gospel accessible to the community, and to celebrate all that happened during the year of HOPE.
  - **67.6%** participated in a Gift of HOPE event
  - **45.8%** agreed that HOPE had changed the way that their church normally does Christmas
  - Of those that participated, **75%** reported that theirs was a joint-venture involving more than one church.

3. DOING MORE

The number, variety and scope of HOPE projects taking place across the country were unparalleled compared to any other Christian initiative in the UK.

- **86%** of those polled indicated that their church is doing more as a result of HOPE. **No one** reported doing less in 2008 than in previous years.

Groups reached

• **When Champions were asked** to indicate people reached by their HOPE activities, secondary-school aged children and families each attracted **85.7%** of the responses. This was followed by primary school children (**74.3%**) and young people (**62.9%**). Besides parents of children, the main focus on adults was on singles (**54.3%**) and retired people (**57.1%**). Some HOPE projects were aimed at school leavers (**14.3%**) and university students (**22.9%**).

Words and actions

• **More than half** of those polled – **57.6%** – reported an increase in their church's engagement in **evangelism by words**. **No one** thought engagement had gone down.

• **91.2%** of those polled reported an increase in **evangelism by action**.

• **67.7%** indicate an increase in levels of volunteering in their church. **60%** report that their church's attitude towards poor, vulnerable and marginalised groups has improved.

• Close to half – **45.7%** – of respondents report that their churches are praying more than before as a result of their engagement with HOPE. **No one** thinks participation prayer went down during the year of HOPE. HOPE was **publicly launched** at a Trumpet Call prayer event in Birmingham in 2006 in front of an audience of 3000–4000 people. Prayer triplets and groups formed to pray for HOPE continue to meet.

4. DOING IT TOGETHER

Churches

• **88.2%** report that as a result of HOPE their church's attitude towards other Christian groups and denominations has improved. In areas where inter-church partnerships were already in place, **71%** thought that these working relationships were strengthened. **No one** thought attitudes had got worse as a result of HOPE.

Whatever you do, the aim is that relationships are built, people's needs are met and the church is engaged with its community.

91.2% of those polled reported an increase in evangelism by action.

• **91.7%** of those polled indicated working with **Baptists** of various affiliations, 88.9% worked with the **Church of England** and 77.8% saw **Methodist** involvement. Other denominations and the response rate they attracted include **Roman Catholic** (58.3%), **Salvation Army** (55.6%), **United Reformed** (50.0%), **Assemblies of God** (41.7%), **New Frontiers** (41.7%) and **Elim Pentecostal** (38.9%). 'New' and 'Independent' churches were significant partners in HOPE projects, registering 47.2%. Amongst others this category included **Brethren, Vineyard, Community** and **House** churches.

Associate Groups

• **The Church denominations** and para-church agencies which accepted the invitation to partner with HOPE were known collectively as **Associate Groups**.

• **155** of these organisations registered with HOPE.

• **100%** of Associates surveyed agreed that HOPE was a good fit for their organisation. **100%** think that the continued association with HOPE was a good one. **None** of the Associates polled thought that HOPE had a negative effect on their organisation's work.

• **Prominent partners** include **Soul Survivor, Message Trust Trust** and **Youth For Christ**, each of which donated generously and released Mike Pilavachi, Andy Hawthorne, Roy Crowne and other staff to do the work of HOPE.

• **Other organisations** also released key personnel to be on the HOPE Board and Leadership team: **Bible Society** (Rob Cotton); **CELL UK** (Laurence Singlehurst); **Make It Happen** (Matt Bird); **The Church of England** (Paul Bayes); **Oasis** (Clive Dudbridge); **Street Pastors** (Eustace Constance); **World Prayer Centre** (Jane Holloway) and **Pioneer** (Steve Clifford).

• **Other collaborations** at the national level include: **ABA Design, Associated Bus**

Ministries, Authentic Media, Christian Enquiry Agency, CPO, Evangelical Alliance, Urban Saints, MEMO, New Life Publishing, Scripture Union, RUN, Kingsway Communications, Fresh Expressions and Vivid Broadcast.

• **Alpha, Big Idea, Book of HOPE, CARE, Compassion, Spring Harvest, the Methodist Church, Saltmine, UCB, Elim Church** and **New Wine** were amongst organisations who dedicated significant resources to HOPE and to the promotion of HOPE throughout the year.

• The **Girls'** and **Boys' Brigade** gave their summer camp a strong Acts of Kindness dimension in partnership with the HOPE on the Streets High Point.

Young People

• **HOPE Champions** report that the **majority of people reached by their HOPE activities were under 20 years of age**.

• **Throughout the UK,** young people also took active roles in leading HOPE events.

• **HOPE Revolution** was the official youth arm of HOPE, and chose not to use the '08' in its logo – HOPE Revolution remains the most active network of Christian ministry in the UK.

Government, Police and Media

• In June 2008 **Prince Charles** hosted a reception at Clarence House for the organisers and volunteers of HOPE. In December 2008, **Prime Minister Gordon Brown** honoured HOPE workers at a reception at 10 Downing Street.

• HOPE gained the early support of stakeholders such as the **Association of Chief Police Officers** (ACPO), the office of the **Metropolitan Police Commissioner** and the **Department for Communities and Local Government** (DCLG).

Prince Charles hosted a reception at Clarence House for the organisers and volunteers of HOPE.

• Many **MPs** gave their public support during the early promotion of HOPE.

• A number of regional police forces officially included HOPE in their community strategy documents.

• **61.8%** of HOPE Champions agreed that their church's relationship to secular institutions overall has improved. **No one** reported having a worse relationship with these groups as a result of HOPE.

• **68%** saw specific improvement in working relations with **local government**.

• **67%** agreed that relationships with the **police** had got better.

• **59%** found that their church's relationship with the **local media** had improved as a result of HOPE.

Strong partnerships were forged with **Christian media**.

• **16 publications** agreed to devote regular space to HOPE stories.

• **A number of national publications** published HOPE stories on a case-by-case basis.

• **HOPE's Communication Officer** wrote articles for Christian publications as well as denominational literature including calendars, prayer leaflets and promotional literature.

5. HOPE MATERIALS AND RESOURCES

HOPE produced a high quality promotional **DVD** featuring stories, ideas and words of endorsement from leaders of denominations and organisations across the country.

- **22, 800** copies of this DVD were given away.
- **100%** of HOPE Champions polled reported finding this resource 'Useful' or 'Very Useful'.

There were three main parts to the HOPE family of **websites**

- **www.HOPEnews.co.uk** provided a platform for broadcast reports, E-news stories and user-generated content.
- **www.HOPEinfo.co.uk** (created and maintained by Christian Enquiry Agency) was designed to be the public face of HOPE. The site won the 2008 Christian Web and Blog Award for Best Christian Social Action Website.
- **www.HOPE.com** was the inward-facing website, intended primarily for participants and organisers of HOPE activities.
- **The websites** attracted a combined 'Useful' or 'Very Useful' mark of **94%**, while **88%** found the E-news service to be of use to their projects.

The Resource Book was the major material production to come out of HOPE. It was published by Authentic in 2007 and it featured extensive resources and ideas, with chapters devoted to every key feature of the HOPE Year.

- **91%** of HOPE Champions polled found the Resource Book 'Useful' or 'Very Useful'.
- By the close of 2008, **29,420** copies had been sold.

> A new model of mission seems to have emerged across the UK in recent years combining words and actions.

6. RECOMMENDATIONS AND REFLECTIONS FOR FUTURE HOPE PROJECTS

- A new model of mission seems to have emerged across the UK in recent years combining words and actions, being good news as well as proclaiming good news. HOPE has been an important champion of this change.
- Grass roots collaboration between local churches served by national agencies allows the empowerment of Christians to serve their communities in ways which are appropriate to their situations.
- Non-prescriptive models of mission allow a flexibility of approach within a national vision. A give-away 'brand' creates an expression of unity in the midst of a diversity of activities.
- The small scale, relatively low cost administrative base provided limitations to the support of the HOPE initiatives. An earlier employment of a key administrator and detailed, planned database would have helped both communication and evaluation.
- Black Majority Churches represent a vibrant and growing part of the UK church scene. An earlier consultation and opportunities to shape the vision might have resulted in an even greater buy in from this part of the church.
- HOPE's use of new technology (web/email/text-messaging) assisted communication in ways unthinkable previously. It is anticipated that future initiatives will further benefit from technological change.
- Target setting for initiatives such as HOPE has always proved challenging. Certain targets, such as the number of locations adopting HOPE, were outperformed by a factor of 3:1, while other targets proved more difficult to either achieve or monitor.
- Large 'successful' churches sometimes find it difficult to see the benefits of an association

with national initiatives such as HOPE. Future planning should consider articulating the vision of large churches serving smaller churches as an expression of their commitment to the wider body of Christ.

• The HOPE high points provided a helpful model for churches to plan their diaries, reflecting on both the churches calendar and the rhythm of everyday lives.

• The *HOPE Resource Book* provided an invaluable resource, enabling churches to access creative ideas and resources with which to deliver their HOPE initiatives. A number of networks and denominations invested in the book as an expression of their commitment to HOPE and desire to resource local churches.

• Engagement with local councils and police has many positive advantages. Early approaches are both appreciated and will result in greater opportunities for joined up activities. Mutual understanding of the different cultural environments between the church and state agencies takes time to develop.

• The intentional use of villages as the first part of the HOPE strap line, 'HOPE in our villages, towns and cities' was clearly appreciated, but much more could have been done. There is a need for increased understanding of rural church life when nationwide initiatives are being planned.

• There are a tremendous number of excellent resources widely available to help churches engage more effectively in their communities. The challenge for everyone is to remain aware of these and make good use of them.

7. CONCLUSION

Considering the deliberately scaled down model and the 'give-away' nature of the HOPE initiative, the success that HOPE enjoyed across the country is all the more remarkable. The amount of churches and regions which signed on, the new community projects that began and which look set to continue, and the strong partnerships that HOPE participants made with each other, with local government and with the police is testament to the strength of the vision guiding HOPE. HOPE has undoubtedly left the UK in a better state than it found it, by doing more, by doing it together and by doing it in word and action.

HOPE has undoubtedly left the UK in a better state than it found it, by doing more, by doing it together and by doing it in word and action.

Church Urban Fund Faith in action

'They helped me to achieve goals I wouldn't have been able to before'.

Beryl is one of thousands of people we support every year, through funding projects which bring hope for the future to people who otherwise feel they would have little or none...

Church Urban Fund does this by working through a network of churches who are supporting their local communities.

In 2009 we are launching our **Seeds of Hope** campaign, which will run over the next three years. This is our direct response to the recession, raising money to change lives. We would love you to pray, act and give to enable us to bring new hope to England's poorest communities.

For more information: **www.cuf.org.uk** or phone us on **020 7898 1667**

Church Urban Fund is a company limited by guarantee Registered in Cardiff No: 2138994 Registered charity number: 297483

You know your church needs to engage with your community...

You know that family issues are a key way to achieve this. But where do you find the resources you need to help you?

Engage is an initiative from Care for the Family to equip churches who are meeting the needs of families in the wider community – and those who would like to start.

Discover the range of resources which you can use to engage with your community.

- Ground-breaking family-strengthening community courses
- Realistic, practical resources
- Support for toddler group leaders
- Specialist bereavement ministries
- Support networks for families in challenging circumstances

Find out more at
www.engagetoday.org.uk

Care for the Family – a Christian response to a world of need.

110-09 HOPE09 01

CHAPTER 7

THE BIG HOPE

EASTER

Liza Hoeksma, Soul Survivor

Easter is the most significant time in the church calendar. As individuals and churches we spend the 40 days of Lent preparing our hearts to think again about Jesus' sacrifice for us on the cross and to celebrate the amazing victory that he won for us when he rose to life. Over the Easter weekend we come together to reflect and to rejoice again on the story of Jesus' death and resurrection that is central to our faith. Despite all that Easter means to us, to those outside of the church it can be just a long weekend away from work and a chance to eat chocolate eggs. HOPE has been encouraging Christians everywhere to not just celebrate the joy of Easter inside the walls of their churches and homes, but to see what a fantastic opportunity the festival provides for evangelism and mission and to take the good news out to their communities.

Many churches have been embracing this idea for the first time through HOPE, others have been using it as a chance to work more closely with other denominations in their area or to increase what they were already doing. Overall the challenge to bring the 'Big Hope' of Easter out of the church was taken up in some creative and amazing ways!

Use these stories and ideas to help you think about what you could be doing in your neighbourhood next Easter and in the years to come.

The challenge to bring the 'Big Hope' of Easter out of the church was taken up in some creative and amazing ways!

An Easter Wave of Blessing – Leamington Spa

Where? Leamington Spa, Warwickshire.
What did it look like? Between 300 and 400 people took part in an 'Easter Wave' walk through the high street giving out free chocolates and balloons, followed by a short outdoor service that included escapology. Rev David Banbury was fastened into a straightjacket by two volunteers to represent Jesus in the tomb. Each strap also represented things that bind us in everyday life and stop us experiencing the hope intended for us. He then escaped, showing the power of the resurrection of Jesus to overcome everything and give us an eternal hope.
Why? As Churches Together in Leamington Spa we wanted to bring HOPE to our town and put on an event that could be built on in future years. Previously we had done a Walk of Witness on Good

Friday but we wanted to make the event more colourful and joyful to really celebrate the good news of Easter. The idea was to make it a 'wave of blessing' hence the name 'Easter Wave' rather than Easter parade.

How did it work? We talked to all of the local ministers to get an idea of what was happening in the area and what people would be interested in getting involved with.

On the day we met at one of our churches to give people instructions, etc. and gave out the 300 helium balloons that had our web address and cards attached to them, ready to be handed out during the walk. We had asked people to bring their own chocolates to give away.

The Salvation Army band led the way and we carried a large 'HOPE Leamington' banner so it was clear who we were. As we walked we had teams of people who stopped and chatted to onlookers, handing out our goodies and cards. We also had a team who went inside the shopping centre to see the shoppers and workers there so they didn't miss out.

We gave out leaflets that said 'with love from Leamington churches' during our walk. We didn't want to be heavy handed or put across any agenda other than blessing people but we wanted people to know who we were.

The outcome

We had some great conversations and one old gentleman told us we had made his week as he'd never seen anything like this before. One of our team was approached in the shopping centre by a security guard questioning whether she had permission to collect money. When she explained she wasn't collecting anything, just giving things away for free, he was astounded!

Top tips for if you'd like to do something similar:

• Meet with the Police beforehand. Because a parade holds up traffic we made sure they were aware well in advance what we had planned and they were very helpful and supportive.

Between 300 and 400 people took part in an 'Easter Wave' walk through the high street.

• Have teams of people who can go and visit shops and shoppers who aren't on the main walk route to make sure as many people as possible are blessed.

• Be prepared for any weather – we did the wave in hail!

Lessons learned

• We had to compromise on the date of the walk. Though we would have preferred to do the parade on Easter Sunday to celebrate the day of Jesus' rising, the shops weren't open that day and we felt we would have missed the event by waiting until the Monday. This of course meant we had to put aside the fact that the Saturday is still a more solemn part of Easter for the church in order to meet people where they were at.

• It was great to do something with lots of churches joining together. That took a lot of planning and meetings to make it happen but it was worth it and hopefully even more churches will join in events in future years now they've seen what we can achieve together.

• The sound for the outdoor service wasn't very good and so didn't draw a very big crowd. Next year we'll change that so that more people can hear what is going on.

• Don't be afraid to just go for it! We didn't feel we knew what we were doing but the event turned out really well and we'll be better prepared for next year!

Did you know that over four million people tuned in to watch each episode of *The Passion* on BBC1 during Holy Week? The Churches Media Council provided advice and support for churches to maximise the opportunities this brought about. Look out for similar programmes and resources at www.churchesmediacouncil.org.uk.

The churches in Coventry went to town with their Easter activities!

• Christ in the Precinct has been running in Coventry city centre for a number of years, so for 2008 they focused on the theme of HOPE. Over three days they offered free face painting, balloons, chocolate eggs, and shoe shining. There were performances from gospel choirs, screenings of the BBC's *The Passion* series, a wooden cross where people could put their prayers, and they even had an outdoor Communion service on Good Friday. In the weeks and months leading up to the event, they videoed hundreds of people asking them what their hopes, dreams and prayers for Coventry were. The resulting video was shown on a large screen to shoppers and passers-by over the weekend.

• In South Coventry HOPE organisers said a survey uncovered local people wanted more of a community spirit. A free festival seemed like the natural response so on Easter Saturday they held a festival on the green – opposite a shopping centre with marquees, a free hog roast, a bouncy castle, market stalls, kids' crafts and a stage for bands.

An exhibition of Hope

A village in Cambridgeshire used the theme of HOPE for an exhibition in their church over the Easter weekend. They covered topics that are very much on people's minds like climate change, parenting, debt and life after death, and they looked at what hope there is within these areas. Visitors were then able to make a practical response through information provided on organisations like Tearfund, Care for the Family and a local debt counselling service. There was also room for feedback so that members of the community could say if they'd like the church to provide any courses on the topics throughout the year. What a great way to get people talking about these topics and to find out how the church can bless them!

> We wanted to get out into the community to show people Christians are just ordinary people.

Getting stuck into community projects in Herne Bay, Kent

Who? Christ Church and St Andrew's in Herne Bay, Kent.

What? A day of community work, blessing four existing local projects with practical help such as painting, gardening and cleaning.

Why? We wanted to get out into the community to show people Christians are just ordinary people; we're not as scary as some think!

How did it work? Members of our congregation suggested projects they thought might need our help, including an Age Concern Day Centre that is next to one of our church buildings, and three local nurseries. We contacted them and asked how we could help.

On the weekend we met at 9.30am for a short time of praise before heading out to our projects and ended the day by meeting back at the church for another time of praise.

At the Day Centre we painted 13 rooms in one day! The nurseries asked us to help with some gardening, cleaning up the kids' outdoor toys, renovating a play area, painting fences and sheds.

Between the two congregations 50–60 people got involved, young and old alike, and between them they gave 180 hours of kindness.

Top tips for if you think this could work in your town, city or village:

• Build relationships with the people you are trying to help. Get in touch with them well ahead of the day so they have time to think about how you can serve them and to get ready for your visit. Keep that contact up as well so they know you really will follow through.

• Learn to listen, whether it be to what kind of help they're really asking for or their questions and concerns about faith.

• Members of the church who are less physically able can still be a vital part of the work. We had an organised prayer rota so that the whole event was covered in prayer.

• Make sure someone in each team takes responsibility for the quality of work being done and the safety of participants.

• Make sure you have enough paint, paintbrushes, cleaning equipment, etc. for the day's work. If you need volunteers to bring anything themselves, make sure they have plenty of notice.

The outcome

The people at the nurseries and Day Centre were really grateful for our support and even came along on the Saturday to say thank you. The projects brought everyone in church a lot closer, too; it was a great chance to build and deepen friendships plus as a church HOPE has helped us be much more outward looking.

For loads more hints and tips, see Chapter 8 on social action projects completed as part of HOPE on the Streets.

The Big Picture of Easter

Churches in Loughborough made a huge impact with their Easter activity by getting the community to complete an 80m-wide and 8m-high painting of the Easter story! Find out more in Chapter 14.

Making a Splash

On Easter Sunday hundreds gathered to see Archbishop of York, Dr John Sentamu, baptising 25 new believers outside St Michael-le-Belfry in York. What a fantastic way to take the celebration of Easter and the gift of new life out onto the streets for all to witness!

Prayer Point

Local churches in South Manchester worked together over the Easter period to send out 20,000 cards to homes in the area wishing them a Happy Easter. Each card had a detachable form asking for any prayer requests which could then be sent back to either their local church or a central collection point. A HOPE Prayers service was then held at St James' Church, Didsbury, where each person attending was given a prayer request card that had been received and was asked to pray in response to it. The service was moving and symbolic with about a third of all requests received being for physical healings. Delivering the cards by hand was also a great way to meet members of the community and to engage in conversation and the churches are keen to repeat the activity as it can be done at any time of year.

The projects brought everyone in church a lot closer, too; it was a great chance to build and deepen friendships.

Egg Rolling Extravaganza!

Seventy volunteers from eight local churches offered face painting, temporary tattoos, refreshments and a big balloon race to the crowds that converged on Avenham and Miller Parks in Preston, Lancashire, for the council-run egg rolling race. The churches joined together to see what they could add to the event and were amazed at the response. A prayer space was offered and visitors left them nearly 50 prayer requests, some of them 'heart-breaking'. *'People were astonished and really taken aback that everything was free,'* said local vicar, Joe.

Great Idea For Your Village – Free Hot Cross Buns!

After their traditional Good Friday Breakfast and Walk of Witness, The Junction (a youth group from Folksworth) toasted hot cross buns and gave them out to passers-by during the morning. This was followed by an outdoor service in the centre of the village to make more villagers aware of the importance of Good Friday and show that Christians aren't only found in church!

We heard loads of other great ideas that we've listed below. Which do you think might work in your village, town or city?

- Having a sunrise service (St Mary's in Peterborough).
- Holding an Easter egg hunt after church on Easter Sunday (churches in Wansford, Cambridge).
- At Moreton Baptist Church, children and parents enjoyed a free screening of *Miracle Maker*.
- A family fun day drew the crowds in Aberdeen.
- Doing a prayer walk on Good Friday (churches in south east London). They stopped and had a picnic on the way, then ended their walk with a time of acapella worship.
- The churches in Sevenoaks, Kent, held a card-making event on the high street a few weeks before Easter.
- Inviting school children to church to do a walk through Holy Week – see Chapter 13 for more details.
- Doing a passion play on the streets like the churches in Bradford and Edinburgh who wanted to bring their celebrations out into a public place.
- Nottingham University Student Union teamed up with local churches, Student Community Action and the local council for a Great Big Student Gardening Week.
- Churches in Coventry put on a showing of the critically acclaimed *Son of Man* film at the Warwick Arts Centre. The film tells the story of Jesus through a tale of corruption and redemption in modern day Africa. See www.sonofmanmovie.com for more details of the film and how you can use it.
- Just before Easter, Newbury Methodist Church contacted people who had past links with them. They invited them to a special 'welcome back' service – with cream teas and prayer stations based on the HOPE 08 prayer.
- Young people from churches in Newark, Nottinghamshire, planted Easter baskets which

Nottingham YFC offered to take lessons in schools covering the events of Holy Week.

they then distributed to older members of the community and to a local peace hospice.
- Churches in Watford, Hertfordshire, held an art exhibition on the theme of HOPE at their local shopping centre.
- Holy Trinity Bradley Stoke in Bristol had a pancake party.
- Churches in the Black Country encouraged believers to sacrifice a day's holiday to serve their community whilst thinking about Jesus' great sacrifice for us.
- Nottingham YFC offered to take lessons in schools covering the events of Holy Week.
- Members of Unity, a Christian Entertainment Group, put on three performances of the musical *Jerusalem Joy* at a nearby school. They charged a £5 entrance fee and gave all the proceeds to the local children's hospice.
- Churches Together in Bromsgrove, Worcestershire, delivered 20,000 Easter cards with details of church services and upcoming HOPE activities.
- Churches in Consett, County Durham, and Rushden in Northamptonshire gave out Easter eggs to local families.
- St Polycarp's Church in Sheffield invited 250 junior school children to their church and took them through a re-enactment of the events of Holy Week. See Chapter 13 for more details.
- You could encourage church members to give blood – visit www.blood.co.uk, www.scotblood.co.uk or www.welsh-blood.org.uk like Congregational Church, North Walsham and churches in Edinburgh did.
- Use the Lent period to go through a course with your church. Churches Together in north Bristol found the Faithworks i-church course incredibly helpful as they thought more about how they could have a positive impact on their community.
- Letchworth Garden City attracted more attention than usual for the Walk of Witness by having everyone wear something red!

YOUTH

Cambridge YFC worked with local church St Andrew's in schools for two weeks in the run up to Easter taking a drama group called Lifeforce in with them. They finished with a gig. St Andrew's Youth worker Dan said, *'Cambridge schools are very sensitive when it comes to the faith issue – we've been going around trying to build a few bridges. We've actually seen massive breakthrough these last two weeks in schools that haven't let Christians in for the last ten years.'*

We've heard about young people raising money in their churches to buy boxes of Cadbury's Creme Eggs. They've then handed them out at school with the simple explanation that as Christians they believe God loves each person and wants to bless them, not least of all with a free chocolate egg!

EASTER IN YOUR COMMUNITY

What has your church done to celebrate Easter in the past? How could you have an even bigger impact on your local community at this special time of year? Think about:

- Joining up with other churches to make your Easter celebrations bigger, better and more unified. Start talking to each other early, sharing ideas and making plans so you're well prepared when Easter comes round.
- Trying something new or adding a new twist to your traditional activity. It doesn't have to be expensive or take lots of time to prepare – have another look through this chapter for ideas you can adapt for where you live.
- Encouraging the young people in your church to come up with some ideas and supporting them as they put them into practice.

How could you have an even bigger impact on your local community at this special time of year?

RESOURCES

CPO (Christian Publishing & Outreach) produces a wide range of posters, banners, invitation cards, booklets, tracts and other outreach resources specifically themed for use at Easter and have specific HOPE branded resources available from www.cpo.org.uk/hope. A team of outreach advisors are available on 01903 263354 to help suggest the most appropriate resources for local needs.

Easter Cracked is full of ideas for Easter celebrations, evangelistic outreach for the whole family, craft, drama and events. There are ideas for all-age events for Passover and Good Friday plus assembly outlines and ideas for working with youth and the under-five age group. £9.99 from www.scriptureunion.org.uk. For resources from Scripture Union Scotland see www.suscotland.org.uk, for Scripture Union Northern Ireland see www.suni.co.uk.

The **Easter SONrise** booklet is an evangelistic resource explaining the truth and significance of Easter as well as outlining the history of many Easter traditions. Price 99p for a single copy, 30p if you buy 100+ at www.philotrust.com.

Easter SONrise DVD: A live-recording of J.John speaking at Hillsong London explaining the truth and significance of Easter. £9.99 from www.philotrust.com.

Love Life Live Lent family book contains 40 great ideas for adults and children to help transform our world locally, nationally and globally. From just £1 at www.livelent.net.

www.rejesus.co.uk has many Easter-themed resources. See their website for more details.

CHAPTER 8

HOPE ON THE STREETS

PENTECOST

Dan Etheridge, Soul Action and Liza Hoeksma, Soul Survivor

HOPE has given churches across the country an amazing opportunity to show their communities what they are all about. We know that our actions speak louder than our words and whilst we want to make sure we tell people the good news of Jesus verbally, we also want to make sure we shout it out loud with our actions too! Words alone can be empty so we need to demonstrate God's kindness. Running social action projects, big and small, means that communities have seen, experienced and heard what the church is for: love, compassion, meeting needs, building community and changing lives!

The HOPE on the Streets 'high point' is based around the Church's celebration of Pentecost. With Pentecost we remember the outpouring of God's Spirit upon the first followers of Jesus. With events like HOPE on the Streets we act out what it is to be a people that are filled with God's spirit . . . we speak life and truth to those around us in a language that is understandable, real and relevant to them. For many in our communities the language they hear from the church can be alienating and confusing but churches that seek to

Just check out the stories over the next few pages and see if you're inspired about anything else your church could be doing to let your actions speak louder to your community.

serve, meet needs, bless and love the communities of which they are a part, speak a language of hope and life.

It's important for us to remember that social action initiatives like those that happened as part of HOPE on the Streets are concerned with evangelism, but they may not end in hundreds of new Christians. Most significantly they are part of a process in which the church strives to live out its call to be a community of life and a community that reveals the loving God. For some, HOPE offered the chance and inspiration to run social action events for the first time around the May Bank Holiday weekend. For others, the national initiative has given the impetus to scale up weekly, monthly or annual projects, so churches across a town or city have worked together to serve their communities. What's becoming clear is that many churches are making social action projects a regular part of their church calendar which is brilliant!

Just check out the stories over the next few pages and see if you're inspired about anything else your church could be doing to let your actions speak louder to your community.

Double The Noise!

Churches in North Bristol have been running 'Noise' projects (see Resources to find out more about The Noise) in their community for seven years. For HOPE 08 they decided to kick things up a few gears and get double the volunteers so they could commit to double the amount of projects and cover double the geographical area! They took the HOPE strapline to heart and decided to 'do more and do it together' – getting lots of local churches involved.

What? Over the May Bank Holiday weekend we ran free kids' clubs, held banquets for senior citizens, did free car washing, we cleared up gardens and public spaces, scrubbed off graffiti, re-painted walls and re-planted gardens and flower beds. We even had a creative team that painted murals on walls of a local school playground and a 'Detached youth team', reaching out to the young people on the fringes of our community.

How? We spent a lot of time in the run up to the weekend networking and asking local community groups how we could best serve them. We also got in contact with lots of local churches and encouraged more Christians to get involved.

We publicised the weekend by doing a door drop of flyers to 10,000 houses. We also had a website for volunteers to sign up and one for the local community to see what we were planning as well.

Every day we had a free fun afternoon with a barbecue, bouncy castle, cafe and face painting.

This year we had a small team of people praying for healing which was well received by the community. We didn't make a big deal out of it as we wanted it to be a natural thing so we could meet people where they were at and not scare them.

Top tips

• It was great to get the whole church behind The Noise and not just run it as a youth thing. I would say encourage as many people as possible to get involved as everyone has a part to play.

• If you're growing your projects don't take everything on yourself – get different people leading different areas. Encourage younger people to be leading and overseeing different areas. Take a risk on them.

• Plan early. In the autumn term start thinking about what you can do next year,

> Make sure what you do isn't a one weekend 'hit and run'.

get networking and speaking to lots of different community groups and churches to get them on board. It may mean you attend lots of meetings but it will be worth it!

• If you've never done a Noise project before, try and see one in action to help you get a better idea of what it can look like (find project details at www.soulaction.org/thenoise).

• Make sure what you do isn't a one weekend 'hit and run' – the best projects are ones that can be sustained in some way throughout the year but the Bank Holiday weekend is a great way to raise the profile of the work and get more people involved.

• If you're a small church, link up with other churches in the area to make a bigger impact. If you're part of a big church, try and get smaller churches involved too. Together you can make the biggest Noise!

Lessons learned

• The more you take on, the more efficient your administrators need to be! There's a lot of preparation work needed to make a Noise weekend happen.

• Be aware that not all your volunteers are likely to turn up – don't over commit to projects, and have a back-up plan for if lots of people don't show. Likewise think about what you can do if people finish their projects early – get them prayer-walking around the area for example.

• You can't really depend on the good old UK weather so you need to be flexible! Try and think of good projects that aren't reliant on dry/sunny days.

The impact? Offering to serve really opens up doors to local community groups and is such a blessing to local residents. It totally changes people's perceptions of the church when you're doing something nice for them and not asking for anything in return. This year we managed to reach a whole new estate – Southmede – and they were overwhelmed, saying they'd never seen anything like it before. Churches who got involved for

the first time were really positive, too, saying it was amazing to be a part of getting something happening in the community again.

In **Swindon** one lady came to church after a conversation in B&Q while the YFC team were buying things for their HOPE on the Streets project!

Whitton Baptist Church, Ipswich: Last year the team made contact with a family who sadly later had a death in the family. The church was able to offer support and comfort due to the relationship formed over the HOPE on the Streets activity.

In **Meanwood, Leeds**, churches offered to pray for an elderly lady whose garden they had been doing. She suffered from arthritis but since has said that after prayer she has been able to move more freely than she has done in years!

First Shouts

For the churches in Lichfield, HOPE was a great chance to get started on some community work in their local area.

What did the weekend look like?

Saturday: We started off the weekend with a free car wash, and then went on to do a free barbeque and family fun afternoon at a local church with lots of free face painting and balloon modelling.

Sunday: On Sunday the young people led the service at our church, to let everyone know what had been going on.

Monday: We started Monday morning by painting a local community building, it was hard work (we didn't realise quite how big a job it was before we started!) but we were really proud of the results. We spent the afternoon face painting, balloon modelling, hairbraiding and playing games with children in the park. This was really popular and we had lots of good feedback from the parents and children. We then finished off the weekend by having a meal together, sharing stories and watching the video from the weekend.

> Have a variety of projects so that people can choose to get involved in something that appeals to them.

The results? It went much better than we'd expected for our first try at some social action projects! Although we had a relatively small group I think everyone worked really hard and it is definitely a positive step in terms of working with other churches and putting faith into action. Mostly we had very good feedback from the public, although lots assumed that if things were free there must a catch!

Top tips

- Talk to your local council about your plans and get them on board. Make the most of secular organisations that have expertise in this area.
- Get young people involved and leading things from the start.
- Have a variety of projects so that people can choose to get involved in something that appeals to them.

Lessons learned

- Because the young people were involved in running it, we didn't have enough adult support. In future we'd make sure all ages of the church both knew about the event and got involved if possible.
- We'd also try and communicate better with other churches and get more people involved.

Swansea: A team of 300+ people from churches and the community took part in a Love Swansea weekend where, with council support, they cleared Crymlyn Bog (the largest in the UK) to restore this naturally beautiful area that had been ruined by dumping and fly tipping.

Cotgrave, Nottingham: A team of ten people had a busy 90 minutes in Cotgrave and were amazed just how much litter they collected! The Borough Council supported them by loaning hi-visibility jackets, pickup sticks, bags and gloves. They had a number of comments from folk including, 'Thanks,' 'Who are you?' and 'Are you paid for this?'!

While people were having their car washed for free at **Cottingham Road Baptist Church** in Hull they were invited to come in for coffee, take a free book and have a piece of the church's 80th birthday anniversary cake!

Why not give one of these ideas a try as part of your HOPE on the Streets projects?

- Give a giant hamper to your local homeless kitchen like Blackhill Baptist, Consett.
- Give away free energy saving lightbulbs.
- Run a little nail bar and pamper the local girls.
- Get all sporty and hold a five-a-side footy tournament down at the local park (see Chapter 19 for loads more sports ideas).
- Feed the five thousand (or fifty) with a summertime barbecue.
- Litter pick a public area like a park or estate.
- Run an *X Factor* style talent show, hosted by some musically minded chaps from church.
- School the younger generation and hold DJ, dance, sport or other creative workshops.
- Get all arty and paint a mural in a local subway or school.
- Soul in Dinas group in Wales had some great ideas. They:
    - Had an open air service at the end of their activity and gave out fliers inviting people while they worked.
    - Got 'Keep Wales Tidy' to support their litter picking by supplying them with graffiti cleaning kits and other materials.
    - Had people in the teams who didn't do practical work, they were there purely to chat to those having the work done, get to know them and provide a listening ear.
- Churches in Heathfield, East Sussex, used Pentecost as an opportunity to hold a special joint service at the local community college. They commissioned the new Street Pastors who were about to hit the streets (to find out more about Street Pastors see Chapter 16).

Rough structure of the weekend . . .

There's no right or wrong way to run a day or weekend of church-based service in the local community but some of the following might help you plan yours. Many churches choose to run events over a weekend as they can build the multiple projects or activities they organise into a climax with the last afternoon of the weekend culminating in a big party! This has been anything from an informal meal at someone's house, to a full-on street carnival or massive barbecue. Not only is it great fun, but you also get to invite all the people you've served to come along and hang out.

To illustrate how this tends to look check out the weekend schedule here. Obviously adapt this to suit your own needs, but make sure that people doing the serving have plenty of time to grab some food and get a break! Also, *do* factor in lots of time for prayer, and have people in each project who are available to chat and build relationships with the people your projects serve. In this way those you are serving will perceive the projects less as a free service run by the church, and more as a way of connecting with new people.

Time	Friday	Saturday	Sunday	Monday
9am				
10am		Morning team meeting, 10–12	Morning team meeting/ Church Service 10–12	Morning team meeting, 10–12
11am				
12pm		Lunch, 12–2	Lunch, 12–2	Lunch, 12–2
1pm				
2pm		Projects, 2–5	Projects, 2–5	Projects, 2–4
3pm				
4pm				Community Party, 4–6
5pm		Regroup	Regroup	
6pm		Dinner	Dinner	Dinner
7pm				Regroup and Review Projects
8pm	Evening Celebration/ Outreach/ Team Meeting, 8–10	Evening Celebration/ Outreach/ Team Meeting, 8–10	Evening Celebration/ Church Service/ Outreach/ Team Meeting, 8–10	Evening Celebration/ Outreach/ Team Meeting, 8–10
9pm				

Do it your own way . . .

No town, village or city is the same. In fact no street is the same. Every community is different, full of a glorious mix of diverse people, with different interests and commitments. What works in one place may not translate to another, so the ideas here are all suggestions. You, yes you reading this, are the expert as to what would be useful, helpful or a blessing in your community . . . you're the expert because you live there, you know the people, the area and the issues!

The key to effective social action projects is to run activities that are relevant to those you hope to serve. It may be worth spending a few evenings knocking on doors of people in your area, explaining you're from the local church and asking them what they think the greatest needs in the area are. From this you can build a picture as to what people perceive problems are, and the church can be involved in finding solutions, offering alternatives and leading the way. You may not be able to do everything (like build a swimming pool or new community centre) but you may be able to offer a youth club for local kids who have nothing to do on the weekends or provide gardening services for elderly people who are still waiting for someone from the council to help them out!

Every community is different, full of a glorious mix of diverse people, with different interests and commitments.

Prayer Point
It's a great idea to have a team praying and walking round the streets while you're doing your social action projects. Maybe swap people in and out of other teams. You could offer to collect prayers from the people you are serving as you go round and offer to pray for people you meet on the streets too.

Global Day of Prayer

In 2008 the UK joined with 213 other nations to pray on 11th May – Pentecost Sunday. Around 60 locations across the UK took part continuing to lay the foundation of prayer before continuing on with mission. See www.globaldayofprayer.co.uk for details of future events including the 2010 day which will be held at Wembley.

RESOURCES

If you're keen to run a social action project or event in your local community then you might want a bit more advice and help. These products and organisations should be able to help!

Express Community and **Express Community Through Schools** by Phil Bowyer. In these inspirational and practical guides, Phil Bowyer gives young people the methods and principles needed for social action. Suitable for youth, student and young adult groups plus teachers and schools workers, these book shows how evangelism and social action are inextricably linked. Authentic, £8.99

GO:LOCAL: This CD-ROM from Soul Action gives you loads of practical advice if you want to get stuck into your community, bless and serve those around you. £5 from shop.soulsurvivor. com.

Moving into a new mission field? The Message Trust have inspired hundreds of missionaries to move into some of the toughest estates in Manchester to live and breathe the good news. As a result, the areas have seen churches growing and crime coming down. If you're thinking about doing something similar and you'd like advice, resources or any help, please contact eden@ message.org.uk.

Free **NOISE** resources: There are loads of free things you can download on the Soul Action website that will help you get your social action projects up and running, including all those vital forms such as consent forms for under 18s, volunteer application forms, child protection documents and an information sheet for volunteers. All can be adapted to suit your needs – just go to www.soulaction.org and head for The Noise pages.

Working in Wales? GWEINI (the council for the Christian Voluntary Sector in Wales) provides an umbrella organisation and resources for churches who want to get involved in longer term community projects. See www.gweini. org.uk and the book *The Naked Church* for more details. GWEINI, £6.50.

Organisations That Can Help

Besom

Got time? If you have a few spare hours Besom will put them to good use whether it be sorting through donated goods or picking up and delivering items in a van to those in need.

Got skills? Can you paint, cook, teach, do DIY or carpentry? Besom can put you in touch with someone in need of your skills.

Got old goods? Things you don't need lying around at home like clothing, crockery, toys, baby equipment, linens or curtains? Pass them on to Besom and they'll be given to someone who is in need.

Find out more and get involved at www.besom.com.

Faithworks

Join with thousands of others who are motivated by their Christian faith to serve the needs of local communities and to positive influence society as a whole by joining the Faithworks network, either as an individual (for free) or as a church (£20 annual fee). You can then access a library of information, training and resources to support you in your community work. See www.faithworks.info for more details and to get involved.

Don't know where to start? Volunteer bureaux across the country will help match the skills and time you have available to the needs of the local area.

Volunteer Bureaux

Don't know where to start? Volunteer bureaux across the country will help match the skills and time you have available to the needs of the local area. Try:

www.timebank.org.uk
www.scvo.org.uk (the Scottish Council for Voluntary Organisations)
www.nicva.org (the Northern Ireland Council for Voluntary Action)
www.wcva.org.uk (Wales Council for Voluntary Action)
www.volunteering.co.uk (Volunteer Development agency)

HOURS OF KINDNESS

Collated by Fritha Washington, HOPE

Right across the year we encouraged churches to think about their acts of service as clocking up 'hours of kindness' to their communities. There were some pretty imaginative ways that people chose to be a blessing. Check these out:

• Painting the children's equipment at five local parks. **St James', Southam** (200 hours).

• A 'Street Cafe' in front of a church, offering an afternoon for families with free refreshment, food and drink, kids' games and activities, colouring, paddling pools and face painting. **St Paul's Church, Hainault** (9 hours).

• Breakfast, shower, laundry and 'new' second hand clothes for homeless people in Doncaster on a weekly basis. **Bread of Life Breakfast Service, Hall Gate United Reformed Church in Doncaster** (516 hours).

• Various 'Practical Actions' for people who needed them such as lifts to hospitals, gardening, hanging curtains and house cleaning. **St James', Southam** (80 hours).

• Volunteers made greetings cards (such as birthdays, Mothering Sunday, etc.) for the prison chaplain to give to prisoners so that they could send them to family and friends. **Upton by Chester United Reformed Church, Chester** (100 hours).

• Refurbishing football training areas for the local community. **Seacombe United Reformed Church, Wallasey, Merseyside** (100 hours).

• Painting the fence at Sandbach Community Primary School in Cheshire. **CTS Sandbach/ Sandbach Baptist Church** (80 hours).

• Photography studio with free photos at Prestwich carnival. **St Paul's, Kersal, Salford** (30 hours).

• At **St John's Church, Charlesworth, Derbyshire**, the young people set up a stall outside the church and gave away food, drink and things they had made like bookmarks (75 hours).

• Jennie Frost and Claire Dean from **All Saint's Marple** and **Heaton Moor Evangelical Church** in Stockport asked their churches to donate beauty products (shower gel, bath foam, make up, perfume, moisturiser, etc.) after Christmas. Then a group of five friends helped make up gift bags of 'pamper packs'. They made 120 complete bags and also ribbon-wrapped children's clothes which they donated to two local women's refuges to help women when they first come to the refuge (25 hours).

• Bike clinic in **Disley, Cheshire** (4 hours).

• An 'ice the biscuit' stall was held at Intag Summer Festival in Ingol, Preston. People were invited to come and ice a hand-made biscuit and take it away (all for free) and were given bookmarks advertising all four churches in the Ingol area. **Ingol Methodist Church, St Margaret's and Holy Family in Ingol** (50 hours).

Breakfast was delivered to 60+ market stallholders in Frodsham market, Cheshire.

• Served drinks to thousands of cyclists on London to Brighton bike ride. **Turners Hill Free Church, Sussex** (11 hours).

• Breakfast was delivered to 60+ market stallholders in Frodsham market, Cheshire by **Main Street Community Church** and others (2 hours).

• Baked cakes for a cake sale as a fundraiser to purchase paint, etc. for decorating specific homes of refugees and others in need. **Members of Mrs. I. Smith's and Mrs. L. Wooldridge's small group in Crawley** (5 hours).

• 110 young people cleaned six beaches in Newquay for a day and then provided a free community barbecue organised by **Love Cornwall, Newquay** (700 hours).

• A group from **Frome, Somerset**, worked with local police providing hot drinks in the town centre at night (16 hours).

• Monthly youth fishing trips for local non-Christian children. **Frome, Somerset** (40 hours).

• Car marshalling, litter picking and clear up at a music festival. Handing out sweets to students revising for exams. **Loughborough churches, students** (59 hours).

• Handing out creme eggs around school. **Gordano Christian Union, Bristol** (1 hour).

What great ways to show God's love to our communities!

CHAPTER 9

HOPE EXPLORED

AUTUMN

Steve Clifford, Evangelical Alliance

The Christian faith stands up to examination and, for many, the best way to explore faith is by means of a relaxed yet structured course which covers the key areas of our faith in an environment where questions can be asked and there is no pressure to have to agree.

Over the last few years courses such as Alpha have been a key resource in the church's outreach (over 2 million people have been through Alpha in the UK alone!). While many run all year round, September has, for a large section of the church, proved a great launch time. The summer holidays are over, Christmas is three months away, children are back at school, colleges and universities are open for business and for many it feels like the beginning of a new year. For churches engaged with HOPE-style mission, the summer has provided some great opportunities for connecting with their communities. Relationships have been built, through fun days, kids' clubs, and community projects (see Chapter 20 for loads more ideas!). September is a great time to build on these relationships and offer an invitation to explore the Christian faith.

September is also when Alpha do a huge advertising push across the country to raise the profile of the course using bill boards, cinemas, national and regional press, radio, buses and taxis to get the message across to millions. And, of course, many churches maximise on this by adding their own regional and local publicity campaigns,

> Over the last few years courses such as Alpha have been a key resource in the church's outreach.

kicking off their courses with launch parties, lunches, suppers and dinners which are a great opportunity to extend the invitation far and wide.

Of course Alpha is not the only way of developing the HOPE Explored theme. Other courses have emerged as highly successful resources, while in other settings a different approach is required. (See later for more details.)

However, three main common elements have proved effective and therefore should be included:

- A relaxed and informal atmosphere, perhaps aided by refreshments or a meal.
- An encouragement for conversation where there is no pressure to have to agree, but a genuine opportunity to engage in an exploration of the Christian faith.
- The conversations are open to all, whether they have faith or not.

Some places started an Alpha-style course for the first time during HOPE, others used it as an opportunity to build on the work they were already doing. Looking for fresh inspiration for what you could do in your town, village or city? Check out these great ideas!

A Bradford Banquet

In Bradford, the HOPE team decided to put on a high-profile event to back up what the churches were already doing in the autumn. They wanted to support churches and attract more people to courses like Alpha and Start! (see Resources) through the event so they knew they needed a big venue, some food and an interesting speaker who could deliver the goods in a non-cringy way. They were also keen to make sure that as many non-Christians were there as possible and it wasn't just a nice event for the churches!

So using their contacts at Bradford City Football Club (namely the chaplain) they negotiated for the hire of the banqueting suite on an otherwise quiet weekday evening. The hope was that the venue would appeal to people who liked football . . . or food . . . or a cheap night out . . . and especially to men. With seats for 600 they knew the club would make good money on the bar if the place was full. The food was to be prepared and served by club staff as part of the cost, leaving the team to concentrate on the rest of the evening. Bradford City's former player-turned-coach Wayne Jacobs is a Christian and agreed to share his story and, as he is really well-known in the area, it was clear he would be a draw. Comic evangelist Mark Greenwood from the Forty Three Trust (www.fortythreetrust.com) went along, too, to provide some light entertainment for the evening. Musicians were arranged to sing some familiar songs (no hymns or worship songs) as people came in and waited to be served, to help make people feel at ease.

HOPE Bradford Co-ordinator Marianne Clough said, *'The next bit of the operation was inspired – I'd like to say it was my idea but I'd be lying – we asked*

Looking for fresh inspiration for what you could do in your town, village or city? Check out these great ideas!

churches to book whole tables of ten, selling tickets as cheaply as we could at just £10 a head. It meant churches could look after the people they brought and be in charge of the seating plan etc. We stressed to them that at worst we wanted half Christians and half searchers at each table. The churches that really got the bit between their teeth were the ones who gave the responsibility to cell groups/house groups to book a table each, which definitely brought out the competitive element in some people! Some individual churches booked as many as six tables. Others just brought a few people along and ended up sharing a table with a neighbouring church. In all, more than 30 churches brought guests resulting in 57 full tables. It was a real mix of people including couples, singles, older people, ex-addicts, businessmen, members of church walking groups, passion play actors and a few people who had simply read about it in the local paper and wanted tickets.'

How did it go?

'Our speaker, Wayne, was amazing. We had not expected him to generate the warmth of support in the room that he did. He spoke between courses and one wonderful moment was seeing the serving staff (maybe 15 of them) all young people, lined up waiting to serve the dessert, all agog at Wayne's words. He had a clear testimony of how God's love had been there in the good times and the bad times. The applause for him went on for ages.

'Mark did exactly as we'd asked, too, with some great jokes, finishing up with the unforgettable line: "afford the luxury of finding out about Jesus for yourself". Wonderfully, a member of his family was in the crowd that night and gave his life to Jesus the following Sunday!

'Typical comments on the night from non-churchgoers were, "It's really made me think," "It's really nice to come along even though we don't usually go to church," and another person said that afterwards they couldn't stop thinking about what Wayne had said. One church guy told us they hadn't planned on holding a course but after chatting with their guests found there was a great demand for one!

'The downside was that it cost more than we had anticipated (hence some of the advice below) but God is good and we've been able to cover the costs thanks to some wonderful donations.'

Advice we'd give to others planning something similar:

- If at all possible, use a central venue to sell tickets and make them available on-line.
- Be ready for people to get cold feet at the last minute and also for some to decide to come at the last minute!
- Be clear about what you're doing so the guests are clear about what they are coming to.
- Have a clear cut-off point for churches to pay up, the date determined by the venue and their requirements of notice re catering.
- Make it clear churches will still pay for a full table if their guests don't come.
- Have a dedicated prayer team to cover you throughout.
- Have something ready for people to take away with them. For us, churches did their own follow up, most with courses. Each table also had a list of all the courses going on around Bradford, including those of churches not represented on the night. It was a pretty impressive list!

Make Alpha a part of your summer fun day!

Chesterfest, a group of three local charities and 22 partnership churches in Chester, decided to have a summer celebration week in July as part of their HOPE activities.

The week culminated with a free entry fun day which over 12,000 visitors attended, so they decided to have an Alpha tent and give an invitation to every person at the event to a city-wide Alpha celebration supper. The supper took place on September 25th at the Queen Hotel – a high-quality venue with good food, live music and an interesting speaker. They booked a function room that could hold 200 people and set the room for a banquet with tables of 10, each with a host.

The greatest challenge is still the need for Christians to invite and bring non-Christian friends or family.

They decided to do a table plan and encouraged people to book in and give their names so that they could allocate the tables and evenly spread the non-Christian guests with the Christians. They charged only £5 per ticket (which was a third of the actual cost for each person) to encourage more people to come. Co-ordinators said, *'Leading up to the evening was quite stressful particularly as 10 days before the event we had only secured 25 bookings! After a week of frantically ringing round our partner churches and much prayer, on the evening we had 211 guests at the event of which 50% were non-Christian! It was a great success and as a result we have over 40 people on Alpha courses running across the city, plus a number of the guests on the evening were individuals who had done an Alpha course in previous years and so we have 12 people on a follow on course.*

'It was quite an expensive evening to run, but we were blessed to have a local Christian underwrite the event financially, so this gave us some breathing space in our planning and budgeting for the evening. The greatest challenge is still the need for Christians to invite and bring non-Christian friends or family, but we did have quite a few guests, some via the link with the Chesterfest summer celebration week.'

DOES ALPHA FEEL 'OLD HAT' TO YOU?

Many of you have been involved in Alpha-type courses for years. Need some fresh inspiration? See what these groups did to bring some fresh flavour to their course for HOPE:

Be re-inspired!

In preparation for the autumn Alpha Invitation and the season of HOPE Explored, 130 delegates from 22 churches from all over Coventry and Warwickshire got together for an 'Equip and Refresh day' in May. Equip and Refresh is an Alpha conference to inspire and refresh course leaders and helpers so that they are enthused to either keep going or to start afresh. The title of the day was 'Alpha out of the Box'; new ways of doing what is old hat to many.

They now have 18 courses running in the area and a new local website www.coventryalpha.com. They found their numbers on their regional Holy Spirit away day doubled from 150 to 300! This meant having to change venue three times to accommodate the numbers – what a brilliant problem to have!

Try a new venue!

A Baptist church on the edge of Coventry has been running Alpha courses in homes and on church premises for the last 14 years. When they found the church premises were booked when they needed it, they decided to move to the local Campanile Hotel. With good food, good parking and in a well-known location, it was an easy threshold for a guest to cross who would otherwise be put off by a church or home venue. Organisers have also found that they're meeting the guests in the hotel, too, many of whom are there week-in week-out, and at least one has joined in with the course!

After asking his friends (who weren't churchgoers) where they would feel comfortable doing Alpha, Rev Vaughan Pollard from Spalding approached the local bookshop. The owner was amazed, he said, *'She'd just been at a conference where she met a Scandinavian man who was telling her all about his recent enrolment in an Alpha course. She was blown away and said, "I found out about Alpha last week and now you come and ask to come and hold it in my shop!"'*

Churches Together in Spalding also found that their acts of kindness throughout HOPE warmed people to exploring the faith. Members of local churches decided to adopt Spalding train station, tidying flower beds, hanging baskets of flowers, binning rubbish and sweeping floors. When the station manager saw Alpha posters nearby he asked if the work had anything to do with the course. The group explained the connection and to their delight the station master asked if he could attend the next course!

'I found out about Alpha last week and now you come and ask to come and hold it in my shop!'

How about using a cafe?

The team from Cafechurch network have been working hard in recent months to develop an agreement with Costa Coffee and other major coffee shops to allow a relaxed, informal evening, which includes a talk, followed by lively discussion fuelled by coffee and cake. Permissions have been granted and a support structure is in place. To find out more look at: www.cafechurch.net.

Or if a coffee shop isn't right for your area how about the local pub? A back room could be a great area for a Lyfe course!

Up your publicity!

HOPE Explored is a key part of the strategy for churches in Cambridge, with Alpha and Christianity Explored courses running right across the city. They publicised centrally with the distribution of 45,000 leaflets to every home in Cambridge and the surrounding villages!

For churches in Dinas, their social action week was a great chance to give out invitations to their Alpha celebration supper and four churches – why not have something ready to leave with people after you've served them?

OTHER GREAT IDEAS FOR HELPING PEOPLE EXPLORE CHRISTIANITY

Schools

ExploRE (based on Youth Alpha) is a 12-week programme providing an overview of the Christian Faith. It is designed to be used by teachers, youth workers and church workers who want to take the message of Jesus into schools. Leaders have the opportunity to outline what they believe and students have the opportunity to explore and discuss their own views, as well as listening to those of others. Written by experienced teachers and filled with fun activities, it fits seamlessly into the national guidelines for teaching RE at Key Stage 3 and has gained government support as part of the National Curriculum. For more details check out www.exploreforschools.co.uk. For loads more ideas for working in and blessing schools see Chapter 13.

Showstopping Holiday & Mid-week club resources from Scripture Union

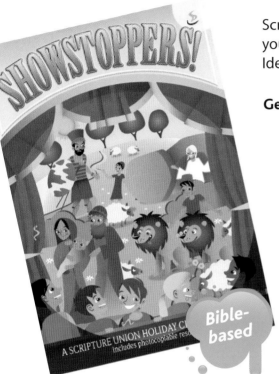

Bible-based

Scripture Union holiday and mid-week club resources will equip your church to run a complete 5-day club for children aged 5 to 11. Ideal for use with children with no church background.

Get ready to lift the curtain on the greatest show on earth!

Use performing arts to explore the stories of creation, David and Goliath, Daniel in the lions' den, Jesus' birth, and his crucifixion and resurrection, as featured in the *Must Know Stories* books. Everyone from the experienced actor to the stage-shy musician will enjoy *Showstoppers!*

The accompanying DVD will bring the Bible stories to life, and the *Showstoppers! Cast List* provides the text of the Bible stories, plus puzzles and games to give the children a take-home souvenir to help them remember *Showstoppers!* all year round.

And for the encore...

Now that the main stage has been set for God's plan for salvation it's time for the *Dress Rehearsal*. Keep in touch with all the children that attended your holiday club with this fantastic mid-week follow-on programme, which can also be used as a stand-alone club.

Explore the stories of Noah, the good Samaritan and the prodigal son from the *Must Know Stories* books which were not covered in *Showstoppers!*, together with three more stories that help children examine what it means to live God's way.

Action-packed

Prices from only £9.99
Additional downloadable materials available online

Fun-filled!

To find out more:
Visit your local Christian bookstore
Shop online www.scriptureunion.org.uk/holidayclubs
Call Scripture Union Mail Order on 0845 07 06 006 quoting 'HOPE09'

Scripture union

Youth Groups

How about getting your youth group to text or email their friends, inviting them to come for a pizza and do a Youth Alpha? It's great material for the young people of your church and a wonderful opportunity for their friends to come to Christ. For more details see www.youthalpha.org.

Workplace

For many of us the workplace is where we spend a high percentage of our lives and while the workplace these days comes in all kinds of shapes and sizes, wouldn't it be great to see short, sharp lunchtime or after work get togethers, where discussion takes place and faith can be shared? Some of the resources in the Resource section lend themselves to such a use. See Chapter 17 for more thoughts on evangelism in the workplace.

Your Street/Neighbourhood

'Loving our neighbours' comes in all kinds of shapes and sizes – a summer barbecue, mulled wine at Christmas, a chat over the garden fence or an exchange of pleasantries as you meet on the stairs. But maybe there is an opportunity for more – how about a specific invitation to explore faith – an Alpha-style course on your street or in your apartment? Book clubs or film nights are increasingly popular and provide a great opportunity to get together with friends and explore some of the big issues of life. The Bible Society's *Reel Issues* magazine might well help you discuss the faith elements of current cinema releases.

Story Telling Evening

Why not consider getting someone with a great story, which is personally relevant and glorifies God, to tell their tale (either in a home or at the pub – whatever would work best) and then with a group of friends open up the discussion and talk about it?

The motto for Back To Church Sunday is 'success is one, success is one big church'.

Back To Church Sunday

Back To Church Sunday www.backtochurch.co.uk is a simple invitational idea which began in Manchester in 2004. Since then over 70,000 people have come back to church on a single Sunday in each year because their friends invited them. But the big numbers aren't the true story. The motto for Back To Church Sunday is 'success is one, success is one big church'.

What does this mean? Well 'success is one' is about one person inviting one person. For many people evangelism seems so far away from their own lives. But this, the shortest step in evangelism, simply involves asking someone you know to something you love. And in 2008, 37,000 people did just that!

The motto 'success is one big church' is where the Back To Church vision overlaps with the HOPE vision of 'Do more, do it together . . .' Anglican, Baptist, Salvation Army, Methodist and many other churches are now part of the Back To Church family. They all aim to invite their friends on a single Sunday at the end of September, using common publicity and a common theme, so that the nation can recognise Christians as belonging to the 'one big church' of Jesus Christ. Media coverage has been fantastic because all churches work together. And the DNA of invitation becomes deeply grafted in to local churches all over the country.

HOPE and Harvest

For many churches, especially in our villages, Harvest Festival remains a key event in the church year. This fits very well with the 'invitational season' in the autumn, when the Alpha course, Back To Church Sunday and other initiatives have a high profile. So people can be invited to church at Harvest and can hear about God's invitation and also hear about God's call for a harvest of justice. This fits so well with the HOPE theme of doing more in word and action.

This holistic mission is happening at Harvest all over the country. Traditional churches find it easy and natural to use Harvest to move the mission of God forward where they are. Listen to this church in West Sussex, bringing evangelism and community outreach together with a passion to help the poor, locally and in the two-thirds world: *'Here at Lyminster we are having a Harvest Family Communion as the focus for our Back To Church Sunday. Apart from collecting goods for Worthing Churches Homeless Projects and Littlehampton Homelink we are giving our collection to our Diocesan African Appeal. (And Africa is the theme for our Harvest meal at The 6 Bells on Wednesday evening.)'*

Slum Survivor

Autumn is also a great time to get your young people looking outwards and thinking about the realities of life for people in developing countries. Soul Action have come up with a fantastic initiative called Slum Survivor where groups spend a weekend living in the slum-like conditions that one billion people face for a lifetime. See www.soulaction.org/slumsurvivor for everything you need to run one of these events.

As you can see, there are lots of ways of getting involved with HOPE Explored. Hopefully these ideas have sparked your imagination for what you could be doing in your community next September.

RESOURCES

Evangelistic Courses and Resources

1. Alpha

The Alpha course is designed for people who don't go to church and aims to bring the good news of Jesus Christ to people in a way that is relevant to them. Churches and individuals of all denominations are using the course as a way to share their faith with those around them. The courses are normally 10-weeks long with a weekend or day away in the middle. It is based around small groups of 12 people and most begin with a meal or refreshments. Each week, the talk looks at a different aspect of the Christian faith, followed by discussion in the small groups.

There are around 7,000 churches running Alpha courses in the UK, many of which are run in homes or churches, cafes or other local venues. An increasing number of courses are run by people in their workplaces, universities, residential homes, youth groups and parent and toddler groups, or are linked to social action projects and outreach activities.

For all the latest information about Alpha – news stories, up-coming events, Alpha Advisers, free advertising downloads, course registration and links to the different Alpha ministries – please see www.alphafriends.org.

Youth Alpha is specifically designed for young people between 11 and 18 years old. It is run in the same way as Alpha and aims to be friendly and fun – see www.youthalpha.org.

Student Alpha courses are based on the Alpha material but aimed at students and take place on campuses, in student houses, in churches, at pubs, in cafes and even in a McDonald's! See www.alphafriends.org/students.

Alpha in the Workplace is designed to fit into busy working schedules and so sessions tend to be shorter to fit into a lunch time or even breakfast meeting timeframe offering an opportunity for those in the workplace – of whatever type – to engage in meaningful dialogue with colleagues.
See www.alphafriends.org/workplace.

2. CaFE

Catholic Faith Exploration is a programme provided on DVD for use in parishes, schools, colleges and prisons. It's a fresh modern approach with easy-to-run courses that are fun and inspiring and will help people young and old to grow together in faith. The courses are flexible and can be adapted to suit the individual needs. A wide range of supporting material is available.

For more information see their website www.faithcafe.org.

3. Cafechurch

Cafechurch is the fresh expression of community on the high street. It brings communities into the relaxed cafe atmosphere of Costa Coffee, Gloria Jean's Coffees (and other coffee shops) to deal with issues such as stress, adoption, parenting, debt and divorce, from a faith perspective. Everyone is welcome whether a churchgoer or not.

Churches interested in running a Cafechurch in their local Costa Coffee or Gloria Jean's Coffees should go to their website www.cafechurch.net to register and attend one of their training days, which are filled with worship, teaching and workshops to equip churches to run a Cafechurch.

4. Christianity Explored

Christianity Explored is for anyone who wants to investigate Christianity informally with a group of other people. Whether you have previous experience of church, Christians and the Bible, or none at all, this course is for you. It is different from other courses as it focuses on Mark's gospel with its emphasis on who Jesus was, what his aims were and what it means to follow him. It lasts 10 weeks, including a weekend (or day) away when you can explore other areas such as the Bible, the Holy Spirit, prayer and the church. To find out more information, or if you are a leader and would like to run the course yourself go to www.christianityexplored.org where you can purchase all the materials you will need.

5. Emmaus: The Way of Faith

The Emmaus course aims to encourage non-believers to become Christians and get involved in the life of the church as well as nurture new Christians and inspire life-long discipleship. Based on the model provided by Jesus in the story of the Emmaus Road, it progresses through three stages – contact, nurture and growth. It begins, in Contact, by encouraging the vision of the local church for evangelism

> Christianity Explored is for anyone who wants to investigate Christianity informally with a group of other people.

and giving practical advice on how to develop contact with those outside the church. The full programme includes a 15-week Nurture course that covers the basics of the Christian life and four Growth books that help Christians to deepen their understanding of Christian living and discipleship. There is also a Youth Emmaus course for 11- to 16-year-olds.

For more information and to download/purchase resources see www.emmaus.org.uk.

6. Essence Course

Essence is a six-session interactive programme to stimulate a deeper spiritual life, drawing from the teachings of Jesus and the Christian mystics. It is designed for all who recognise they are on a spiritual journey and who have a desire to travel further on that journey. Written from a Christian perspective, the programme aims to encourage all fellow travellers on their pilgrimage, both within and outside the church community. The hope is that all who participate will deepen their spiritual life and come to a richer understanding of the God whose glory is revealed in a woman or man who is fully alive. To download the relevant documents go to www.emergingculture.co.uk/essence.

7. Evangelism UK

Evangelism UK serves the network of church leaders with a national role and responsibility for evangelisation in the four nations – England, Ireland, Scotland and Wales. www.evangelismuk.typepad.com.

8. Lyfe Course (Bible Society)

Lyfe is a fresh approach to getting to know the Bible better by meeting regularly in small groups in informal settings (such as a coffee shop) to discuss passages of Scripture and how they relate to everyday life. Lyfe aims to transform your life by connecting you with God and your world. It can be used by anyone, even non-Christians. To download a free copy of the Lyfe special edition welcome pack go to their website www.lyfe.org.uk which gives you all the information you need to start a group and discuss passages from the Bible. Published by the Bible Society.

9. NOOMA DVD

NOOMA uses the medium of short films on DVD, with communicators who really speak to you, to provide spiritual direction in a real and meaningful way. Each NOOMA touches on issues that we care about, and want to talk about and provokes great discussions in any group of people. See their website www.nooma.com for more information. You can buy the DVDs, published by Zondervan, from most major UK Christian bookshops and websites.

10. ReJesus

ReJesus is a website which aims to be a 'buzzy', talked about website that is a key evangelistic resource on the Internet for individuals and churches to share information about Jesus with those who have little knowledge of him. It's easy to use and enables people to find out more at their own pace. The site has five sections: the story of Jesus and his followers; explains how Jesus is alive today and how we can meet him; provides an opportunity for online discussion; has an art and poetry section; gives suggestions for prayer and reflection. For more details see www.rejesus.co.uk.

11. RUN *iMatter* DVD

Chris Stoddard, the director of the RUN (Reaching the Unchurched Network) has worked in partnership with HOPE on a ten-minute DVD called *iMatter*. It is designed to be used as a free give-away by churches, groups and individuals to those within their communities and has been priced accordingly (the more you buy, the cheaper it becomes). It is both a tool that will help open up dialogue with people who feel they may like to explore faith and an invaluable introduction to how they might develop their spiritual journey further. It asks lots of questions and explores hopes, dreams and aspirations. For more information see www.run.org.uk/R/imatter.

12. Start!

Start! is a basic six-session introduction to the Christian faith for use in small groups of 5 to 10 members with 2 leaders. It is primarily designed for people with no previous knowledge of

TEN is a DVD series which explores the relevance of the Bible's message today.

Christianity and works well with baptism families, wedding contacts, bereaved families, parents of children and teenagers, and people intending to do an Alpha course who are new to the church. The format for the sessions (which aim to be informal and enjoyable) includes the use of videos and allows time for discussion and reflection. The venue can be decided according to the nature of the group. To order a Start! pack costing £39.95 with everything you need to run the course (including a DVD, course leader's handbook and a CD-ROM) go to the CPAS website www.start-cpas.org.uk/overview.htm or ring 01926 458400.

13. Just 10 – J.John

Just 10 is a DVD series which explores the relevance of the Bible's message today. The series includes ten programmes in which J.John presents the Ten Commandments in a positive light, showing that far from being a set of rules to oppress us, they are the key to finding freedom in life. The DVD box set can be bought on the Philo Trust website www.philotrust.com and comes with a study guide which can be used at home or in cell groups, in your church or in wider partnership with other churches and organisations. It is ideal for use in an evangelistic setting, while benefiting both Christians and non-Christians alike. Authentic, £39.99.

14. Y Course

The philosophy behind the Y Course is simple – everyone has the right to encounter the good news about Jesus in a setting where they feel at home and in a way which is relevant. The Y Course is an eight-part evangelism series on DVD answering the questions on everyone's mind and focuses on Jesus rather than the church. All the course materials come in the DVD pack on CD-ROM.

The Book of Y (the revised version of *Beyond Belief*) by Peter Meadows and Joseph Steinberg forms the basis of the Y course. Authentic, DVD £29.99 and book £7.99.

CHAPTER 10

THE GIFT OF HOPE
CHRISTMAS

Andy Hawthorne, Message Trust

Most of the year it can feel as if we have to duck and dive, encourage and cajole people to have any chance of them coming through our doors and hearing the best news in the world. At Christmas time it seems they are banging down the doors! The reality is that with so much amazing work going on in communities throughout the year, and so many great relationships built, churches found their pews overflowing again in 2008 at the end of the first year of HOPE.

Christmas is also a great chance not just to invite people in to church but for churches to serve the community, helping people at a time that can often be stressful and stripped of the joy that is supposed to surround the season. Loads of churches took up the HOPE challenge and used Christmas to be imaginative, creative and bold with their plans. They made the main focus not the congregations who hear the good news week by week but the millions who come across our path this one time of the year and who desperately need to see the good news demonstrated and hear it proclaimed in language they can understand.

We want to encourage local churches to keep their foot on that gas in every corner of the British Isles as we move beyond the first year of HOPE and look to the future. See what you think about these great Christmas ideas and whether you think they could work in your community.

> Christmas is also a great chance not just to invite people in to church but for churches to serve the community.

Operation Rudolph

Who? More than 200 volunteers from churches across Watford, Hertfordshire.

What? Operation Rudolph – an initiative that has been running in Nottingam since 2002, delivering good quality Christmas hampers to disadvantaged families and individuals.

Why? As a way to bring all the churches in Watford together to do something practical to bless the community and to bring some unexpected joy and hope to those in need.

How did it work? The previous December a small group visited Operation Rudolph in Nottingham to see how it all worked and to pick up some vital tips on how to co-ordinate the project. A short DVD was made from their visit to be shown at church services from October onwards to share the vision and let people know how they could get involved. Volunteers were required to help pack the hampers as well as distribute them, and church members were also asked to sponsor a hamper for £25 (or to join together with members of their cell group to cover the cost). Goods were gathered ranging from staple foods to Christmas treats, and the 400 boxes were made up by 200 volunteers over two sessions. Each volunteer signed a card to wish the recipients a happy Christmas. The Operation Rudolph organisers contacted the local council and other organisations such as a local homeless charity to find the people who would most benefit from receiving a hamper.

The Results? Rev Chris Cottee, who led the project, said, '*It has just been amazing to see how people from so many different churches, businesses and agencies have worked together to make this happen. The atmosphere on the production line was cheerful and the comments coming back from recipients are truly inspiring. We're planning an even bigger project for next year now!*'

Erica Tuxworth, newly appointed pastor at the Woodside Church of the Nazarene said, '*The response we got from people was tremendous. They were overwhelmed, tearful and invited us in for tea and cake. One man asked who the hamper was for thinking it was being given to someone else and when we told him it was for him he said, "No one's ever given me anything before." There were genuinely lovely stories and the volunteers came back emotional and blessed themselves.*'

In Manchester two churches, Ivy Manchester and Altrincham Baptist Church independently approached The Trafford Centre to see if they could host their carol services in The Orient, their massive food court complete with large stage and video. The Centre was delighted and encouraged them to do a rolling programme of music featuring gospel choirs, hip hop music, drama, testimonies and short Christian messages on their two busiest Sundays of the year, the 14th and 21st December. Literally thousands of shoppers stopped and joined in and invitations to Alpha and free copies of *The Gift of Hope* booklet were distributed (see Resources for more details).

If we are sensitive all the evidence is shopping centres will welcome churches in and how great for

How great for the good news of Christians to be in the market place rather than behind our church walls!

the good news of Christians to be in the market place rather than behind our church walls!

In Loughborough churches took part in a Star Service run in the market place in conjunction with their local council at the start of December. A 16-foot tree was donated and there was opportunity for those who had lost loved ones to place a star with the name of their loved one on the tree as an act of remembrance. The following Sunday they took part in an International Day run by the council to celebrate the fact that the town has become a melting pot of many nations. The event, again held in the Market Place, was designed to celebrate the diversity of the church in the town in the context of Christmas. There was music from South Asia, Africa and China together with testimonies from those parts of the world about what Christmas and the Christ of Christmas means to them, as well as readings of the story of the Wise Men coming to visit Jesus in 17 different languages. It was a great opportunity for ex-pat Christians to build links with their fellow countrymen and invite them to Christmas events going on in the churches.

In Glasgow a local church sent out Bags of Hope – bags full of food and drinks – to individuals and families in various parts of the city. This was not a ministry only to the poor but a message of hope to friends, neighbours and colleagues of church members. Quality items were brought in to a storehouse ready for the bags to be filled. The colourful bags, labelled with the tagline 'Jesus adds colour to the season' were filled with the groceries then some Christmas crackers and a copy of *The Gift of Hope* (see Resources for more details).

Church members registered how many bags they would like to fill and distribute, and others donated financially so that the church could give Bags of Hope to members of the local community. Each mother at the weekly mothers and toddlers group also received a bag. In all, nearly 150 Bags of Hope were distributed and the message of hope touched many families. Here are what some had to say:

'*I couldn't believe that a Church would do something like this.*'

'When I gave one lady the bag and explained it was a free gift from the church, she began to cry and said she really needed hope this year. I cried, too.'

'Money is tight and the things in the bag were all the things I needed. It's like everything was hand-picked for me.'

At a time when many were losing jobs and were uncertain about the future, God used this initiative to help men, women and children in this community find hope in Jesus Christ.

A similiar project was run in **Birmingham** where, as one of many acts of kindness, a team of 100 volunteers from a number of local churches delivered 1,000 parcels of essential food items to the Ladywood estate which has been highlighted as 'the epicentre of child poverty in the UK'. Patricia Hoskins who co-ordinated the project said that *'Many families in Ladywood will go without at Christmas. Our aim was to make a real difference in an area of great need and give people the opportunity to do a practical act of kindness in this season of goodwill.'*

The churches also held a free outdoor community Christmas Carols evening lead by the Agape Gospel Choir, BBC West Midlands presenter Nikki Tapper switched on the Christmas lights of an 18-foot Tree of HOPE donated by the projects, and people were given the opportunity to write their hopes, dreams and prayers on cards which hung on the tree.

In Macclesfield they held a 'HOPE Christmas Wrap' in their local shopping centre and offered to wrap people's Christmas presents for free.

They also asked people if they had any prayer requests and took them to the prayer tree (not pear tree as some thought!). They received many requests for loved ones who were sick, who had just found out about having cancer, a daughter who has Parkinson's disease, and many more tragic cases.

Many ministers from the town centre came down and had a great time of fellowship and shared with the shoppers the good news.

It was a great time and there was a real sense that the conversations and prayer requests wouldn't have happened if they hadn't been wrapping Christmas gifts and giving away leaflets with the Christmas message on.

> ### Prayer Point
> In Penicuik, Midlothian, the local Tesco and Somerfield supermarkets agreed to give churches space for a prayer box during December. Dozens of prayer requests were received from young children to old people ranging from very general (war/peace, the world's financial situation, etc.) to very personal and moving requests. Existing prayer groups agreed to pray for these requests during the week and all the churches in the area got involved. The group are now planning to offer this at other times of the year, like Easter, or even on a year round basis.

In Prestwich 49 Santas, aged from 5 to 75, invaded the streets of Prestwich and Kersal in Greater Manchester one Saturday for a two-mile fun run. The event was organised by Geoff Williams from St Paul's, Kersal, and St Andrew's, Carr Clough, Prestwich. Runners were sponsored in aid of the Christian charity Barnabus which works with homeless people in Manchester city centre.

Geoff said: *'We really wanted to do something positive in this HOPE year to highlight and support the excellent work that Barnabus does with homeless men and women in Manchester. The Santa fun run was a great way to do this, to raise much needed funds and to have a lot of fun at the same time!'*

Runner and mum Ruth Saunders ran with her children, Alice, aged 7, and Jacob, aged 9, all dressed as Santa of course. She said, *'I was a bit embarrassed about being seen out in public dressed as Santa but motorists just kept beeping their car horns and waving, there were even whole busloads of passengers waving as they passed us – it turned out to be a really good laugh and the atmosphere was brilliant!'*

Rector of the parish, Rev Lisa Battye, who is always game for a laugh, happily swapped her clerical robes for a Santa suit to join the fun. She said, *'There was a real spirit of joy throughout the entire event. It was a great way of demonstrating God's love for the world, by supporting those in greatest need whilst enjoying a good laugh with friends old and new.'*

Have these ideas sparked your imagination for activities your church could be doing around Christmas? We heard lots of other great initiatives – big and small. Take a look at this list to see what could work in your area:

• Churches in Penicuik, Scotland, hired the Town Hall to do a joint carol service which they packed out with people who don't usually go to church. They used different versions of the Bible for their Scripture readings, had a sketch and a two-minute sermon given by a puppet!

• In Herne Bay, Kent, Christ Church offered mince pies to shoppers while they wrapped their presents on their behalf. Children could contribute to a nativity collage while they waited too!

• Sevenoaks Vineyard Church in Kent put on a 'Carols with Fun' night one evening a week for four weeks in the run up to Christmas. On the last evening everyone invited friends and family along and the group met on the Green with torches and had a good sing-song before returning to one member's home for refreshments.

• Churches in Uckfield did carol singing in various outdoor locations for three nights in December. They gave out helium-filled balloons with the HOPE logo on them, and leaflets with details of local church services. As a result they have been asked to sing at one of the residential homes for the elderly next Christmas.

• BCC Youth from Beverley, Yorkshire, went into all their local primary schools to deliver a Christmas assembly and then a Christmas lesson, leaving each school with a 'VeggieTales' Christmas DVD to play, too. See Chapter 13 for loads more ideas for working in schools.

• Young people from churches in Newark, Nottinghamshire, took part in practical

'When I gave one lady the bag and explained it was a free gift from the church, she began to cry and said she really needed hope this year. I cried, too.'

workshops during their autumn weekend away and then showed off their new dancing, drama and song-writing skills at a Christmas showcase for parents and friends.

• At St Martin in the Bullring, Birmingham, Christian Aid hosted an ecumenical evening inviting people to reflect on the Bethlehem of the Nativity, in contrast with the unrest that exists there now. Guests included a local school choir, the Birmingham Poet Laureate, the president of the Birmingham Organists' Association and Nader Abu Anusha – Director of YMCA Bethlehem.

• Leicestershire Churches Media Trust with local Churches Together groups and BBC local radio organised a community initiative where over 130 venues tuned in to a *Sing Christmas* broadcast. Carols were played and song sheets were available on the Internet so that everyone could sing along. Some churches held their sing-alongs in their own buildings, while others chose to do their outreach in pubs, clubs, care homes and even in a supermarket!

• Along Brighton seafront, 'Beyond Church' hosted a real-life, interactive advent calendar. On each day of December a new beach hut was opened with a different theme and an opportunity for visitors to engage with the Christmas story. This project drew to a close in spectacular fashion when around 250 people turned up to celebrate Christmas Eve.

• A homegroup from Holy Trinty Church in Boston, Lincolnshire, put on a Christmas Cheer event with mulled wine, mince pies and carols. A local coffee shop donated a basket of goodies to be raffled and overall the group raised £500 for John Fielding Special School!

• New Life Church in Woking organised a Christmas Day dinner for anyone in Woking who would otherwise be on their own on that day. A present and Christmas card conveying the significance of Christmas was given to the 70 guests, as well as to the 30 who could not come but received 'Meals-on-Wheels' on that day. The mayor and mayoress of Woking attended the event, shared in the splendid Christmas dinner and joined in the carol singing and entertainment. About 50 volunteers got involved to help cook and serve the meal as well as transport the guests.

• Kilmington Baptist Church and St Giles, Kilmington in Devon sent the 250 homes in their neighbourhood a Christmas card with a free Christmas CD (sourced for 50p each from www.beaconmusic.co.uk).

• In Lutterworth, Leicestershire, two local artists created a nativity picture, which was divided up into much smaller canvasses (A3 size) for school children to paint at a series of workshops. All the pieces were then glued together on a backdrop (18ft high by 6ft wide), and the final picture was hung from the Town Hall for all to see. It graced the Town Hall for the whole of December and well into January.

• Churches in Heathfield, East Sussex, delivered Christmas cards to every home in the area with details of their Christmas services.

• Portadown Christian Centre, Northern Ireland, received an arts grant for their youth group which they used to purchase puppets. They taught the young people how to use the puppets and then put on a well-attended nativity play for the local community.

RESOURCES

Evangelistic resources to give away

The Gift of Hope is an evangelistic booklet, written by Andy Hawthorne, exploring why Jesus is the greatest gift of hope. Available from CPO (www.cpo.org.uk), prices start at 80p for 2+ copies.

God With Us is a slim publication telling the Christmas story in the Bible's own words. Suitable to give away at services and events. There is space to write your own message or to add your church details and it can be given away as a Christmas card. See www.sgmlifewords.com/christmas.

More than a Christmas Carol, **It's a Wonderful Life, Christmas Treasures** and **What's the Point of Christmas?** are a set of mini books by by J.John's Philo Trust exploring themes of Christmas using well-known Christmas films and traditions. Authentic, £1.99 each.

More to Christmas DVDs from Viz-a-Viz come gift-wrapped and contain stories of eleven people for whom Jesus is making a real difference in their lives. At just £2 a copy this is an affordable and quality evangelistic tool, also available as a magazine for £1. See www.vizaviz.org.uk.

Events

Check it out at Christmas is a professionally produced, action-packed multimedia event ideal for 11- to 18-year-olds. Viz-a-Viz will provide speakers, hosts and a theatre group to perform as well as multimedia material for this two-hour production. An ideal opportunity to work with other churches in your area to hire a neutral venue such as a school hall or theatre. To find out more and discuss costs, contact Viz-a-Viz via their website www.vizaviz.org.uk/checkitoutatchristmas.htm or by calling 01268 530531.

General

Christmas Unwrapped DVD is a live recording of J.John speaking at Hillsong London, unpacking the true meaning of Christmas. Aimed at the unchurched but enjoyable for everyone. £9.99 from www.philotrust.com.

CPO (Christian Publishing & Outreach) produces a wide range of posters, banners, invitation cards, booklets, tracts and other outreach resources specifically themed for use at Christmas and have specific HOPE branded resources available from www.cpo.org.uk/hope. A team of outreach advisors is available on 01903 263354 to help suggest the most appropriate resources for local needs.

SGM Lifewords: creative resources for faith-centred living: SGM Lifewords is part of a global family of organisations working for the common goal that the Bible's life words are seen, heard and experienced as an essential part of everyday life. Their range of booklets, toolkits, and new media resources help tell the Bible's story and involve others in the conversation. All SGM Lifewords' materials are designed for you to use and adapt to connect life words in your own culture, in your own world, in your own way. Order, download, share ideas, and join the conversation at www.sgmlifewords.com/christmas.

www.rejesus.co.uk have many interesting and innovative Christmas specific resources such as an overview of the Christmas story, karaoke carols, nativity puzzles, prayers and meditations and a look at the Father Christmas tradition.

Publications

Christmas Wrapped Up and **More Christmas Wrapped Up** are two publications from Scripture Union that are bursting with ideas for all ages for outreach and celebration at Christmas. Visit www.scriptureunion.org.uk for more detail and to order. For resources from Scripture Union Scotland see www.suscotland.org.uk, for Scripture Union Northern Ireland see www.suni.co.uk.

Together for a Season All-age Material for Advent, Christmas and Epiphany by Gill Ambrose, Peter Craig-Wild, Diane Craven, Mary Hawes. A practical resource book full of creative ideas to transform the seasonal liturgy of Advent, Christmas and Epiphany into a multi-sensory and interactive worship experience for all ages. It includes: fully worked out services, step-by-step instructions on ways to introduce creative elements into services, and suggestions on how to use the ideas in group work, homes and outreach activities. £22.50 includes free CD-ROM from www.chpublishing.co.uk.

Cool Christmas is a booklet from J.John's Philo Trust helping children aged 3 to 6 discover what Christmas is all about. www.philotrust.com.

CHAPTER 11
REACHING YOUNG PEOPLE

Gavin Calver, Youth For Christ

For far too many young people today, God is irrelevant and church is a completely alien concept. Teenagers face a reality that often involves bullying, knife and gun crime, sexual pressure, break up of families, the strain of exams. These young people need to know hope; they need to know that God not only exists but cares about what they're going through.

We have an incredible challenge before us to reach a whole generation of young people, to help them to see that God is not only real but can make a difference in their lives. Statistics tell us that 75% of Christians make their commitment to Jesus before they are 21[1] so this is not an area we can choose to ignore without putting the future of the church into peril. The way to do it? Through other young people. The HOPE Revolution is about two things: firstly getting young people in church excited about their God and their mission field. Secondly it's about equipping them with the ideas and skills so they can reach other young people for Jesus.

Since the HOPE Revolution kicked off, we've been amazed and delighted at how many young people have signed up to say they want to be part of Jesus' Revolution (over 7,000 within the first 12 months!). Over the next few pages you'll find some inspiring stories of what they, and others, got up to, with encouraging tales of innovative – or just plain simple – ways young people and their churches found to reach out to young people in

> Young people need to know hope; they need to know that God not only exists but cares about what they're going through.

[1] P.Brierley, *Reaching & Keeping Teenagers: Report of the Evangelical Alliance Commission on Evangelism* (London: Scripture Union, 1968)

their area. Be inspired and think creatively about what you could be doing in your neighbourhood in the years to come!

The HOPE Revolution Website

The Revolution has a dedicated youth site (www.hope-revolution.com) that provides resources, material and inspiration to young people. It's an interactive site where HOPE Revolutionaries can submit what's going on in their part of the country through the 'My Area' section of the site, as well as getting Weekly Challenges emailed from the HOPE team that focus on the key aspects of the Revolution: 'Change Me, Change My Friends, Change My Community and Change My World'. Multimedia testimonies, Bible studies and other features all seek to encourage, equip and inspire Revolutionaries to stay in touch and these have been well used. Over 1200 young people have signed up for the weekly updates giving challenges, encouragement and stories via email.

Additionally, thousands of young people have been socially networked through a Facebook profile and group (1700+), a MySpace profile (720+), YouTube stream (750+ channel views) and Bebo account (120+) to promote and share events to draw young people back to the main site as a vehicle for information sharing.

What teenagers have said about the HOPE Revolution . . .

'HOPE Revolution, I salute you! This is awesome stuff! You've inspired my Christian Union . . . We have trebled in size this year and hope for even more in the coming year. Keep up the good work!' John, 15

'The HOPE Revolution day in Sheffield was awesome. I went and had one of the best days ever. I will now live differently in every way!' Rachel, 14

'This year I shared the gospel with some of my mates on msn. It wasn't as scary as I thought it would be and one of them even became a Christian. He came to New Wine with me this summer.' Paul, 16

'I would like the project we ran as part of HOPE Revolution to happen again because it's made a huge difference in my area and three of my friends became Christians and loads of people saw God's work in action through us. Can you ask for much more?' Sarah, 15

'Last summer we went as a small group from our church to Soul Survivor for the first time, there were about 15 of us max. This year we took a coach.' Ethan, 16

'On the last day of our HOPE Revolution mission eight of my friends became Christians and loads of other people became Christians too. It was awesome!' Lizzie, 17

What else have HOPE Revolutionaries been up to? Here are just some of the stories we heard . . .

Hungry to help others

HOPE Revolutionaries at Cottingham Road Baptist Church, Hull, decided to fast for 24 hours to raise money for essentials for the Hull Homeless and Rootless project. The aim was to raise £400 but they raised a massive £750 which they donated to this charity who were, quite understandably, bowled over. The young people involved commented that the fast was a way of them empathising and trying to understand something of the every day conditions and struggles of homeless people.

> 'The HOPE Revolution day in Sheffield was awesome. I went and had one of the best days ever.'

> 'On the last day of our HOPE Revolution mission eight of my friends became Christians.'

Crowthorne, Berkshire

Before they began youth outreach in their local area, members of churches in Crowthorne, Berkshire, went into the schools and ran assemblies for each year group by way of introduction, so that when they went out on the streets in their bright red 'HOPE Youth Team' hoodies, everyone would already know who they were, and what they were about. They said their work has given them real opportunity to develop authentic relationships amongst the 'hard to reach' youth and that the project has the full support of their local police.

A Great Start to the Year

A number of churches in Bradford realised that if they wanted to put on a really credible event for young people, the best thing to do was to work together and pool their resources.

What did it look like? The first of these HOPE Revolution evenings took place back in January, and saw more than 200 young people gathered downstairs in Bradford University's student nightclub. These young people were all from churches across the city including St John's Great Horton, Buttershaw Baptist, New Life Christian Centre and Abundant Life. There was a guest speaker, live hip hop tunes and powerful, hard-hitting, upfront testimonies from the band 29th Chapter. This was just the first of many youth events organised throughout Bradford alongside many other church and community social action projects taking place under the banner of HOPE Bradford.

But why? Working together allowed the churches to put on bigger, better and much more relevant events than they could do working alone. Local Baptist minister Stuart Gregg said that, 'The event came from a greater desire to see more co-ordinated, impactful youth work, especially in the south side of Bradford. We knew that we didn't need to rely on the nearby cities of Manchester, Liverpool and Leeds to put on big events for us; by working together we had enough resources to host something locally.'

The outcome

Local vicar Nick Jones said, *'Until now, there hasn't been an opportunity for Christian young people to come together and bring their friends for a fantastic night where they'll also hear the gospel. We were thrilled to take nearly 30 people – most of them totally unchurched – to HOPE Revolution. They were well up for the message and the challenge of becoming revolutionaries. Seven responded and became Christians, and we are setting up a nurture cell for them; praise God! We want to see our city turned around and, with the help of the Holy Spirit, it's our young revolutionaries who are going to do it.'*

He continued, *'It was also immensely encouraging to see many young people symbolically stand up that evening, declaring their desire to be revolutionaries living "all-out" for Jesus. There was an opportunity for young people to receive group prayer afterwards, to unpack the evening's teaching and reiterate the "DNA" of a revolutionary: God changing and using them to articulate their own stories of faith; to talk, listen and pray for their peers, and through personal testimony, courageous witness and creative mission, carry the hope of God's story throughout the year of HOPE and beyond.'*

Top tips for if you'd like to do something similar:

- Work with other churches in order to pool resources, budget and foster ownership.
- Plan well in advance for an event of this size.
- Pick a venue that's neutral and where young people feel comfortable, such as a nightclub or sports hall.
- Underpin everything in regular prayer.

Newmarket

A group of young Christians in Newmarket made the local papers when they decided to run a series of events for local sheltered-housing residents in Mildenhall. Organising tea and coffee mornings with 'sing-alongs' to 1940s music, these young people made an impact not only on the residents, but also in getting alongside local people and being an active presence in changing their communities.

> Work with other churches in order to pool resources, budget and foster ownership.

They also took part in a 'litter and leaf' clean-up in the local park. Local spokesperson, Alison Reid, commented: *'The youngsters really enjoyed themselves. Not only did they learn from the residents, they also got to mix with other young people. The older generation really appreciated it and it showed them young people in a positive light.'*

HOPE in the Park

Young people often hang around the park in Horsforth near Leeds, so local Christians decided to make this a focus of their summer's activity. A group of adults and young people ran lots of activities including sports, games and craft, all on a youth bus, with an additional tuck shop, prayer tent and sumo wrestling. Young people from the team went to the skate park and showed off their BMX skills and had fantastic conversations about their faith in Jesus. At the end of each afternoon the young people boldly shared their own story of why God was important in their lives. Dave, 17, said, *'It was good to show young people that we weren't the stereotypical "geeky Christians". We had great opportunities to get talking to people and even managed to talk to some of the "big hard" lads about God. One woman didn't think she'd be welcomed at church but thought differently after she had met the people from the local churches.'*

A Banquet of HOPE

In an event designed to bring together youth from right across the local churches Kingston YFC's Oxygen project helped host a HOPE Revolution banquet. The young people got the chance to dress up in posh frocks and suits, and enjoy a bit of a fun, formal, glitz 'n' glamour for a night centred on the theme of hope. As well as the speaker's challenge to the HOPE Revolutionaries, each table was named after someone that had themselves changed the world for Jesus such as Martin Luther King, Edith Cavell and William Wilberforce.

Oxygen director, Richard James, summed up the evening: *'We were really encouraged by these young Revolutionaries' reaction to the evening, with around a quarter of those who were there responding positively*

to the evening's closing challenge. It was a memorable evening, not just in being a great event, but because it has definitely sown the seed and inspired many young people to give their all in living for Jesus this year and beyond.'

Prayer Point

24-7 Prayer is a great way to get young people excited about the power of prayer. Visit www.uk.24-7prayer.com to find out more information about how to run Boiler Rooms and 24-7 Prayer event.

Taking HOPE to Nottingham

Five days of community mission saw around 50 university students from Nottingham join up with The Family Church to help decorate the premises of the Asian Women's Project and a local shop. They cleared rubbish, visited and created activities for residents in an assisted-living home, supported the tidying of city allotments and local government rubbish clearing initiatives. They also supported The Family Church's 'Sports Challenge' for local un-churched kids who are 'challenged and encouraged to build character', plus another local church's holiday club for children. In addition, they set up a website and PowerPoint for a school in the Philippines, and visited a young offenders institute amongst other activities. All within five days! The mission was motivated by a desire to offer hope through acts of kindness. The students financed themselves and gave up their free time to support the HOPE Mission. Here's just a few comments made by those involved:

A Young Offenders Institute inmate:
'I was just sat there wishing someone would come – I can't make sense of the fact that my mate committed suicide two days ago. Then your friends turned up and offered to pray for me . . .'

'I was impressed by the attitude of the students and appreciative of the practical help they had been able to give.'

The Chief Executive of the Asian Women's Project:
'I was impressed by the attitude of the students and appreciative of the practical help they had been able to give.'

An Allotment Committee member:
'Thanks to all the volunteers and The Family Church team for their input . . . Great people, and we recognise, even if some of us are hairy (or shaven-headed) heathens, why they wanted to demonstrate their faith in a practical and tangible fashion. I think they succeeded!'

Shackles off

In the Cumbrian coastal village of Seascale, HOPE advocate Lyn Edwards is working towards fulfilling a dream: *'In my dream I saw a cafe full of young people chatting – young people who had formerly been "chained and burdened" on the streets of the village. The cafe was called Shackles Off.'* Whilst plans are underway to turn a shop into this cafe and drop-in centre, Lyn has teamed up with two friends, to turn a Citroen Picasso into a 'HOPE Mobile'. They've stacked it with snacks and use it to get around so they can build good relationships with local teenagers who told them they didn't have anywhere to go or anything to do. Lyn's aim is to provide a place where they can come and find 'security, purpose, fulfilment and a God who loves them' and alongside plans for the drop-in centre is working on developing a facility to help young people get access to education, training and employment. The Rev Philip Peacock says that the level of support for the project is very high, and that *'this is a positive fruit of HOPE that will extend beyond this year'*.

Resonate Youth (part of Riverside Church, Exeter) took a great step to loving their global neighbours by sponsoring a child through the Christian charity Compassion. Their sponsored girl is called Shabnam, who lives in India and is as old as the youngest members of the youth group so that they could, year by year, grow up with her.

The young people raise funds for the sponsorship through a range of activities including the 'Jar of Shabnam' which appears at all their weekly youth programmes so people can drop in spare change and pocket money. They usually exceed the sponsorship costs which means they can then send a little extra to Shabnam on her birthday and at Christmas. A sponsored 'Slum Survivor' event (see Chapter 9 for more details) which raised £800 meant they could buy a new roof for Shabnam's family home!

The group receive regular letters from Shabnam, and they respond, too, with letters and photos of their own. Finding out more about Shabnam's life and family situation has had a real impact on all of the group. They said, *'Having regular contact with a young person in a different culture to your own has a really positive impact, and certainly extends our global awareness. It also gives us a personal perspective into the challenges faced by others around the world.'*

If you'd like to get your youth group sponsoring a child visit www.compassionuk.org or call 01932 836490.

'Having regular contact with a young person in a different culture to your own has a really positive impact.'

We've heard about many other great ideas that have taken place, including these listed here. Which do you think might work in your village, town or city?

• The streets of Peterborough were invaded by 80 young people engaging in social action and evangelism projects after having worship, workshops and seminars each morning. Each evening they invited people to come to their club called The Zone where the gospel was presented and many young people gave their lives to Jesus. The following week a gig was held and another 30 young people became Christians!

• Warfield churches got local non-churched young people involved in a 'Battle of the Bands' competition. Eight bands performed in the

preliminary rounds and then a final was held at their summer HOPE in the Park day. See Chapter 20 for more details.

• Churches and the County Council in Billericay got together to kick off a weekend of social action by turning a town centre church into a nightclub for young people with an MC, a non-alcoholic bar, and breakdancers who shared their testimony.

• In Littlehampton young people took a day out of their camp to do a day of mission and evangelism in the town. One group went to an elderly people's home, one group did Random Acts of Kindness and others looked for specific opportunities to tell people about God. Between them they helped out in shops, did some busking, prayed for people and gave out flowers.

• After conducting some research, Christians in Aylesbury set up six youth cafes and have seen a massive decrease in anti-social behaviour as a result.

• Around 23 teenagers from Prestbury Methodist Church, Bollington Air Cadets and St. Peter's at Prestbury, got stuck in and cleaned rubbish out of the Prestbury River one day over the summer. They cleaned out loads of rubbish including a wheelbarrow, an estate agent's board, road signs, and much more!

• A Friday night cafe for young people was started by churches in Chatteris, funded by Chatteris Action For Youth with gifts of cakes, drinks, etc. from church members. There are games, magazines, music, jewellery-making kits and nail-painting goodies for the young people to enjoy.

• The young people of Knightswood Congregational Church spent seven days making over an old cloakroom at Bankhead Primary School, turning it into a library area. They then helped Yoker Primary School by painting their assembly hall.

The first year of HOPE has been truly amazing, yet it really is just the start.

Or how about . . .

• Using sports as a way to reach young people? See Chapter 19 for loads of ideas and resources.

• Reaching young people through schools? See Chapter 13 for everything you need to get you started!

• Getting your young people involved in social action projects such as The Noise over the May Bank Holiday weekend? See Chapter 8.

HOPE for the future

The first year of HOPE has been truly amazing, yet it really is just the start. This is all HOPE and the HOPE Revolution were ever intended to be: the start of something big.

Many have had their minds employed, their skills used, their faith stretched, their wallets emptied and their energy sapped during the course of the HOPE Revolution. We think most would agree, though, that their hearts have been changed. They've seen what just a bit of time, effort and commitment can do for a community, when it's done in love and done in Jesus' name. In short, they've been changed as they've sought to bring change to this nation.

And it certainly doesn't stop here. The HOPE Revolution is living on.

Let's be motivated by what we've seen is achievable in just a year. Let's celebrate this amazing first year of HOPE but be ready to move on with lessons learned, faith deepened and renewed purpose, as we shine like stars in the universe, holding out the word of life. But whatever we do let's not stop. Point every teenage Christian that you know towards www.hope-revolution.com. Let it be known that this mission is ongoing, and pray for the Christian young people of Britain that by the grace of God the revolution that we all so desperately need, could one day transform our nation.

RESOURCES

Alove works with young people (primarily aged 12–25), youth workers and youth focused services within and external to The Salvation Army. They put on events, provide training opportunities and their website provides access to cell notes, music, podcasts, book reviews and resource packs. www.salvationarmy.org.uk/alove.

Disappointed with Jesus?: Why do so many young people give up on God? by Gavin Calver. The book outlines many of the issues and suggests ways of reaching teenagers in new ways. Monarch, £6.99.

Fort Rocky is an incredible activity weekend with a clear gospel message for those aged 11–14. For further information go to www.yfc.co.uk/residentials/fortrocky.

Visit **www.hope-revolution.com** which is packed with resources, ideas and inspiration for young people.

For your young people who are Christians there are some great tailor made Bible resources such as the ***Mettle Bible Reading Notes*** at www.cwr.org.uk and ***Word 4 U 2day*** www.ucb.co.uk.

Romance Academy work with youth workers to set up programmes that support and mentor young people, helping to build self-esteem and think through sexual health issues. Find out more at www.romanceacademy.org.

Don't miss out on the opportunity to take your Christian and non-Christian young people to the **Soul Survivor** events over the summer. They are an incredible opportunity to gather with thousands of other teenagers and youth leaders for a unique week of worship, fun and challenge. See www.soulsurvivor.com/uk for more details and to book.

Don't miss out on the opportunity to take your Christian and non-Christian young people to the Soul Survivor events over the summer.

Urban Saints offer many resources on their website http://web.energize.uk.net for groups between the ages of 5 and 18. They also provide training for youth leaders, including free one-day training sessions.

A key resource for reaching young people is **Youth Alpha**. It fits into one term's worth of activity and covers all of the basics of the Christian faith. For details visit www.youthalpha.org.

Youth For Christ offer many resources for reaching young people – check out www.yfc.co.uk/resources including *Rock Solid* (11–14s outreach), RS2 (11–14s discipleship) and *Mettle* (14–18s outreach and discipleship).

CHAPTER 12

WORKING WITH CHILDREN AND FAMILIES

Sarah Bingham and Ro Willoughby, Scripture Union

One stunning global statistic is that 60–80% of responses to the gospel come from those under 18. Statistics show that adults rarely come to faith unless they have significant exposure to the gospel in their childhood. This is a really serious challenge to the church to ensure that the gospel is lived out in the full view of children and young people, accompanied by effective discipleship. Of course, every child is in a family, in some shape or form. So when working with children, it is vital to remember this, respecting the cultural and faith expectations within their family.

Working with children and families must be a top priority for us as the church because every child in this generation needs to hear just how much God loves them. Failure to do so will have long-term effects for the future of our world and of Christ's body. The challenge we're facing today is to make sure that children see and hear the gospel in ways they can understand, in and out of church, in schools, in the community and in the home. The faith of those children who are followers of Jesus needs careful nurture which includes supporting parents to pass their faith onto their children.

> One stunning global statistic is that 60–80% of responses to the gospel come from those under 18.

Uniting in hope . . .

Where? Nottingham.

How? Clare Whittaker, a children's worker at St Nicholas Church, Nottingham, told us how she got involved with ministering to children through HOPE: *'For a while I'd had on my heart the idea of doing regular big Christian children's events in Nottingham, to draw together children from churches across the city. I also wanted to get to know the other children's workers in the city and to start a network of support and encouragement. HOPE gave the perfect catalyst for those ideas! We ended up with a group of seven children's workers meeting together to put on a children's event under the HOPE banner. We decided to call the event "Unite" as our purpose was threefold: to unite children with God, to unite Christian children, and to unite as churches as we worked together.*

'The event took place on a Saturday evening in June. Hundreds of children came together from different sized churches from across the city and they brought their friends. It also brought together an amazing team of Christians, all passionate about children's work. HOPE has been a fantastic catalyst for future activities. We continue to meet together as a core team to support and encourage one another but also to plan for the coming year and future Unite events. HOPE was just what we needed to get the ball rolling.'

Why? Children in church can feel isolated, especially if they do not have many (or any!) other Christians they know at school. They can feel embarrassed about inviting friends to a regular

Sunday event, especially if services aren't child-friendly.

Putting on city/town/borough/rural network focused events allows a number of things to happen:

- A wider team base offers more skills and talents and thus a wider potential range of activities.
- Having a team to plan events takes the pressure off individuals.
- A higher level of funding from several churches enables the purchase of 'big equipment'.
- Children are able to meet other Christians from their own and other schools and can link up with them.
- Children have a great event to invite friends to.

Potentially, this type of event could lead to spin off family events that will network churched and un-churched families in a safe, fun, relaxed environment.

What? The events are run every two months for anyone who is 7–11 years old. Everyone has lots of fun whilst learning more about God, such fun that children often invite friends to come, too. Each event combines silly games, live music with a great band, videos, creative prayer, craft/construction, drama, Bible stories and lots more!

Can I do one? Scripture Union is working with partner churches across England and Wales to develop children's events similar to the Unite event in Nottingham. They go under the banner of 'X:Site', that is, 'the place of the cross'. To find information on this type of event and to see if you can get one happening near you visit www.xsiteuk.org.

The outcome

- A public united service to children and families from a group of churches.
- Better relationships between churches.
- Children discover they are not alone.

Top tips

- Make sure all the team clearly know their role, but be flexible!
- Ensure all churches have agreed a CRB/CP policy beforehand.

> Children are able to meet other Christians from their own and other schools and can link up with them.

- Share out leadership around different churches.
- Prompt all churches to pray in advance, as well as on the day.
- Make sure the team have fun!

Spring Lambs

St Mary's Church in Haughton Green (Tameside) had been running a parent and toddler group called Little Lambs for a couple of years but a few of the mums were concerned that they and their children were not exercising enough. With all the media coverage about obese children, the church decided that a parent and toddler exercise group would be a healthy addition to the parent and toddler format!

One of the team members studied for a qualification to be able to lead and plan sports activities and for HOPE the new, one-hour session was launched. With half an hour of free play, then a themed exercise session e.g. Noah's Ark or Going to the Circus, it involves a lot of fun, singing, imagination and puppets to talk to the children about healthy eating. At the end, healthy snacks are offered and everyone goes home energised, happy and hopefully a little bit healthier!

Holiday Bible Club

Otley 'Churches Together' used HOPE as an opportunity to build on the success of their monthly children's event by running a holiday Bible club called Champions. Held over four afternoons in the local primary school, the club included singing, puppets, games, crafts and refreshments as well as a Bible story, and was attended by around 70 children. The team said, *'Champions was good for the children as they had masses of fun and were gently introduced to Jesus; good for the community as it brought people from all over together; good for the team as we saw our faith grow and were pushed out of our comfort zones; good for the churches as relationships were built and vision for the future shared.'* Ele Booth from the team added, *'There were two children I met who thought church was dull and boring so it was great to show them that being a Christian can be fun . . . they even said they would be willing to give church a try now!'*

Thinking about reaching children through schools work? See Chapter 13 for loads of ideas!

Christmas make and do . . .

Where? West Silvertown, Newham.

What? In Advent, leading up to the first year of HOPE, a community project worker, supported by volunteers from Royal Docks Community Church, ran a series of Saturday events aimed at families. During the sessions there were opportunities to make Christmas crafts or small gifts, to play team games and to socialise over drinks and snacks.

Why? The aims were to give families positive things to do together and help with social mixing within the housing estate where the hall is located. Additionally, parents and children could learn new skills together and make quality gifts to give to each other, friends and family. There were many chances to discuss Christmas and 'the reason for the season'.

How? Use a local hall (community building, school or church) providing free or subsidised materials, refreshments and sports equipment. The team of volunteers needs to be well prepared, although as parents are coming numbers are not limited by the team size. A rough timetable should be planned with flexibility for people to finish crafts without rushing. Advertising should be targeted to those you most wish to attract either by delivery method (via primary school, leaflet drops or posters in public places) or by the style of invitation you design.

The outcome

Families were:

• Able to hear about the meaning of Christmas from Christians.

• Given positive ways to interact.

• Made to feel welcome and wanted.

• Invited to church Christmas celebrations like carol services.

• Able to make things together.

Top tips

• Choose crafts that children can do well, if given a little help.

> Families were able to hear about the meaning of Christmas from Christians.

• Use good quality materials.

• Use the craft skills of your volunteers.

• Build a team from several churches if doing this on a town-wide basis.

• Don't force conversations about faith, let them come up naturally.

• Ensure people are praying for the event(s).

FAMILY FRIENDLY AUDIT

Want to explore family ministry in your church? Try doing an audit like the one offered by Scripture Union which will help you work out where your church is currently at in terms of the number of families it comes into contact with and the services it offers to them, as well as thinking ahead to what you could provide in the future. See the Families section of the Scripture Union website for more details or contact families@scriptureunion.org.uk.

Other great ideas to try in your village, town or city . . .

• See Chapter 15 which has lots of courses that are suitable for parents and families.

• Budding Musicians – percussion, singing and stories with toddlers has been successfully run in a number of places in North Devon.

• When she offered to tell Bible stories at her local pre-school and nursery, Alison Dayer from Bedfordshire found she was welcomed with open arms.

• Run a holiday club to include at least one family night and build a families' programme around that. A church in Littlehampton is developing this idea. Other churches have incorporated a parent drop-in once a month to their midweek club after school or have run an evening midweek club with a monthly family night.

• Do a 'dads and sons' or 'mums and daughters' weekend – or be radical and do 'dads and daughters' or 'mums and sons'! River Church in Canning Town ran an all male version in the summer. If your group is too small, Care for the Family regularly run this type of event. www.careforthefamily.org.uk.

• Organise a picnic in a local beauty spot or park and provide rounders, frisbee, etc. In Cornwall, covenanters groups were invited (with family and friends) to a picnic on a farm and had a scarecrow competition. This could easily be adapted for town or suburban situations.

• A number of churches in Shepton Mallet, Somerset, worked together to organise a local sports day with silly and serious sports and family team games.

• Put on a regular 'family entertainment night' – this might be films, games, challenges, quizzes, whatever your imagination comes up with. In Littlehampton this has included a quiz, Christmas party, picnic and games on the Green. They also involve parents in the holiday club (see above).

• Develop cross-age specialist clubs such as drama, chess or knitting – using the skills of your congregation. Kevin Moore in East Anglia has developed a number of successful chess clubs which cater for all ages.

• Organise a coach trip to somewhere unexpected – very popular in places where families cannot afford holidays. Royal Docks Community Church are organising seaside trips though numbers do not yet require a coach!

> Organise a coach trip to somewhere unexpected – very popular in places where families cannot afford holidays.

RESOURCES

Born for Such a Time as This by Daphne Kirk powerfully addresses the need for us to equip children and young people for mission and evangelism. Kevin Mayhew, £6.99.

Core Skills for Children's Work by Steve Pearce. A practical and creative course to provide training for children's workers through six foundational modules. Barnabas, £12.99.

Detonate by Mark Griffiths. Ideal for use with unchurched kids, *Detonate* is designed to teach, convert and reach a new generation for Christ. Includes over 100 games; 52 unique stories and 52 Bible lessons. Monarch, £19.99.

Fusion: A Year's worth of teaching 5–12s by Mark Griffiths. Fifty-two weeks of teaching materials for local churches who want to reach the vast majority of 5- to 12-year-olds who currently have no contact with church. Monarch £19.99.

50 Five Minute Stories by Lynda Neilands. Fresh ideas, parables, true stories, once-upon-a-time stories communicating values and ideas in a palatable, non-threatening way. Kingsway, £8.99.

100 Instant Children's Talks by Sue Relf. This book provides 100 ideas for talks that are easily altered in order to make them suitable for the age and background of the children and the situation in which the talk is to be given. Kingsway, £8.99.

Let's Grow by Daphne Kirk is an eight-unit foundation course for discipling children. It takes child and adult together through the fundamentals of the Christian faith. Kevin Mayhew, £29.99.

Messy Church by Lucy Moore. Overflowing with creative ideas to draw the community together for fun, food, fellowship and worship, this resource book contains 15 themed programme outlines. Each outline has ideas for creative art and craft activities, meal plans and recipes for eating together and family-friendly worship. BRF, £8.99.

Parable Fun for Little Ones by Renita Boyle. Explore Jesus' parables with under 5s, using these 10 sessions of pick-and-mix stories and activities. Includes stories, songs, crafts, games and role play. Barnabas, £11.99.

Scripture Union's midweek club and **holiday club** resources are easy-to-use programmes for children aged 5 to 11, many with an accompanying DVD and linked to a holiday club resource. They are for use with churched or non-churched children in midweek clubs, special events or as a follow-up programme. Every midweek club programme is packed with ideas for games, listening to the Bible, relationship building, prayer, craft, small-group discussion and lots more! See www.scriptureunion.org.uk for more details.

The **Top Tips** series, from Scripture Union, which includes *Top Tips on Welcoming Children of Other Faiths* or *Growing Faith with Families* (£2.99) are 32 pages of distilled wisdom tackling contemporary issues. They are pitched mainly for those working with children or young people, but would also benefit parents and pastors.

Other organisations that may help

Arise is a joint initiative between Viz-a-Viz Ministries and The Girls' Brigade England & Wales that is helping churches to reach out to children in their community. Their website gives details about activities and events and provides resources, ideas and support to equip you as you minister to children – www.ariseministries.org.uk.

Barnabas Bible Reading Fellowship (BRF) seek to find new ways to engage people of all ages with the Bible, both inside and beyond the church, through publishing, training and quiet days. Their website offers some helpful resources for schools work – see www.barnabasinschools.org.uk.

Children Worldwide is a growing, pan-denominational membership organisation of independent children's workers with a vision to train, disciple and encourage children to be enthusiastic about starting and developing a personal relationship with God through Jesus, and enable them to become an effective part of the church. www.childrenworldwide.co.uk.

Dave Godfrey offers a variety of sessions to challenge, encourage and equip children's workers in their ministry. Dave is also available to lead praise parties which incorporate music, drama, puppets and game shows to communicate the good news of Jesus in a visual, interactive and child-friendly way – www.omegazone.org.uk.

Organise a picnic in a local beauty spot or park.

Doug Horley is available for conferences, praise parties, church weekends, Sunday services and other events for action songs, dance tracks, tricks, illusions, puppets, praise and worship all geared towards kids and families – www.duggiedugdug.co.uk.

www.familyministry.co.uk is a website with three separate areas for family ministry, children's ministry (0–13) and teens ministry, filled with information and resources to inspire and equip those involved in evangelism, discipling and teaching in these areas.

Urban Saints is passionate about working with children and young people who have no church connection, helping them to realise their full God-given potential as they journey from childhood to adulthood. They hold weekly youth groups, special events, holidays, community projects and training programmes for young people aged 5–18. Their website provides details about their Energize package which, from £17 per month, provides Internet access to teaching and activity ideas for youth and children's groups, free access to their events and ongoing advice and training to help you run your group effectively. www.urbansaints.org.

CHAPTER 13
HOPE IN SCHOOLS AND UNIVERSITIES

Dave Newton, Youth For Christ (Schools) and Rich Wilson, Fusion (Universities)

HOPE IN SCHOOLS

If you're looking to connect with young people in your community then one of the most obvious places to start is your local school – after all, that's where they spend most of their time! Teachers and schools are often over-stretched and under-resourced meaning there are a great multitude of ways we can be good news to our community by serving them and offering a helping hand.

Community Cohesion is the phrase buzzing around schools at the moment, which means a desire to see schools pivotal and influential in the life of a community, so schools are actively seeking ways to engage with the communities to which they belong. As churches we have the privilege and opportunity to serve and invest in the lives of young people to see boundaries broken down, stereotypes challenged and potential reached.

We heard about loads of churches that were inspired by HOPE to get stuck in at their local schools and made a big impact. Read some of their stories over the next few pages and you can see that no matter how much time you have or what your skills are, there's probably a way you can bless your local school!

Hopes and dreams

Walsworth Road Baptist Church in Hitchin, Hertfordshire, asked children in five local primary schools to enter a competition to express their hopes and dreams in a piece of art work. The church promised to display every single piece produced in their building – a promise they kept even after they received over five hundred entries!

The exhibition made waves beyond the school community with over a thousand people coming to view the artwork. The three judges were an art shop owner and two local artists who were absolutely bowled over by the exhibition and the response to the competition. *'It was a great experience,'* said Andrew Henton Pusey, minister of Walsworth Road Baptist Church, *'and one really enjoyed by the schools and by the wider community too.'*

Singing HOPE

In a project run from the Liverpool Lighthouse by Love and Joy Ministries, young people from many schools across the city were united in a mass gospel choir, culminating in a spectacular event in the Liverpool Metropolitan Cathedral.

Some lessons when engaging with schools . . .

Participation – Look for ways to get young people involved and give them a chance to display their hard work and achievements in a way that impacts the wider community.

Partnerships – Don't assume partnerships with school begin overnight. Look for simple and authentic ways to engage with your school, some projects may stay small, others will grow year on year.

Presence – Involvement in your local schools shouldn't be hit and run. If it is a short-term project make it clear to the school from the start.

Painting, gardening and more!

Who? HOPE team from Crowthorne alongside Vineyard church members.

What? Helping out in schools by painting and gardening.

How did it work? When the HOPE Crowthorne team contacted their local school to offer to help, a very grateful headmaster, Bob Elsey, asked if they would help the Parent Teacher's Association (PTA) prepare and paint one of the science blocks. With help from the local Vineyard church who meet in the school, the HOPE team got stuck in and the headmaster estimated that their three hours' work saved the school a massive £2000! Mr Elsey said, *'Friends of ours from the Wokingham and Vineyard church and HOPE have really helped to bolster our numbers and our spirits by coming along to work alongside us. I know I speak for all of us when I say how much we appreciate their support.'*

Look for ways to get young people involved and give them a chance to display their hard work and achievements in a way that impacts the wider community.

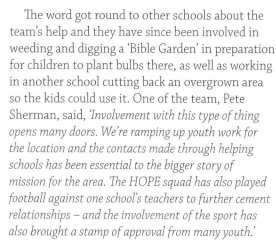

The word got round to other schools about the team's help and they have since been involved in weeding and digging a 'Bible Garden' in preparation for children to plant bulbs there, as well as working in another school cutting back an overgrown area so the kids could use it. One of the team, Pete Sherman, said, *'Involvement with this type of thing opens many doors. We're ramping up youth work for the location and the contacts made through helping schools has been essential to the bigger story of mission for the area. The HOPE squad has also played football against one school's teachers to further cement relationships – and the involvement of the sport has also brought a stamp of approval from many youth.'*

Lessons learned

• PTAs are screaming out for participation in this type of activity so contact either the PTA chair or the head teacher to offer your services.

• Have a 'tell us what to do and we'll do it' approach.

• Working together with the teachers and governors is a great chance to build relationships and to ask them about other ways you can help out the school.

• Bring some tools for the job.

• Have someone ready to do a trip to the rubbish dump at the end of the session.

• Once you've got involved, you'll find you're invited back again and again!

Top tips

• The local press love to cover this type of thing, so it's worth getting the PTA to invite them along, or suggest that you'll do it instead. HOPE T-shirts are great for the photos and be ready to explain why you're doing it – if you think it through in advance you can deliver a 'sound byte' type reason to make it a little slicker. See Chapter 22 for more media suggestions.

• Bring some food with you; it's a great excuse to get all the family helping out and never hurts to have a little bribe for volunteers!

Look for ways that your church can organise or sponsor activities to bring life and hope into your local school. Find out what is already going on and look for ways or people who can enhance it, offer support, advice or an extra pair of hands.

Take a lesson: More and more schools are being forced to provide a high range of curricular activities for all pupils but don't always have the specialist staff to deliver it. What specialism do you have? Can you give an hour a day or a week to help out in your local school? Whether it's RE, Geography or PE, an expert in the field is often welcome in any school. Find out who is already involved in your local school and seek to work with them and support them. If there is no obvious involvement, approach the school via a teacher you know or a letter to the head of the department you are keen to work with.

Book a team: Lots of organisations offer teams who could come and add impact to your current schools programme – see Resources for some ideas. A team could visit for one day or for a whole week, working with you to arrange a full timetable of activities including assemblies, lunch clubs and after school clubs. To make sure this isn't a 'hit and run' activity, it's best to have a local team who are able to follow up after the event by running a drop-in club or a discipleship course.

Start a club: The extended schools programme has increased opportunities to run after school, lunchtime and holiday clubs for all ages. Looking for ideas/material? Check out The Crux 'YFC's Extended School Resource' which can be delivered by teaching professionals or local volunteers. There is an accompanying DVD and the resource contains five components: Risk IT where pupils work towards producing an animated version of the Nativity story; Cre8iv which explores the biblical themes of conflict and forgiveness through dance; Sports looking at teamwork, trust and perseverance; Express, a fun programme based around games and small group discussion; and Discovery, a discussion-based programme that looks at current affairs, allowing students to debate and reflect on a Christian response to issues such as fear, justice and trust.

Engaging schools in the Easter story

Who? St Polycarp's Church, Malin Bridge in Sheffield.

What? An exciting walk through Holy Week to engage 250 junior school children in the story of Easter.

How did it work? Two church leaders went into four local schools to teach them some songs, make palm leaves and to choose the 12 disciples. Then, on the day, groups of 60 Year 5 and Year 6 pupils arrived at church and heard and saw the beginnings of Palm Sunday events, so they sang and waved their palm leaves as Jesus (one of the church leaders) arrived, followed by the chosen 12 disciples. After a re-enactment of Jesus overturning the temple tables and an explanation that he stood for justice and truth, the children broke into two groups: one group did Easter crafts, the other went to an inside gazebo where they shared a Passover meal and Jesus washed the disciples' feet.

The next corner was Gethsemane where the school children watched a video of Jesus at prayer and heard the story of the soldiers arresting Jesus. He was marched off to another corner, which was draped in black, with a large cross. The church's Lay Reader dressed in a centurion's costume, dramatically told the story of the crucifixion. He ended with the striking words, 'Despite all I had done to him, the beating, nailing him to the cross, he looked at me with such love.' After such a powerful moment the children went off quietly for refreshments and then to the crafts. The other group then participated in the events of Maundy Thursday and Good Friday.

For the final scene, the front of the church was transformed into the empty tomb with two leaders explaining that they were going to anoint Jesus. Then Mary saw the risen Jesus – the church erupted into celebration, dancing and singing 'Jesus is alive' with all the kids joining in!

The outcome

There was very positive feedback from the pupils and teachers and the schools have asked whether they can come back next Easter!

For lots more ideas of what you could do around Easter see Chapter 7.

Prayer Point

The Schools Prayer Network exists to stimulate and encourage committed Christian prayer for every school in the UK, and to provide a means of communication and support for those concerned. To get help starting a prayer group for your local school visit www.schoolsprayernetwork.org.uk.

> Have a 'tell us what to do and we'll do it' approach.

In the Spotlight . . .

What? Over the last seven years Rhema have taken a unique blend of music, theatre, action and fun into schools across the country to present Christian teaching in an accessible and engaging way. In response to HOPE they decided to act in faith and put two children's companies on tour with Rhema shows for the whole year instead of just at Easter and Christmas.

They were able to reach more schools than would have been possible with just one team and were also able to take part in a HOPE Fun Day held in their area, receiving fantastic feedback! Not wanting this to end, they've decided to keep the two companies running into their new school year too!

Why? Schools are increasingly open to welcome non-teachers to deliver curriculum requirements. This is especially true of RE, where many non-specialist teachers have to teach RE and most agreed RE syllabuses require at least some opportunity to meet people from faith communities. Using the arts is a great way to explain the Christian story (either the Bible, a historic figure or personal faith).

How? Rhema are professionals, but a local church or several working together could put a drama group together who offer to take collective worship once a term or get involved in special cross-curriculum days at schools. This involves developing links with the school(s) to build up quality relationships. In areas where there are dedicated Christian school trusts, it would be worth engaging in their work to see what opportunities there are for the arts.

The outcomes

- Careful presentations of the Christian message in educational settings.
- With local teams, the building of relationships between schools and churches.
- An opportunity to serve without a hidden agenda.
- Potential (with the permission of the head teacher and governors) to use the school to invite children to midweek or holiday activities.

Top tips for working in schools:

- Build a relationship with schools first.
- Ensure the team perform 'professionally'.
- Follow any guidelines given by the school.
- Ensure you are thoroughly rehearsed.
- Be prepared for the unexpected – including heckling!

Great ideas

- A group in Bath launched a 'Hope in Our Schools' initiative getting 400 people giving £5 per month so that a full-time secondary schools worker could be employed to develop mission in local schools.
- Warfield churches contacted every school in their area and asked what they could do to help. This led to a team going to Garth Hill College in Bracknell to redecorate classroom areas, paint the perimeter fence, and do general site work. Similar work was done at local primary schools including the Pines Infants School and Fox Hill Primary School, where they helped resurrect overgrown wildlife area and gardens. In the future they're hoping to get more of the pupils involved in their work. Find out more about how they reached young people through a 'Battle of the Bands' in Chapter 20.
- The Christian Union in Gordano secondary school in Portishead, Bristol, gave out mince pies to pupils at Christmas and Creme Eggs at Easter!
- Ravensworth Road Methodist Church in Bulwell hosted their local junior school, Rufford, for their harvest festival, and presented the school with 30 Bibles at the service. The money was raised by giving the profits from a mid-week service and soup event, and the balance was made up from church funds. They also supported the school as it went through a re-organisation, writing to the City Council to voice their appreciation of the work that the school does.
- Sister church, Aspley Methodist Church, made links with Bethel School in Ghana, and raised £200 from a sponsored walk in a local park. Ravensworth also supported the school

In areas where there are dedicated Christian school trusts, it would be worth engaging in their work to see what opportunities there are for the arts.

by sending donations from its Christmas tree festival to swell the funds. Aspley Methodist Church also regularly take assemblies at Rosslyn Primary School, quite close to the church.

- Sheffield 6 Youth Network / Hillsborough Churches Network organised a Year 6 leaving ball, and went into all the local primary schools to give away the Scripture Union *Moving On* booklet.
- Many LEAs have a 'Place of Worship Week' so why not make your premises welcome for children with activities or a snack? Claire Clinton, an RE advisor, initiated this in Newham.
- Churches in Slough invited local schools to presentations about Easter and Christmas and the idea has been picked up by many other churches across the country.
- The Community Church@Greenway has a team of people who are committed to giving one hour a week to hear children read. It can make an amazing difference to a child's confidence and skills as well as helping out overstretched schools.
- Regularly deliver nice coffee and cake to the school staffroom. Schools workers in Fleet have 'adopted' schools to bless in this way.
- With the head teacher's permission, run a drop-in 'coffee spot' for adults dropping off or picking up children. In Bedford, some Christians were encouraged to set up a drop-in coffee spot for parents in the church next door, and later were offered use of a mobile classroom. Parents and carers love both the coffee and the chat.
- Churches in the Medway area of Kent offer to talk to school groups about surviving World War 2 and their experiences of the 30s, 40s and even the 60s in their history lessons!
- Why not get involved in Open the Book which offers a free programme to schools of themed and dramatised Bible stories to fit into assembly times? A schools trust in Sudbury used it and found the response from the schools was so encouraging they took on an additional part-

time worker to develop its use. Go to www.openthebook.net for more info.

• The Government-driven Extended Schools and Every Child Matters initiative provides many church opportunities to get involved with schools and children – see www.everychildmatters.gov.uk.

RESOURCES

Top Tips on Developing Partnerships Between Church and School from Scripture Union – a must-have for all those wanting to work within a school context and the extended schools opportunities, £2.99.

Great resources to buy for your local school

50 Christian Assemblies for Primary Schools by Chris Nicholls. Fifty assemblies that will expose children to Christianity so that they can explore it for themselves and make up their own minds but are structured in a way that stays within educational guidelines and the law. Kingsway, £8.99.

Care for the World by Chris Stafford. Combining facts, faith and fun, a resource for use throughout the school year, covering Harvest, Christmas and Easter, local and wider environmental matters, relationships, community and responsible citizenship in a worldwide context. Kevin Mayhew, £16.99.

Complete Primary Prayers by Tony Bower helps raise pupils' awareness of the Bible through prayers based on selected psalms and other parts of Scripture. There's also a special section with ideas to inspire children to pray their own prayers as groups and as individuals. Kevin Mayhew, £6.99.

Explore is a 12-week programme of study for 11- to 14-year-olds that fits in with the framework for teaching RE at Key Stage 3 – see www.exploreforschools.co.uk for more details.

The Christian Union in Gordano Secondary School in Portishead, Bristol, gave out mince pies to pupils at Christmas and Creme Eggs at Easter!

Express Community through Schools by Phil Bowyer is a book and CD-ROM that has five sessions to help students engage with their community in ways that will challenge, inspire and excite them. Authentic, £8.99.

Get Ready Go for children about to start full-time education – available as singles or bulk orders, to give to a local school, £2.99 or 5 pack £10.00, Scripture Union.

Hit the Ground Running – Assemblies by Denis Orgorman. 50 ready-to-use acts of collective worship for primary schools with a theme. Suggested visual aids, songs and prayers are also provided. Kevin Mayhew, £10.99.

In the Bag 2 – Primary School Assemblies by John Wright. Ready-to-use assemblies for the year, designed to help children learn about God, to pull something 'out of the bag' to grab attention, to get the children doing and not just listening, and to reinforce the message with just the right amount of repetition. Kevin Mayhew, £9.99.

Into the Bible: 101 Routes to Explore is a programme to teach the Bible component of the primary RE syllabus. Twenty-four lesson outlines with downloaded resources on a CD-ROM to use on an interactive whiteboard plus a book for children with 101 key Bible extracts – available in various formats and bulk orders available – see www.scriptureunion.org.uk/intothebible (book £8.99 or bulk buys for less).

It's Your Move for children about to move to secondary school – available as singles or bulk orders, to give to a local school, £2.99 or 10 pack £12.00, Scripture Union.

Life Actually for those in Year 11 making decisions about the future – available as singles or bulk orders, to give to a local school, £2.99 or 5 pack £10.00, Scripture Union.

Lifepath is a Scripture Union initiative where churches provide a programme for schools in a local historic place, such as an abbey or monastery, to explore the life path of the relevant Christian historical figure, the life path of Jesus and their own life path – see www.scriptureunion.org.uk/lifepath.

The Message Trust works in schools, local communities and prisons, to improve the lives of young people in Manchester. Through their Eden youth projects, over 100 volunteers live and work in tough urban contexts and, using two high-tech mobile youth centres, they provide a safe 'off the street' environment for 500 young people. They also have three bands that perform and take lessons across the region's high schools, promoting self-respect, good citizenship and the Christian message of hope. For more information contact info@message.org.uk.

NGM – Since 2005 NGM has been touring the UK with its *Luv Esther* musical, using a Biblical backdrop to tell an exciting story. NGM also run Inspire – a national charity with the aim of reaching children and young people through music, inspiring them to realise their potential, be creative and live their dream. They also have a variety of speakers, bands, artists and DJs, available for events. Contact NGM for more details info@ngm.org.uk.

Pure Creative Arts is a dynamic and multi-faceted company who work through music, theatre in education and workshops to challenge young people to discover their individual worth and potential. Contact info@pure-potential.org.

Saltmine Theatre Company presents the gospel in churches, schools, colleges, prisons, youth clubs and universities, touring with a wide range of productions. They also run summer holiday initiatives. For more information email mail@saltmine.org.

Springs Dance Company offers inspiring performances for churches and schools to suit all tastes and contexts. They also offer workshops for all ages in churches, and in schools will tailor-make workshops to link with the curriculum. Contact info@springsdancecompany.org.uk or call 01634 817 523 or visit www.springsdancecompany.org.uk.

> The Message Trust works in schools, local communities and prisons, to improve the lives of young people in Manchester.

Youth For Christ offer a number of teams to come into schools including:

- **Crux Media** – a film and media team.
- **Crux Theatre** – offering performances and workshops aiming to inspire and empower young people to achieve more, to increase their self-confidence and self-belief, and to take responsibility for their actions.
- **Nomad** – a sports team who work in schools and community settings using either a giant cage (see Chapter 19 for more details) or sports tournaments to build relationships with the young people – see www.yfc.co.uk/schoolsresources for more details.

If you'd like to take lessons in school around the topics of sex and relationships, there are some great resources to help you:

- **CARE** provides three age-appropriate programmes called 'Evaluate – informing choice', helping young people to make healthy choices. Training for volunteers runs twice a year to equip you to deliver the programme in schools – see www.evaluate.org.uk for future dates, email info@evaluate.org or call 01525 375210.
- **Christians in Sport** have assembly outlines that you can download for free from www.christiansinsport.org.uk on themes like celebrating good times and living life to the full.
- **Oasis** provide OASIS Esteem – a four-day course designed to give you resources to help young people work through issues surrounding early sexual activity – see www.oasisuk.org.

HOPE IN COLLEGES AND UNIVERSITIES

Universities are often one of the largest employers in a town or city. Specialising in creating the future, they develop people and, through research and innovation, dozens of new businesses and thousands of minds every year. The microcosm of the lecture theatre and research lab infects the rest of society for decades to come.

Consequently, student mission needs to be viewed as long term and holistic, reaching the whole university: staff to students and professors to pot washers. The infrastructure for 21st century hope-affirming student mission requires both on-campus Christian groups and the surrounding local churches to play their part.

Each three-year cycle, 2.3 million students pass through the university gates. What is at stake?

- Sharing the gospel with the country's largest unreached people group: students.
- The discipleship of millions of students beginning the journey of their working lives.
- Character and leadership development for future leaders in the church and society.
- The growth and effectiveness of the local church: reaching and keeping 18–30s.

loveyouruni – Loughborough University

Where? Loughborough, Leicestershire.

What did it look like? loveyouruni in Loughborough was less of an event and more about many lifestyles filled with compassion. (Compassion being what love looks like in public.) It began with students carrying out simple acts of service; helping direct traffic for Loughborough Student Union's annual music festival followed by litter picking afterwards. A team of people (Bag Angels) helped carry the bags of new students as they moved into halls. It meant giving out bottles

Each three-year cycle, 2.3 million students pass through the university gates. What is at stake?

of free water to drunk students outside the Student Union. It also meant being inside, staying up late, praying with, talking to and holding a bucket under inebriated students on the biggest SU club night of the week.

Why? Open Heaven Church has a passion for students. It partners with other churches in Loughborough, runs Fusion Cells and has seen over 700 students in the last 12 years reached, discipled and equipped for a life of service. It has been over a decade in the making, through prayer and relationship building and, during the first year of HOPE, many areas of breakthrough occurred. It demonstrates the effectiveness of a local church being involved in student mission and their commitment to consistently loving the university, the Student Union and the students.

How did it work? 21st-century student mission means going to people, being prepared to build relationships and understand where they are coming from. Where possible, over many years, Open Heaven has sought to build relationships with University authorities, the Chaplaincy and the Student Union. It worked through being willing to develop these relationships and put time, effort, energy and money into acts of service.

The outcomes

Club Mission started as a simple idea to serve drunk and distressed students on the Student Union's biggest party night of the week. The Student Union now backs the initiative financially and logistically. It recognises Club Mission as an essential part of the event, caring for the pastoral, emotional and spiritual needs of students.

'This year, Club Mission was so well received; it's become an official part of the Student Union, working alongside the security staff. We've also been given a room to pray in as well as having a mobile prayer team walking around the venue,' says Paul who is a student at Loughborough University and leader of Club Mission. So far there are 37 members on the Club Mission team. *'A lot of the success has been down to continuing favour with Loughborough Student Union who have been amazing.'*

Due to the service that Open Heaven student society and Fusion Cells have been providing, the Student Union offered to deliver a Student Alpha invite to every student room on campus. That's every single first year student being invited on an Alpha course! Not surprisingly, Loughborough has run its biggest Student Alpha course to date!

Lessons learned

• Releasing students to operate with the full support and mentoring of church leaders makes a huge difference to the quality of initiatives and the character, leadership and development of individual students.

• There were many more possibilities through partnership than we could have imagined.

• We were not ready for how quickly things could scale up and more helpers were needed for Club Mission and Student Alpha.

Top tips for if you'd like to do something similar:

• Be prepared as a church to build relationships with the university and Student Union over the long term.

• Seek to understand the needs of universities and where local churches can serve and enhance the student experience and what the university needs from the community.

Here are some other ideas from churches, small groups and students who have been loving their university through HOPE – what might work in your area?

Join a non-Christian Society – Engaging with students around mutually shared interests presents opportunities to share faith in an authentic and unforced way. For example Imperial College London/Every Nation Church said, 'One of our

Be prepared as a church to build relationships with the university and Student Union over the long term.

campus workers directed an official play for the drama society with 20 freshers as the cast. This led indirectly to a regular small group discussion where five members of the cast (none of whom were Christians) voluntarily got together to discuss the purpose of life, including exploring this from a Christian perspective. One of these students has even moved from being vehemently atheist, to just agnostic!'

Hosting International students – In Medway, Kent, international students were told by the university that their accommodation would not be ready until September 21st though they were expected to report on the 18th. Medway University and churches jumped to the rescue: 'We took the challenge of believing God to feed and accommodate them by mobilising churches in Medway towns. None of the students went without accommodation or food. Believe it or not, just by us being there for them, a lot are even attending churches.'

Summer mission – 'In July, as part of our HOPE summer plans, we gathered a team of over 100 students from churches across York, and from universities across the country, for a mission to the city called Summer Soul. For a week we ran a cafe in St Michael le Belfrey Church open 12 hours a day with live music and testimonies, free tea, coffee and cake and student hosts to chat to visitors. We had 4,412 people through the doors during the course of the week! We also went out onto the streets to ask people questions about faith and spirituality, which led to some amazing conversations with people about Jesus.' (York University, St Michael le Belfrey)

Spag Bol for 6 – The student population acutely feels the need for community and as God said, 'It is not good for the man to be alone' (Genesis 2:18, NIV). 'Campuses have enormous potential for community at its finest – living, working and socialising with the same people,' say members of Guildford University and St Saviour's Church. 'However, we often choose individualism, refusing to share life with one another. In an attempt to bless people in the opposite spirit, a group of our students headed to Tesco and bought 140 packs of dry spaghetti.' They designed a flier with the recipe of 'Spag Bol for 6'. This was given out on campus along with free packets of spaghetti in a bid to bless students and inspire them to cook a lovely meal for their housemates! *'It was great to imagine 140 meals happening across the campus and the town as a result of our small act. The spaghetti was very popular; we got rid of all 140 packs in about 20 minutes!'*

Free Water – Lots of Christian students up and down the country are giving out thousands of bottles of water to drunk students at the end of nights out. Nerve in Loughborough is one such initiative. Why? *'Because God cares so we care but instead of just saying that we care, we show that we care.'* What starts as an act of kindness, can end with a life being saved.

Amy, a student at Loughborough University said, *'Nerve . . . I still don't completely understand what it is but I know one thing: if I hadn't met Corinne who was working with Nerve giving out bottles of water outside our Student Union, and if she hadn't taken the time to explain to me what she was doing and actively invite me and welcome me into her life and the life of the Open Heaven Church, then I'm not sure that I would now be involved with a church and engrossed in the learning and love of Jesus that I now feel.'*

The Tent – Last year, the student team at The Journey in London were thinking of ideas to bring God's love to the Royal Holloway campus in Egham. Gradually, the idea of The Tent was born. Every Tuesday, a group of students from Christians Together (the Christian Union) gather in a tent outside the Students Union building armed with lots of cakes and biscuits which they give out free to the students that they see. The vision is really to show people God's love – whether that's just through a cake and a friendly face, or whether they then get to chat to people, offer them support and pray for them.

'God has blessed us so much with a great relationship with our Students Union, and it is only because of this that we are able to do The Tent. They actively support us and encourage what we are doing. The Tent has been advertised in the SU magazine and on their radio station, all with our input, so that the message of God's love is being spread around the campus.'

UCCF: The Christian Unions
By Pod Bhogal

Students reaching students
UCCF: The Christian Unions is made up of thousands of students and more than 130 Christian Unions, working with hundreds of churches, 120 full-time staff workers and volunteers and many more thousands of supporters. We exist to give every student in Great Britain an opportunity to hear and respond to the gospel. CUs are led by students and unite around the essential truths of the gospel, bringing together students from all kinds of churches who share a passion to make Christ known.

Living for Jesus, speaking for Jesus
Christian Unions are on-campus mission teams committed to a loving and Christ-honouring lifestyle and engaging, creative and persuasive proclamation of Christ crucified. Demonstrating Christ's love through individual acts of sacrificial service and proclaiming his love through over 90 university missions each year, CUs give thousands of non-believers an opportunity to engage with Jesus. Since 1993 over two million gospels have been put in the hands of non-Christian students. This year CUs across Great Britain will distribute another 400,000 copies of a student-friendly version of Mark's gospel to their friends through relational evangelism, lunchtime events and small group seeker courses.

Working with local churches
Thousands of non-believing students have come to faith through the personal witness of CU members and the CUs' planned missional activities and have then gone on to become committed members of local churches. Christian Unions promote involvement in a local church as the life long and primary place of Christian discipleship, teaching and pastoral care.

Getting connected
If you are a new student or, if you know any school leavers going to university then get connected with your CU via our online freshers link-up at: www.uccf.org.uk/freshers/link-up. There is a CU in almost every higher education establishment in Great Britain, so the CU is a great place to be welcomed by friendly Christian students, introduced to a local church and plugged into a supportive community from the off. To find out more about UCCF, Christian Unions or gospel projects visit www.uccf.org.uk.

Other great ideas

There are loads of other brilliant ideas for reaching universities in the name of Jesus, have a look at these and see what inspires you!

- **Art exhibition** – Students from Fusion Cells in Cambridge hosted an art exhibition illustrating people's testimonies and gave out free meals.
- **Fancy a chat?** – Students from Submerge in Guildford dragged a sofa onto the street to be a place where students could talk about 'stuff'. Many great conversations happened.
- **Bag Angels** – A team of students came back to Loughborough University early to help new students move into halls for the first time. Bag Angels makes an easy relational connection to many new students and serves the felt need for moving heavy bags and, in some cases, removing heavy anxiety. A number of students who had their bags carried have subsequently become part of the church.
- **Chaplaincy Partnership** – Holy Trinity Church, Leicester, teamed up with the university Chaplaincy to run Student Alpha.
- **Non-alcoholic cocktail bar** – Promoting safe drinking in conjunction with the SU's drink awareness campaign, the loveyouruni guys and girls in Swansea University set up their very own 'bar' complete with parasols, straws and mini paper umbrellas.
- **Student prayer rooms** – Alongside the Christian groups on Surrey University campus, the Matrix Trust student team arranged a 24-7 Prayer Week during Freshers' Week – in a tent! They were situated right in the centre of campus so it was fairly difficult to miss them and they had dozens of students pop in to find out what it was about.
- **Dirty hands** – Students from York University went out into one of the poorer areas of York to pick up litter and clean graffiti. Cambridge students cleaned the local night shelter.
- **Love your uni societies** – Churches across Liverpool have started a loveyouruni society at each of the universities in Liverpool.
- **Lost and Found** – This Way Up, a youth project based in Solihull, ran a Lost and Found course in two south Leicestershire community colleges for students who had recently lost someone close to them. Participants said the course was really helpful and that it was really good to be with other people who understood what they were going through. For more details of the course visit www.realityyouthproject. co.uk.
- **Globe Cafe** – New Life Church, Lincoln, welcomes international students and gives them a weekly crash course on British culture. An endorsement from the SU means numbers increased from 5 to 36 and from across 12 different nations.

RESOURCES

Agape are passionate about every one of the two million students in the UK hearing the gospel and learning how to follow Jesus. They take student teams away each summer as part of their discipleship programme as well as running an annual National Student Conference. Find out more at www.agape.org.uk.

Christians in Sport have a whole section of their website dedicated to students. They have university groups all over the country who have weekly meetings supporting Christians to **pray** for their team mates, **play** in a way that honours God and to **say** something about the good news of Jesus when they can. Visit their website to see if there is already one operating at your university or to find out how to go about starting one yourself if not. You can also find loads more of their resources there too – see www.christiansinsport.org.uk.

Contact **Fusion** (www.fusion.uk.com) who are working with hundreds of churches and individual students who are involved in student mission and also provide the following resources:

· **Student Link-up** – connecting school leavers to a church in their place of study is the most important preparation a new student can have. Fusion can contact you to tell you about what's going on before you arrive so you can choose a church and check it out in Freshers' Week. You can also chat with students starting at the same university as you and student workers from the Fusion Connection churches at their forum at www.fusion.uk.com/studentlinkup.

· **www.loveyouruni.org** – dozens of locations are loving their universities through words, works and wonders and using this website on stickers, banners and T-shirts. The website features two tracks: one for Christian students to get inspired and involved, the other for students who have been impacted and want to find out more. It also offers links to local churches.

Fresh: Bite-sized Inspiration for New Students

by Krish Kandiah. Daily inspiration and challenges for new students looking to make the most of their faith, relationships and studies. IVP, £6.99

Loving Words – Student Lyfe is a new resource from the Bible Society that connects God, us and everyday life. It's about encountering the Bible with your heart and mind, in a fresh and vital way. It is designed to be used down the pub or in a cafe so would work brilliantly for university students – see www.lyfe.org.uk for more details.

Loving Works – Tearfund, Samaritans Purse and World Vision all have campaigns aimed at engaging students with issues that God cares about. See their respective websites for more ideas www.tearfund.org/students, www.comingtogetherforgood.org.uk, www.worldvision.org.uk.

Dozens of locations are loving their universities through words, works and wonders.

Student Alpha has been very successful in reaching students. See www.alpha.org/students for resources and check out Chapter 9 for more details.

StudentNAVS (part of the Navigators) helps people investigate the Christian faith, to study the Bible for themselves, to live out their faith and to help others do the same. They provide a number of resources on their website including group and individual Bible studies, devotional materials and audio talks. Visit www.studentnavs.org/resources for more details and to download materials.

Find more **UCCF** resources including talks to download, articles to read, Bible studies, videos to watch and book reviews at **www.uccf.org.uk/resources**. **www.uccf.org.uk/students** has tons of useful ideas and resources for CUs to use including a short film about making the most of your time whilst at university – **www.uccf.org.uk/students/give-what-youve-got.htm** – while **www.bethinking.org** is UCCF's apologetics website, helping students engage with questions related to faith, world views and culture.

God's Word
Every Child
One Child
at a time

The Book of Hope is free to schools, churches, teacher's, youth groups and individuals. There are five age-specific versions and a DVD version. Each version of The Book of Hope addresses topical and sometimes difficult issues that are relevant to the age of the reader.

1 *Primary School Edition Teacher's Manual*, is written for teacher's, Sunday School teacher's and parents and works well alongside the *Primary School Edition*. It is ideal to use in children's groups, school classrooms and one to one at home with your child.

2 *Primary School Edition* is written for 5 - 8 year olds.

3 *The Children's Animation Edition Teacher's Manual*.

4 *The Children's Animation Edition* is written for 8 - 12 year olds.

5 *The Story Edition* is written for preschool children. A helpful tool to use alongside the animated film The GodMan or on its own.

6 *The GodMan DVD The GodMan is a powerfully animated version of The Book of Hope £12 from UCB2GO.CO.UK or 08456 188 315.*

7 *The Teen Edition* is written for 15 - 20 year olds. We are very excited about this edition! It has been thoroughly tested and approved by teens across the UK. This book is designed to challenge and provoke thinking on everyday issues.

8 *The Hope Xtreme* is a 44-page book dealing with issues that every child aged 11 - 14 faces and helps to ease the transition from childhood to teenage years with spiritual truth from God's Word, giving youngsters the foundation they need for wise choices.

To find out more visit
bookofhope.co.uk

Book of
Hope
God's Word.
Every Child.

UCB
UNITED CHRISTIAN BROADCASTERS
Changing Lives for Good

CHAPTER 14
ARTS

Rob Cotton, Bible Society

The arts represent a vital shared space for dialogue between those of faith and those with none. From advertising hoardings to Hollywood blockbusters, from magazine articles to community festivals, arts and media remain an open and exciting public arena within which to communicate with people. HOPE has created many opportunities for the church to engage people creatively through the arts, and this chapter provides inspiring ideas to get us all thinking about what else we could be doing.

Arts projects that have already happened under the HOPE banner have ranged from drama to graffiti art, angel-styled Christmas decorations to giant murals, children's 'Images of Hope' art competitions to adult photographic competitions and exhibitions. HOPE has encouraged Christians everywhere to be creative, to engage people in totally new ways in their evangelism and mission, bringing hope to the whole community. The challenge to bring hope to local communities has significantly moved forward our cultural engagement as one leader recently commented, *'HOPE has changed the way we engage our community, it has been one of those defining moments for us as a church.'*

Use these stories and ideas to help you think about what you could be doing in your neighbourhood in the months and years to come.

> The arts represent a vital shared space for dialogue between those of faith and those with none.

The Bigger Picture

Because people often know just snippets of the Easter story but aren't familiar with the full story and its real meaning, Rev Phil Weaver, one of the ministers in Loughborough, Leicestershire, came up with a creative idea to address the issue.

The Loughborough Churches Partnership, involving 19 separate church congregations, came together to paint the biggest paint-by-numbers community picture in the world! The painting depicted the Easter story and in particular the specific events of the Passion Week. It comprised of over 500 ply-board paint panels and each panel was painted by various community groups including schools, churches, families and individuals. In total approximately 2,000 different people from within the community took part in painting the picture. The finished piece of art measured a total area of 460 square metres – at least 10 square metres larger than the previous world record! To give you an idea of what that looked like – it was about as long as a football pitch and as high as a house!

The Bigger Picture reached its peak on Easter Monday with a fun day, barbecue, Easter concert and a large firework display attended by approximately 1300 people. It also included a ceremony for putting the last piece of the picture in place and effectively making a new world record.

Terry Woods, a local artist, was appointed as Art Director and was responsible for designing the piece of art. He admits he prefers to paint on a large canvas – in fact, the bigger the better, so no wonder The Bigger Picture was a project that particularly interested him!

Literally thousands of people took part in creating The Bigger Picture and huge numbers of people from within the community came to view and photograph this extraordinary piece of art. Each person received a souvenir brochure outlining the full Easter story. As Rev Phil Weaver said, *'The Bigger Picture was an ideal opportunity not only to engage the community but also to enable us to retell the life-transforming story of Easter in a creative way and in all its fullness for all to see. It created a great community buzz and captured the imagination of the whole town.'*

Festival of Arts, music and faith – HOPE Nottingham

Who? Churches in the Nottingham area.

What? A weekend of community festivals started in Beeston (on Saturday), followed by a city centre Market Square celebration and festival (on Sunday) including food, street entertainers, stilt walkers, dance, various music styles, a Christian Listening Point, face painting, information stalls and a graffiti art lorry.

Why? To celebrate in unity, giving thanks for the weeks of social action that had preceded the weekend and to publicly demonstrate that the church can be a vehicle to bring hope into the whole community.

How did it work? The Leaders' Prayer Lunch met regularly and shared a vision for a large scale city centre festival, alongside the other HOPE outreach projects that churches were involved in to create a high point for HOPE Nottingham which would impact the city. A small working party was set up to meet with the council, book the artistes and to complete all of the necessary paperwork, which included an Event Manager to oversee the event

> Build relationships with the people you need to liaise with at the local council, police and media.

as a whole. Publicity was circulated in advance by email, letter and leaflet.

On the weekend the preparation in advance was evident and there was a good atmosphere on both days. The graffiti art project, with artists The Love Pusher and Bonzai, was painted on the Saturday with good conversations around The Good Samaritan story, where people watched the art develop and then spoke of their own perceptions of reaching out to those in need today. On the following day people then had the opportunity to do their own graffiti on boards provided in the Nottingham Market Square.

The Sunday HOPE Celebration in the Market Square had 3,500 people present and members of different Nottingham churches joined together to provide contemporary worship music, dance, presentation songs and a speaker. Many people requested prayer or a listening ear afterwards at the Christian Listening Point and Healing stand.

On the Sunday afternoon HOPE Nottingham Festival then featured local Christian artistes with numerous people from the local community passing by (37,000 people go through the Market Square each Sunday) being engaged by the music, dance, interviews, graffiti art, street theatre and by the outreach teams sharing with them.

Think this kind of event could work in your town, city or village? Here are our top tips!

• Build relationships with the people you need to liaise with at the local council, police and media. Get in touch with them well in advance as there will be a number of forms to complete, permissions to obtain and things to get organised. Keep in regular contact so that the relationship develops, good advice can be obtained and problems can be anticipated and resolved.

• Arrange Public Liability Insurance cover, complete a risk assessment which includes health and safety provision. Begin by requesting from the council a draft copy of these documents and by having an early conversation with your church's insurance company.

• Create a timeline, so that your team can clearly see what needs to be done and when.

• Make check lists and task members of the team to action things by a set deadline.

• If there is not the expertise locally to effectively manage the event, consider recruiting an Events Manager.

• Members of the church should be mobilised in prayer for the whole event and consideration should be given to providing a prayer zone and/ or listening point.

More helpful hints

• Make sure you brief artistes, presenters and team leaders in advance of the event (you will have enough to think about on the day).

• Make sure that every team member (and church) understands that the festival is a kingdom venture and is not about promoting any particular church. This can avoid problems later and enhances unity.

• Have helpful literature about the Christian faith available to give to enquirers.

The outcome

The church in Nottingham was able to present a united witness in the Market Square for the first time since the Millennium with a high quality celebration and festival of music, arts and faith. The relationships between key leaders, churches and organisations were developed, through working together to further the mission of the church.

The council's perception of the church changed as a result of the large attendance at the HOPE Celebration and the professionalism of everything that was presented. The media profile of numerous social outreach projects was increased as a result of the interviews, press releases and subsequent coverage of the festival.

A Photo Marathon

Over a hundred people took part in a Photo Marathon run in West Bridgford, Nottinghamshire, where they had four hours to take nine images of the area. A launch was held at West Bridgford Methodist Church when BBC TV

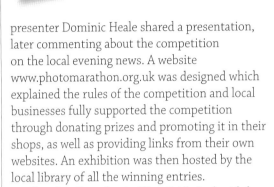

> Over a hundred people took part in a Photo Marathon run in West Bridgford, Notts, where they had four hours to take nine images of the area.

presenter Dominic Heale shared a presentation, later commenting about the competition on the local evening news. A website www.photomarathon.org.uk was designed which explained the rules of the competition and local businesses fully supported the competition through donating prizes and promoting it in their shops, as well as providing links from their own websites. An exhibition was then hosted by the local library of all the winning entries.

Churches Together in West Bridgford said they wanted to deliver a project that offered a low key style of evangelism that could be built on in future years and church members loved the idea because they felt they could invite their friends 'without their toes curling up'!

There were 115 entries in the competition which also provided opportunities for great conversations, media interest and a chance to develop relationships with local businesses and the community. Many people have been requesting a future competition too!

Top tips for if you'd like to do something similar:

• Have a good launch with local celebrities to create media interest.

• Consider setting up a website with links to other local sites.

• Invite local businesses to provide prizes as it creates greater local ownership and encourages people to take the time to enter.

• Organise an exhibition of the winning entries.

An exhibition of HOPE

In one Bedfordshire village, the idea of a photography exhibition first came up at a baptism class when discussing God using our gifts, because of one of the group, Robert Gill's, love of photography. Sadly, Robert was tragically murdered on Boxing Day of 2007 and therefore the exhibition, displaying some of his photos and sharing a little of his story, became a poignant tribute to him, also sharing the hope he had, through his faith.

In preparing for the exhibition the wider village community were invited to submit their own image of 'Hope'. The organisers were blown away by the depth of conversation they had with those who attended. By discussing the images which were on display with those who visited, and the stories that they represented, it was found that people were very relaxed in discussing some very deep issues, which could not have been discussed in general conversation. Of course, people were 'blown away by the photographs taken by Robert that were up on display, but other images had a terrific impact too'. People could see the 'hope' in the eyes of Kenyan children; in the expectation of young people and wrapped up in the arrival of a newborn baby.

This is a very positive example of the church ministering to its community at a difficult time. Plans have already been made for the next exhibition.

Images of HOPE – art competition and exhibition

Great idea for villages, towns and cities!

Who? Schools, churches and community groups all around the country.

What? An art competition for young people and adults where they had to create an image of hope inspired by a Bible story. The winners received a Bible (see www.biblesociety.org.uk/imagesofhope) at a presentation event and the art was then exhibited at a public space.

> People could see the 'hope' in the eyes of Kenyan children; in the expectation of young people and wrapped up in the arrival of a newborn baby.

Why? To offer an opportunity for churches to engage schools and people in the local community with stories of hope from the Bible.

How did it work? The project ran in several settings with over 700 entries in just one competition at Stapleford, but many people were engaged through the exhibition of the art. Presentation events were also a good opportunity for a gospel presentation.

Top tips for if you think this could work in your town, city or village:

- Envision church leaders and school teachers in your church.
- Visit your local head teachers with a leaflet and a copy of the downloaded rules.
- Consider having a presentation event in the church or school.
- Arrange to exhibit the winning entries at a public space such as a library or civic centre.
- Present all entrants with a certificate, possibly with a scanned copy of their art on it.
- Invite the local press to take photos of school children winners.

More helpful hints:

- Involve a local artist in the judging process who can then speak at the awards ceremony.
- Consider having an artist completing an art project as an extra attraction during the exhibition.
- If photographs of children are to be used in publications parental consent must be obtained.
- Have an invitation to your next church event available for guests at the awards presentation.

The outcome

Churches in a number of areas have developed a relationship with local schools and engaged numerous people with stories of hope from Scripture.

We heard loads of other great ideas for engaging communities through the use of the arts. We've listed some more below – which do you think might work where you live?

• When the local cinema closed, Pickering Methodist Church started running a monthly cinema for the community showing mainly family films. They don't charge but work on a donations basis and so far those donations have helped them fund two free family swims and buy a slush machine for cinemagoers! They are now planning on running another cinema slot – this time for those who are retired. They're also developing the church building to be used as a concert venue for local talent.

• Churches in Bradford and Edinburgh took their passion play onto the streets to bring their celebrations out into a public place.

• Winchester Churches Together presented a high profile Community Mystery Play which engaged the whole community, businesses and community groups.

• A Community Gospel Choir met for a number of weeks in Beeston before performing at carnivals and community concerts.

• Carnival events for the whole community can include arts presentations using drama, dance, or music.

• A group of Christians in Bristol hosted the *Unchosen* film festival (www.unchosen.org.uk) against human trafficking after seeing Paul Field's Cargo presentation. Film directors Nick Broomfield and Ken Loach held a question and answer sessions after the film viewing.

• An alternative set of Christmas decorations in a shopping centre using a 'Flight of Angels' made from kites is being explored by churches in Northampton, Sunderland and other areas. See the Resources section if you'd like to try something similar.

• Christians sharing a social concern with others in the community could host a themed festival

When the local cinema closed, Pickering Methodist Church started running a monthly cinema for the community.

on that issue to raise profile, finance and to empower people to respond practically.

• Many schools are open to receive theatre groups for assemblies. Could a group of churches in your area get together to hire a theatre company? Some well-known examples can be considered such as www.ridinglights.org, www.rhematheatre.org and www.saltmine.org.

• Freddie Kofi (www.freddiekofi.com) mentored young singer/songwriters in a BritGos™ academy to present their music in a number of mainstream music contexts. These artists could be available for your event, or see www.ngm.org.uk and www.innervation.org for other examples of bands available.

• You could invite a community arts group to host an exhibition of art or sculptures in your church.

• Churches in Coventry put on a showing of the critically acclaimed *Son of Man* film at the Warwick Arts Centre. The film tells the story of Jesus through a tale of corruption and redemption in modern day Africa. See www.sonofmanmovie.com for more details of the film and how you can use it.

• How about hosting a film discussion evening using website www.reelissues.org.uk where advice and discussion materials are available?

• Churches in Watford, Hertfordshire, held an art exhibition on the theme of HOPE at their local shopping centre over Easter.

• Hope Animation is an initiative that aims to teach biblical truths and encourage people with positive messages by using digital media and animation. The animations, stories and games are available for free at their website www.hopeanimation.com and those behind it have had the joy of knowing that many young people have made commitments to Jesus after watching their work as well as blessing many Christians.

• Host a multi-media presentation such as *Songs and Stories for the Journey* with Paul Field and Dan Wheeler, enabling people to relate their own experiences to Scripture and a faith journey.

• Members of Unity, a Christian entertainment group, put on three performances of the musical *Jerusalem Joy* at a nearby school. They charged a £5 entrance fee and gave all the proceeds to the local children's hospice.

Why not . . .

• Consider setting up a Facebook page or website to promote your HOPE activities.
• Get a volunteer to film your event and produce a DVD record or post it on You Tube.

RESOURCES

www.artisaninitiatives.org is a great organisation for people working out their Christian faith in arts, media, fashion and entertainment industries and provides an opportunity to connect and feel part of a larger network. They advertise local prayer meetings, along with local exhibitions, gigs, etc.

Christian Resources Exhibition – The Arts Zone will be offering an opportunity to experience a variety of theatre, film, fine arts and a rolling magazine programme. See www.creonline.co.uk for more details about the event.

Damaris is an organisation motivated to help Christians to communicate their faith appropriately within contemporary Christian culture. Their website provides free articles on current films, TV shows and books as well as links to books and audio devotionals relating to today's culture, speakers you can hire, and media clips you can purchase for talks – www.damaris.org.uk.

A Flight of Angels – For advice concerning 'A Flight of Angels' or other arts initiatives email luke.walton@biblesociety.org.uk (Arts Development Officer) or call 01793 418100.

> ReJesus website looks at how Jesus has been quoted, misquoted, filmed, reported on, worshipped and argued over.

HOPE Info has been the public face of HOPE, offering a great place for people to point their friends for creative evangelistic tools. Find free downloadable films and much more at www.hopeinfo.co.uk.

Media Campaign – Churches in a town or city could consider sponsoring a billboard or bus panel media campaign, to raise the media profile of mission activities, collaborating with an agency such as Bebo or Bible Society, who have recently been involved in such initiatives.

Reel Issues website provides group materials to discuss the latest talked-about films in the light of the Bible. It's designed to engage people at every stage of their spiritual journey. A 12-month subscription is £21 and you receive a new discussion each month and access to every previous discussion in the archive – www.reelissues.org.uk.

ReJesus website looks at how Jesus has been quoted, misquoted, filmed, reported on, worshipped and argued over. It explores the pictures and words of artists, musicians and writers who have imagined Jesus over the past 2,000 years – www.rejesus.co.uk.

Books

The Bible in Pastoral Practice, by P. Ballard and S.R. Holmes (eds), Darton, Longman and Todd. Essays 17 and 18.

The Creative Gift: The Arts and Christian Life, by H.R. Rookmaker, Inter-Varsity Press. A selection of essays representing Christian thinking on art and creativity.

Using the Bible in Christian Ministry, by S. Pattison, M. Cooling and T. Cooling, Darton, Longman and Todd. Unit 15.

CHAPTER 15
COURSES

Rob Parsons, Care For the Family

Offering a course to your community is a great way to reach out to people. Whether it's looking at marriage preparation, parenting or debt management, you can help people in their everyday lives – and put them in touch with what the church has to offer, too.

The aim is to stand alongside people, draw them in, discover solutions together and let them know that they are not alone in the challenges they face. It's not about pretending we have it all together (which can understandably prompt a negative response from people we invite), it's about identifying with others, telling them, 'I've been there, too, and this is what I've learned.' You'll find they are more likely to open up, share their own story and value what you say.

Some churches ran courses for the first time in 2008 and many others have been inspired by HOPE to develop and expand the courses they were already running. From churches large and small came ideas for courses that would reach people and meet their needs.

Have a look at these great stories we heard – it could be that they'll give you ideas for running a course in your own community!

Parentplay

Where? Leeds, West Yorkshire.

Who? Claire Gooud runs Splashtime, a mother and baby group which meets four times a week at Bridge Street Church in Leeds. In 2007 she

> Offering a course to your community is a great way to reach out to people.

attended Care for the Family's Parent and Toddler Conference and met the authors of a new parenting course, Parentplay. Deciding it looked helpful she bought it and ran it in her church for six weeks in the spring.

There were 12 places on the course, and they filled up immediately. The women who attended were of different nationalities including mums from China, India, Latvia, Ireland and Japan. Only one was a Christian. Some had babies, some toddlers and some both.

How was it run? Claire held the course in the front room of the church's children's centre with other helpers running a crèche in the back room. The mums arrived at 10.30 and settled the children in crèche, and then from 10.45–11.45 Claire ran the parenting principles part of the course.

The 'messy play' for the children (e.g. painted handprints, sand and bubbles) had already been set up and a further 45 minutes was spent with mothers and children having fun together. The morning officially ended at 12.30, although this was flexible. The messy play for the last session of the course was held outside, Claire brought in a cake to share and she prayed with everyone before they left that session.

Claire brought flowers every week which were divided between two mums at the end of each session. It meant that by the end of the course all the mums had left with a bunch of flowers.

If anyone's child was ill and the mum couldn't attend, all the other mums signed a card for her.

Was it successful? The attendance was 11 or 12 every week, out of a maximum 12. The mums got on very well with each other, and all entered enthusiastically into discussions. They learned a lot, made many friends and gained confidence. One of the main things they learned was that no matter where you are from, you all go through the same struggles as parents.

On the feedback forms the mums listed the things they'd learned, such as *'It's OK to have "me" time'; 'It improved my English'; 'I have become more patient; I praise more; I show love more'.* They nearly all said they'd be interested in follow-up courses on self-esteem and on pre-school numeracy and literacy.

Others have now heard about the parenting course, and are interested in attending ones Claire has planned for the future.

Top tips
- Plan ahead. Advertise for half a term before the course is due to start.
- Try to find adult crèche helpers that are already known to the families.
- Prepare in advance and make sure you know what you're doing. For example have the chairs ready so you're not running around still getting organised when people arrive.
- Welcome the mums, make them feel special, praise them.
- Make sure that mums feel it is not a problem if any children are unsettled and need to join them during the parenting principles sessions. It should be easy for the mums to get to their children if they need to.
- Don't be too rigid with the ending time of the second hour of each session – let people go when they're ready.
- Personalise the material and make it your own. Feel able to use the course as a basis adding items of interest to it if you wish – perhaps things you've found on the Internet, or

Plan ahead. Advertise for half a term before the course is due to start.

something that's relevant to your area; perhaps a poem or a recipe.
- Have other leaflets available – from Surestart or Care for the Family, for example.
- Rather than asking mums to fill in the feedback questionnaire at the last session, let them take it home to complete. It gives them more time to think.

Lessons learned
Claire said, *'I tried to run the seven-week course in six weeks so that I could fit it in half of one term, rather than holding any sessions over until the end of the school holidays and losing participants. But putting two weeks' material into one session made it very rushed – particularly because it included a session on discipline. If I was going to run the course in six weeks again, I would combine two different sessions.'*
www.parentplay.co.uk

Supporting parents and young people

To kick off HOPE, Churches Together in Bromsgrove ran two courses for the community. *ParenTalk* is an eight-week DVD- and discussion-based course which gives parents the opportunity to share experiences, learn from each other in an informal atmosphere, and explore some of the principles of parenthood. It ran for three months and at least ten people attended each week. All the course leaders and participants enjoyed it so much that they decided to continue monthly meetings on a Monday night where they discuss one aspect of parenthood and sometimes invite a guest speaker. The churches are planning to keep running the course again, too, for new people to join.

The second course they ran was a basic cookery course for young adults aged between 18 and 25. It ran for four weeks and was particularly aimed, though not exclusively, at young adults who have been homeless and are now living in bedsits or council-provided accommodation, or are in difficult situations.

21st Century Marriage

Where? Isle of Man.

Who? Alan and Enid Quayle attend Marown Church, on the Isle of Man, a church looking at how they could engage with the community around them. Some members of the congregation attended Care for the Family's Engage conference earlier in the year which gives practical insights into how to mobilise churches to get involved with their communities and transform the lives of the people they meet. During the day, ready-made programmes that can be used immediately in churches and communities were featured and Alan and Enid felt drawn to run a marriage course. They had help with advertising and ideas for the course from Carolyn Shipstone, Care for the Family's Isle of Man representative. Posters and leaflets were distributed within the church and local community and also through the local media. Using Care for the Family's *21st Century Marriage* material, the course was run over four sessions on weekday evenings. There was no charge to attend and five couples booked places.

How was it run? The course was run in the church, in a very comfortable small room which fitted in the five couples perfectly. The room was warm, with easy chairs set around low coffee tables. As well as providing refreshments every week (tea, coffee, juice, biscuits and cake), Alan and Enid put bowls of sweets on the coffee tables for each couple. The leaders chose coffee tables because they felt that a large table in front of each couple would have formed a barrier between everyone; and without a table, it would have been awkward to put drinks/sweets on the floor.

They wanted everyone to feel special so on the first evening every woman was given a decoratively-wrapped pink rose on arrival and the men were given a bar of Divine Fairtrade chocolate. They all thought this was a lovely gesture.

The sessions normally started at 7.30pm, but on the first night the church provided a buffet meal and couples were asked to arrive half an hour earlier so they could share this light supper together. This

'It was most helpful to have small group discussions, hearing different people's responses and answers to questions and topics discussed.'

seemed to break the ice as the couples got to know each other before the course began.

Alan and Enid said they found the course easy to run; each evening everyone watched a session from the course DVD together, then individual couples worked through the questions in the accompanying workbook. At the end they got together in small groups to discuss each topic and all participants contributed with enthusiasm.

Was it successful? On the last evening of the course all the couples said they wanted to meet up again as they had formed very supportive friendships. They arranged to have a meal at one of the couple's homes, with everyone taking along something to eat. Two of the couples were also interested in running the course themselves.

Some of the feedback shows what the couples thought: *'A terrific course, thoroughly enjoyed it and got a lot out of it'*; *'Thank you so much, really appreciated this and lovely to do it together'*; *'The DVD was great'*; *'Good humoured and non-judgemental'*; *'It was most helpful to have small group discussions, hearing different people's responses and answers to questions and topics discussed'*.

The leaders were particularly encouraged one week when a participant said she'd been really looking forward to the evening ever since the last session ended. Another said she was thrilled because her husband had attended every week, even though he had been working very long hours.

Top tips
- Make couples feel valued – for example by presenting them with roses and chocolates. Have little bowls of sweets on each table for every couple.
- Consider whether your church could fund the course, so that couples don't have to pay to attend.
- Ask members of the church to cook and serve food for the couples on the first night.
- When the couples go through the workbooks on their own, ensure they are far enough apart from the others so that their discussions remain private.

• Play soft background music on arrival and when couples are working in their twosomes.

• Tell the couples you will start and end on time – and do so! Some may have babysitters waiting. If people want to stay and chat afterwards (and in our case they usually did) that is great.

• The first session can be hard for couples as they meet others on the course. Make sure you greet and talk to everyone as they arrive and do this every session to welcome them.

Marriage and parenting courses in Bedford

Helen Musgrave works for Bedford Community Family Trust. Since 2002 BCFT has held two marriage courses per year; they used HOPE as an opportunity to re-advertise and include more people who hadn't heard of them.

Marriage course: they used Holy Trinity Brompton's *Marriage Course* material for seven sessions over a ten-week period. The course was held in Helen's home – it provided a relaxed environment and separate rooms were used for individual couple discussions. Starting with dinner at 6.45pm and aiming to watch the DVD by 7.30pm, the couples were given coffee and chocolates during the long exercise and departed by 9.45pm for babysitting practicalities. Four couples attended the course and the feedback showed they all benefited. One couple were not churchgoers but the wife became a Christian! Another couple were leaders of a Bedford church who wanted to attend the course themselves before running it.

Parenting course: they used Family Matters Institute's *Parenting Puzzle* material, for five weeks. The Institute's main trainer presented it in the church hall; with chairs around small tables and a white board for discussion points, it was quite formal. It began at 7.30pm with fruit and flavoured water on the tables; coffee and cake was served at 8.15pm, and the sessions finished by 9.30pm. They invited parents from local toddler groups, and advertised on

> Eat a meal together to start with so new friendships can be formed.

the *netmums* website. Seven mums attended and one brought her partner. Two were from local churches but the others were not church attenders. One mum was able to leave an abusive relationship, is regularly attending a church and wants to attend an Alpha course.

As the numbers were small, only two facilitators were needed for each course. One dealt with the practicalities (e.g. washing up) and also prayed quietly; the other ran the presentations.

Top tips

• Eat a meal together to start with so new friendships can be formed.

• Invite people personally – leafleting is not as effective.

• Never be put off if you only start with a small number.

• Be positive about what you are offering – check it out first!

• Try and get people to invite others to attend the course with them – it shows we are all willing to learn.

• Ask people for feedback on how the course could be improved – then do it!

Prayer Point

• Don't forget to include prayer in your planning process.

• Why not ask a few of your friends to be praying for you and the team as you run your course?

• Ask church members or small groups to 'adopt a course' and pray for the participants?

• Keep your pray-ers informed with updates of how things are going and particular prayer points.

Beating Burnout

Through the different church groups he has been involved in, David Judkins, pastor of Andover Baptist Church, has been struck by the importance of work in our everyday lives, and particularly the pressure this can put on people. *'As Christians,'* he says, *'we have so much to offer in this area but we seldom address it.'*

At the start of 2008, David and a friend from his church (an accountant by trade), felt conscious of the many New Year's resolutions being made – and broken! Knowing that one of the main resolutions people make is to deal with work-life-family issues, they thought they would pilot Care for the Family's Beating Burnout course and see if it had anything to say to people in their community.

The course includes a DVD presentation covering topics such as why we sometimes feel we can't cope, financial worries, dealing with difficult people and when it's OK to say no.

They ran the course jointly, hosting it in the town centre to allow easy access to the majority of people. The venue was a Christian cafe/conference venue just off Andover High Street. It was held over the lunchtime period and started with a light lunch and some 'ice-breaking' discussions to help people get to know each other. They then watched a 20-minute section of the *Beating Burnout* DVD followed by group discussion and prayer as appropriate.

The course ran for four weeks which they found just right. It enabled them to start developing friendships and open up in the times of sharing, but was short enough to focus on the main course content and not impose too much on people's busy schedules (*'which is actually the point of the course!'* says David).

The publicity was mainly through the churches in Andover and through posters in the town. It was aimed – to start with – at Christians because they wanted to pilot the material in a 'safe' setting, with people who were familiar with the course format through things like Alpha and Christianity Explored.

> In Hoylake, the HOPE group has launched regular community lunches so that they can listen to what people really need and then decide what courses to run based on their discussions.

Top tips

• *I'd just say: go for it! Even for the small numbers who attended, it was well worthwhile and gives you something to build on.*

• *On reflection, I would probably go for an evening slot, mainly because the working population in the Andover town centre are in the retail sector and wouldn't necessarily be able to spare an hour for lunch. Now we have run the pilot, we would be more confident in opening this to people outside the church.*

We also heard about these great ideas for courses:

• Basingstoke Community Church ran an evening seminar at the church for parents called *Kids and the Internet*. Other people began showing an interest and the seminar was then taken into a local school in December. It is planned to develop this in the coming year.

• Hillview Evangelical Church in Hucclecote, Gloucester, ran Care for the Family's eight-week 21st Century Parent course.

• Manchester Mosley Common ran two courses – one on parenting and another to help people deal with debt.

• Churches in Bedford made sure all their courses were branded with HOPE so that participants made the connection with the other work they were doing in their community. They ran 'HOPE for your marriage', 'HOPE for parenting' and 'HOPE in the workplace' courses.

• In Hoylake, the HOPE group has launched regular community lunches so that they can listen to what people really need and then decide what courses to run based on their discussions.

• In Preston, the HOPE group linked up with the local housing association and the police and, as part of a 'Partnership Action Week', they offered taster sessions for courses on parenting, relationships and financial freedom. Local agencies are now promoting courses that the churches are putting on. The latest course that was run was Celebrating Recovery (a 12-step course) and the churches are developing a course to help people access training and employment.

• Churches Together in the Westbury area, Bristol, made their courses a joint effort. The eleven churches all did a variety of courses, but they chose to advertise them in one leaflet. They offered courses on parenting teenagers and 'noughts to sixes'; debt recovery, 'well-being for older people' and one on how to take time and explore Christian spirituality. They also ran three courses for families – for teenagers, parents and grandparents.

OTHER COURSES AND RESOURCES YOU COULD TRY

MARRIAGE

21st Century Marriage is a DVD-based course including an easy-to-use workbook which can be used by individual couples, as well as being used in a course in church or community. In the DVD, Rob Parsons lifts the lid on eight subjects that can affect everyone, from money and time pressures, to acceptance and love. www.careforthefamily.org.uk.

Connect2 is a five-session course that can be run in your local community or church to support and encourage couples in the early years of their marriage. Sessions include: Love for a lifetime; Communication and differences; Intimacy, romance and sex. It also includes marriage preparation material – www.careforthefamily. org.uk.

Marriage God's Way is a course that can be used by individuals, groups and couples interested in exploring the biblical view of marriage and addressing the biggest challenges relationships face. The pack features two DVDs, audiocassette and one workbook from Selwyn Hughes, £39.95.

The Marriage Preparation Course (for engaged couples) and *The Marriage Course* (for couples who have been married for any length of time) by Holy Trinity Brompton are for any couple that wants to develop or build strong foundations for a healthy marriage that will last a lifetime. Full information and resources for running a course are available from http://themarriagecourse.org and http://themarriagecourse.org/preparation.

FAMILY LIFE

Family Ministry Manual is a practical guide for every church seeking to address the needs of families in their surrounding communities. Written for church leaders by church leaders it addresses the common issues and challenges that leaders might experience as they seek to impact their communities – www. careforthefamily.org.uk.

Family Time is a ten-session course on parenting and family life for those with young children. The course covers areas like the impact of marriage on family life, communication, how to handle other things that influence children such as TV, computer games, school friends, etc.; family values and discipline. All the material you need to run a course is available in the *Family Time* book and you can buy additional resources at www.new-wine.org, by calling 020 8799 3778 or by emailing info@new-wine.org. New Wine also run regular training courses for those wishing to run the course. Five-DVD set with leader's guide is under £40.

From this Step Forward – Stepfamilies are the fastest growing family type in the UK and this resource aims to give them the tools they need to survive and thrive. CD-ROM containing course material is available for £19.99 from www.careforthefamily.org.uk.

Parentplay is a seven-week course which encourages parents to have fun with their children, and to learn some basic parenting principles. The two-hour sessions are planned so that the adults spend the first hour learning parenting principles, while the children are cared for in a crèche. The parents and children then join together for 'messy play'. The course is not overtly Christian and is designed for parents of under-fives.

The Parentplay course, published by Authentic, is written by Rachel Murrill and Rachel Bright. See case study and www.parentplay.co.uk for more details.

WORK

The Heart of Success is a DVD and workbook by Rob Parsons which will enable individuals to explore the best way to find that illusive balance between life and work. £14.99 from Care for the Family.

Love Work Live Life, a book by David Oliver about how to discover your work and career as your God-given vocation – see www. loveworklivelife.com for more information. You can order from UK websites and bookshops. Authentic, £7.99.

You may be able to find some good secular time-management courses too – always popular with today's busy lifestyles!

MISCELLANEOUS

Money

Credit Action: Your Money Counts – a six-week course produced by Family Matters and Credit Action helping churches reach out to those in the community struggling with money issues. Leader's Notes are just £1 and Study Booklets are £2.

Credit Action also provides a number of free downloads and resources to help you help people manage their money better including budget sheets, examples of letters to creditors, information on mortgages, priority payments and County Court procedures. Manuals are available (to buy or download) on a number of issues such as dealing with debt, redundancy and pocket money. See www.creditaction.org.uk for more details.

The Money Secret Adult Education Course – designed for use with the *Money Secret* book or CD, this is a free downloadable resource that can be used by anyone in small group teaching

> Credit Action also provides a number of free downloads and resources to help you help people manage their money better.

sessions, community courses or evening classes – www.careforthefamily.org.uk.

Quidz In gives parents the knowledge they need to talk with their children about money from a very early age. Through an informal and practical course, they'll learn how the world of finance works: everything from budgeting through spending and saving to looking to the future. They don't need to be a whiz at maths – this is about becoming financially aware, understanding how money works and how to get the best out of it. To give children aged 8 through to teens the inside track on money and finance issues, then Quidz In offers parents the information they're looking for. See http://quidzin.org.uk for further details.

Weight/health issues

How about running a Weight Watchers club (www.weightwatchers.co.uk/about) or a healthy cooking course (based on something like Rosemary Conley's *Step by Step Low Fat Cookbook*)?

For teenagers

How to Drug Proof Your Kids (DPYK) – an education, prevention and intervention programme for parents developed by Care for the Family in association with Hope UK, specialists in drugs education. See http://dpyk.org.uk for more information.

Romance Academy is a sex and relationship education programme (as seen on BBC 2) run specifically for teens that has an excellent format and content that could be ideal for your youth group and their friends. www.romanceacademy.org.

CHAPTER 16

HOPE ON THE EDGE

Andy Hawthorne, Message Trust

You don't have to look very far to find large pockets of our society that are riddled with pain and a feeling of hopelessness. Teenage girls find themselves pregnant, frightened and unsure where to turn, young people make bad choices and end up in prison wondering if they've ruined their whole lives, families find themselves in ever-mounting debt and can see no way out. Even a fun night out for young people can end up with them being so drunk they can't get home safely. Unfortunately these circumstances, and many more like them, are all too common these days. Though some of these areas may be ones that the church has traditionally shied away from, unsure of the moral ground, they are actually some of the areas we should be focusing our time and energy on getting stuck into. People who find themselves in these circumstances need somewhere to turn – we can be there, be Jesus' listening ear, be his loving hands, be his kind provision and protection when there is nowhere else for them to go.

We have a fantastic opportunity to break down people's misunderstandings about the church and all that God stands for, too. Many in these circumstances imagine that the church will do nothing but condemn them for their choices, lifestyles and problems – instead we can demonstrate God's love by being right there with them, offering a helping hand and providing

> We can be there, be Jesus' listening ear, be his loving hands, be his kind provision and protection.

support in every way we can.

When talking about the impact of HOPE, the Rt Hon Stephen Timms MP, the Vice Chair for Faith Groups in the Labour Party, said that it really had succeeded in giving people hope. He explained it was, *'not the wishy-washy maybe everything will get better kind of hope but the roll up your sleeves and actually do something about it kind of hope'*. And that has been one of things that has thrilled me: seeing so many individuals and organisations who have been getting their hands dirty in the name of HOPE. Not just satisfying themselves with prayer meetings to pray for those in need, but getting involved in their worlds and bringing hope to what sometimes seemed pretty hopeless situations.

These are just some of the stories of how Christians have been reaching out to those around them. Do any of them inspire you about what might be needed in your community?

Demonstrating the love of God to clubbers in Bath through Street Pastors

Street Pastors is a nationwide initiative that started in 2003 and which many areas have been using as part of their HOPE activities because it is a fantastic way to bless the local community. Eustace Constance from Street Pastors said, *'There is an unprecedented desire from churches to work together in their community and to effect real change at this moment in time. The ethos of both Street Pastors and HOPE is about seeing that happen. The valuable work and success of HOPE has contributed and continues to contribute to the growth of the Street Pastors initiative nationally. Many churches who have worked together through HOPE and are looking for a long term initiative are contacting Street Pastors.'*

We spoke to one group from Bath to find out what happened when they decided to get involved with Street Pastors.

Who? A total of 26 congregations from around Bath have got on board with the initiative, contributing 60 volunteer Street Pastors (ranging in age from 19 to 76!) and 27 prayer partners.

What? Street Pastors is about mobilising the Christian community to address neighbourhood/city centre issues. In Bath they have been going out every Friday night from 10pm until 3 or 4am, talking to people who are on the streets and in night-time venues. They care, listen, offer practical help as needed and enhance community safety.

Why? Having commissioned some research in 2007 to understand the needs of the community, the resulting report suggested that Street Pastors could be an excellent way for the churches to reach out and to be a blessing. Paul Bright, Street Pastors Co-ordinator in Bath said, *'It's all about being modern Good Samaritans, and demonstrating the love of God in really practical ways whether that be providing a pair of flip flops for a girl who has come out of a night club without her shoes on and may cut her feet on broken glass, getting someone safely home in a taxi or offering a blanket to someone who is homeless.'*

How has it been going? Paul said, *'On our first night out we hadn't been going 10 minutes when we turned a corner to come across a lot of people squaring up to each other. We called for the street marshals and police to get the CCTV camera pointing to the location and meanwhile helped to restore calm, getting the prayer going as the street marshals and police sorted out the offenders.*

> **'We've spent a lot of time helping vulnerable drunks and lone women to ensure their safety.'**

'We've spent a lot of time helping vulnerable drunks and lone women to ensure their safety, have picked up endless glass bottles to try and stop any accidents from happening, have helped homeless people and have tried to restore calm when we see potential incidents arising. Prayer partners, whilst monitoring the radio and receiving confidential mobile calls, have prayed about specific situations arising, and time and time again things have been quickly resolved which has been so encouraging.

'We're building up excellent relationships with the police who are very supportive of the initiative, local paramedics, and doorstaff for the clubs and bars. We often get asked by the people we help whether we are getting paid and (as we're not) why we're doing what we're doing. It's a great chance to share with them and, where it seems appropriate, we pray with people, too.'

Top tips

- The Ascension Trust will provide a good deal of guidance and support; however, you need to have a proactive and suitably skilled local management team that will be able to deliver, run and develop the scheme. The Co-ordinator role is key.
- Start small and build things up from there.
- Visit other projects to get an idea of what a night entails.
- Don't be upset about criticism – some people haven't liked the fact that it's only Christians who are involved with Street Pastors.

What are your plans for the future? *'We'll be carrying on with Street Pastors and upping our commitment from just Friday nights to Friday and Saturday nights. Down the line we're also looking at expanding by having a staffed area where people can get drinks and chill out, plus having a Youth Pastors team to patrol earlier in the evening to deal with anti-social behaviour.'*

Think your area could benefit from having Street Pastors? Visit www.streetpastors.org.uk for more information.

TOPS TIPS FOR PROJECT PLANNING

1. Pray! Nothing is more important than prayer. In the place of prayer not only do we receive God's strategy, which is often a bit different from ours, we also receive his heart for the poor, the hurting and the lost.

2. Don't charge anything – Many people have a perception that the church is only after their money, so blessing communities entirely at our own expense sends a powerful message. In many cases local funding pots and parish mission funds will be available to help.

3. Understand your community and think about partnership – If you are struggling to come up with the biggest needs in an area, get in touch with your local council or police. They will help you to do a community survey and audit and also make sure you are scratching where people itch. They will be more than aware of the areas of greatest need in your community and they will also be happy to lend their support to help you tackle that issue. Who are you currently working in partnership with or who could you effectively work alongside in your local community? See Chapter 22 for more details of working with police and government.

4. What about other churches? What other churches are in your area and what kind of relationship do you have with them? Maybe individually you don't have the resources to tackle all you would like to do, but together you do. Or perhaps you could support them in their projects? Your local Churches Together group would be a great starting point to help you find out what others have going on.

5. Think about your own resources – What are the interests of the people in your church? Are there individuals who have a sense of calling to a particular group of people and who could be empowered or resourced to do that?

WORKING WITH YOUNG OFFENDERS
Reflex UK

The door is wide open for Christians to work alongside the chaplaincy teams in our prisons and young offenders institutes (YOIs). Record numbers of inmates present a huge opportunity for the church and to help men and women go from being the problem to being the answer has to be one of the most exciting things in the world. Alpha is registered in 80% of UK prisons (http://alpha.org/prisons) due to prisoner demand and churches are getting increasingly involved with reintegrating people on their release from prison. They often use Alpha's proven Caring for Ex-offenders programme (http://caringforexoffenders.org) or work with the community chaplaincy.

As part of HOPE, the HOPE HMP Tour visited young offenders institutions. Using rap and hip hop music they created a space where young offenders could express themselves, develop social skills and help them re-define boundaries of acceptable behaviour. They also tied these visits into chaplaincy work and hosted services where many young men and women committed their lives to Christ. This pioneering work will now continue to be delivered in YOIs across the nation.

See www.reflexuk.net for more details.

CARE Confidential – Crisis Pregnancy Counselling

An unplanned pregnancy can be a scary and isolating thing. Many women find they face pressure from partners, family and friends and don't have much opportunity to sort through their own emotions and feelings to work out what they themselves want to do. Many Christians are helping these women (and men who are also affected) through 150 CARE Confidential Centres around the country (including Northern Ireland). These independently run centres provide a safe place for women to find the time and space to talk about all the available options, discuss how they feel and make an informed decision. There are loads of ways you could get involved:

• Setting up your own centre – if you have a vision and a passion to bless people in this difficult situation you could think about starting a new centre. Speak to CARE Confidential who will be happy to discuss your vision and the next steps with you.

• You could train as a counsellor either in crisis pregnancy counselling or post-abortion counselling. Training takes place locally over 16 weeks and CARE Confidential provide all the materials to help groups offer their own training.

• Helping an established centre – prayer and financial support are always welcome, or if there is a centre nearby to you, you could offer to help with reception duties or looking after donated baby clothes that are given to new mums.

• If you have experience from a centre you could offer to provide online or over the phone counselling.

• It's not just women who are needed; men can train as counsellors and meet with couples and/or men who are affected by pregnancy and abortion issues.

Find out more at www.careconfidential.com or get in touch via careconfidential@care.org.uk or on 01256 477300.

More top tips
• Don't give up! It takes patience and tenacity to motivate and unite churches and to bring change to our communities.
• Make sure you don't do any 'hit and run' activities – what communities really need are churches that consistently and reliably share God's love.
• Look for the good excuses for a community celebration.
• Young people have amazing energy and talent – take a risk with allowing them to take the initiative and back them all the way! (Even when you don't think it'll work!)
• Often it's the process that yields bigger results than the event itself – don't just use people to get jobs done, use jobs to get people on board.

> Don't give up! It takes patience and tenacity to motivate and unite churches and to bring change to our communities.

• Find the shared values with your community and work together to achieve them – we're all on the same side!
• Always be ready and willing to share your story – the hope you have within you. Often people will ask why you are doing good work in the community. What a great chance to tell people about Jesus!

DEBT COUNSELLING

When John Hughes, the vicar of St John's Harborne in Birmingham, took a sabbatical to Africa he came back inspired by the social action he had seen and the way that the church looked after its local community. *'Let's get more involved in our community as our contribution to HOPE,'* he encouraged the church and they enthusiastically got on board. A shop across the road from the church was up for sale and they snapped it up, knowing it was in an ideal location to reach out to members of the community. They now have five projects running including a Pregnancy Assistance Centre, a Debt Counselling Service, outreach to elderly people in the community, Healing on the Streets (see Chapter 18 for more details of this prayer initiative that's running around the country) and also a Practical Assistance team who offer to help people where needed with things like trimming their hedges or putting up shelves.

The Debt Counselling Service is open two evenings and two mornings each week (including Saturday mornings) and people can make appointments or just drop in. *'Debt is a huge problem in the UK and though there are some organisations that can help, many people find them inaccessible,'* church member Karl said. *'We wanted to provide somewhere people could easily come and get the help they needed.'* The Stewardship Money Team provided training for the team of volunteers and they now have many clients visit them whom they help with things like budgeting, dealing with debts and finding ways to work with creditors. Karl said, *'We can help in quite a few ways but you can't offer legal advice unless you are legally trained so a number of our team are looking into getting the appropriate qualifications to be able to provide that in the future. We're also looking to employ a Lead Debt Advisor – we've found out that if we pay for one then the Christians Against Poverty (CAP) will train and supervise them.*

'We really just want to find ways to communicate with our community that God loves them, wants a relationship with them and wants to do good in their lives. We hope that offering practical help in times and situations when people are struggling will do just that.'

WORKING WITH PROSTITUTES
Hull Lighthouse Project

The Hull Lighthouse Project have been doing some amazing work for a number of years amongst prostitutes in the city. They offer friendship, advice and opportunity for change through a team of trained volunteer staff who run an evening drop-in service and paid outreach workers who give ongoing help during the day. They undertake hospital visits, give support during pregnancy, liaise with social services, help find suitable housing and furniture, provide practical help with budgeting, negotiate repayment of debts, visit solicitors and probation officers, support women during court appearances, give practical help with retraining and education, and deal with issues connected to substance misuse. They have regular peer support meetings at the church centre, have provided computer training, and this year have held an exhibition of art by recovering drug users. Over 40 women have now been helped to exit prostitution and over the last year they have been in contact with 198 women and received over 800 visits to the drop-in.

For the story of what one cell group did to bring HOPE to the women who work in massage parlours see Chapter 23.

Chelwood Baptist Church, Larkhill Estate, Cheadle Hulme

Chelwood Baptist Church met to pray on the local Larkhill Estate and decided to speak to residents to find out what the issues were to fuel their

prayers. This resulted in a realisation of the need for facilities for young people. Even though the church only had around 30 members they had a vision and have created a 5-a-side football pitch and taken over the old Post Office to host a New Life Community Centre. As a result the people on the estate increasingly think of it and call it their church. People have come to faith and significant bridges have been built.

Deprived community or place of HOPE?

Harpurhey, Greater Manchester, has long been burdened with the tag of the UK's most deprived community. But things are changing. For HOPE five local churches hosted a 'Big Up God, Big Up Harpurhey' weekend which attracted 700 vistors and featured an open air service with gospel presentations, followed by a huge picnic. Music was provided by MJK and LZ7 alongside Christ the Vine's youth band and the Pathfinder choir. There was also free face painting, sumo wrestling, bouncy castles and a human table football game! Pastor Michael Brawn from Harpurhey Community Church said, *'It was fantastic to see hundreds of local residents and young people come together in this way; it was a brilliant afternoon, with a positive response from all who came.'*

The council loved it and the process got the churches excited about working together. This led to united prayer gatherings and a calendar of initiatives came about such as New Year

Reach out and bless your community

The Word For Today is an ideal resource for reaching out into the community with the Word of God.

The Word For Today, is a collection of Bible based notes to encourage you each day. They help you to get into God's Word and include references for reading the Bible in a one year.

UCB also produces a contemporary version, the *Word 4U 2Day* aimed at teenagers and young adults.

celebrations, Christmas street parties, Bonfire Night parties, marriage celebrations on Valentine's Day, hanging basket teams and men's quiz evenings in the local pub. As a result there is a new level of faith and the community genuinely feels different.

USEFUL CONTACTS AND RESOURCES

CARE Confidential offers confidential, unbiased pregnancy and abortion counselling through a network of centres located throughout the United Kingdom. They are concerned about the welfare of women and their partners dealing with pregnancy and pregnancy loss, including abortion. Their website provides free downloadable leaflets including 'Making a decision', 'Help after an abortion', 'For men' and 'Adoption'. They have nearly 20 years' experience of helping these centres to support women and their partners with crisis pregnancy and post-abortion concerns. Find out more at www.careconfidential.com and contact them via careconfidential@care.org.uk.

Care for the Family (www.careforthefamily.org. uk) aims to promote family life and help those hurting because of family breakdown. They have a number of quality resources and training programmes for local churches.

Christians Against Poverty (www.capuk.org) Debt is a huge and increasing problem. CAP have over 80 centres based in local churches (and want to open more). They offer debt counselling and a solution to anyone in debt.

Consumer Credit Counselling Service offer debt and money advice training including a free consultation to discuss your training needs. For more info see www.cccs.co.uk and click on the Training link.

Eden (www.eden-network.org) partnerships are now springing up all over the nation as

There are now lots of Street Pastor projects all over the UK as Christians engage with people on the streets.

people choose to live long-term in the toughest communities with a vision of church growth and community transformation.

HopeUK (www.hopeuk.org) offer drug awareness sessions for young people and their parents and train youth, family, and church workers in practical strategies to help.

NCAP facilitates a network to assist groups in providing opportunities for freedom and change for people involved in prostitution. Contact the NCAP office if you are interested in working with grass-root organisations in your local area, or assisting them on a national level. In order to increase public awareness of prostitution and the issues affecting people involved in or exploited by the sex industry, NCAP can provide a speaker or discussion facilitator for your church or small group. You can find out more at www.ncapuk.org and email them on ncap@ncapuk.org.

Redeeming Our Communities (www.citylinks. org) promote prayer and partnership between churches, the police and local authorities to address the causes of crime.

Saltbox (www.saltbox.org.uk) based in Staffordshire have excellent resources to promote, encourage and support churches in the area of community and social responsibility.

Street Pastors (www.streetpastors.co.uk) There are now lots of Street Pastor projects all over the UK as Christians engage with people on the streets often late at night to care, listen and dialogue.

CHAPTER 17

HOPE IN YOUR WORKPLACE

Mark Greene, London Institute for Contemporary Christianity

The workplace is one of the most natural and untapped mission fields in our nation. As a Church of England report concluded way back in 1945:

> 'England will never be converted until the laity (which is Anglican for people) use the opportunities daily afforded by their various crafts, professions and occupations.'

Why? Because if you're in employment outside the home you'll probably spend more than 40 hours and 40% of your waking hours engaged in job-related activities. Compare that with how much time you spend with your best non-Christian friend in a week, a month or even a year? Indeed, the workplace is the place where Christian and non-Christian can't avoid each other. And it's the place where everything is the same for the Christian and the non-Christian – except their relationship with Jesus. The corporate culture is the same, the policies are the same, the pressures, the boss, the food all are the same. And that makes it a place where the non-Christian can see the difference that Christ can make to a life – not for a couple of hours at a barbecue but over a couple of years for 20, 30, 40, 50 hours a week. What's different? Jesus in you.

The workplace is one of the most natural and untapped mission fields in our nation.

Let me tell you a story.

A true story about a young woman we shall call Anita because that is her name and because it means 'grace' and because it is the kind of name that a weaver of fiction would have chosen for such a woman as a clue. But she is real and so the name was well chosen indeed.

And it came to pass that in an ordinary, fairly large company in southern England called Glaxo, Anita would, in the course of her work, walk the office corridor. And from time to time, a particular woman from another department would pass by and Anita would smile. Anita did not know her name and could only guess at her job. And the other woman would smile in return. We will call her Gabriella, though that is not her name but it means 'God is strong' which indeed he proved to be. Occasionally, a little 'hello' would accompany the smile but they had no occasion to pause or chat, for both had work to do and places to go and people to meet whose names they knew. And besides, the work of the one did not touch the work of the other. And so time passed, counted in smiles and little 'hellos'.

And so it was that at the end of an ordinary day Anita was walking to her car and there, coming towards her, was Gabriella. And Gabriella stopped and they began to talk. And she told Anita that her four-year-old child was chronically ill with asthma and eczema that would not go away and that she wanted to leave her husband. And Anita listened and asked if she could pray for her and if her home group could pray for her child. And the woman said 'yes'. And Anita offered her a Bible from the box of Bibles in the boot of her car.

The next day they met for lunch. And Anita prayed. And her home group prayed.

And within six months Gabriella's son was completely healed of his eczema and his asthma had subsided significantly. And Gabriella did not leave her husband but drew close to him and to Christ and to his people.

Is that too small a tale to tell of how an occasional smile was the soil in which trust grew, comfort was offered, secrets were shared and the good news offered and received? A tale of how a hurting woman had seen something in a Christian colleague she passed in the corridor that led her to trust her with her deepest anguish?

Certainly, there are many aspects about evangelism and witness in the workplace that are different from evangelism in other contexts but the fundamentals don't change:

- Praying for people
- Caring for people
- Sharing good news with people as opportunity arises and
- Seeking ways to provide contexts in which they can explore further.

Sometimes, as in the story of Anita and Gabriella, the opportunity seems to come out of nowhere, with a person that you may not have been praying for or even know. More often, however, opportunity comes with people that you've known over some time.

THE GREAT MISSION FIELD

Right where you are?

The reality is that God loves our co-workers. Didn't Christ die so that our co-workers might be freed from the power of sin, Satan and death? And freed for a life of purpose, adventure and fruitfulness now and in eternity?

Of course God is concerned about the spiritual welfare of the people where you work or where the people in your church work. And that means that

> *God is concerned about the spiritual welfare of the people where you work or where the people in your church work.*

it is highly likely that he is already working in their lives, both inside and outside the workplace. And it's also highly likely that he might actually want to work with you, and through you, to communicate his message to the people around you, right where you are.

For too long, many Christians have felt that they are 'wrong where they are', that God is sitting up in heaven looking down on them, wishing that they were really somewhere where they could do something more significant for him in a more strategic context.

Oh, whoops, there you are in TK Maxx. Meant you to be in a church office.

Oh, whoops, there you are in the Crown Prosecution Service. Meant you to be in jail.

Indeed, Christians have often been exhorted to go out into the highways and byways of our land to talk to people they do not know, when in the workplace they already know scores of people, some of them really very well.

Still, in my experience very few people are actually praying for people on their front line or asking others to do so. And not many church communities have seen what an extraordinary opportunity their people already have right where they are.

Love in the office?

It all happened in those wonderful days when I used to work in advertising.

I was deeply single at the time. And Jill was too. And she was, as far as I was concerned, sumptuously attractive. There were, however, three obstacles to my pursuit:

1. She wasn't a Christian
2. She worked for me
3. She had a boyfriend

Still, God is a God of miracles and however mixed my motives for prayer might have been, boy, did I pray for her. I suspect there's probably a technical term to describe this kind of ministry but I call it 'hormonic evangelism'. In any event, week by week we worked together and went to see clients together. Occasionally the question of faith would somehow come up.

Eventually, I invited her to read a psalm with me once a week before work. Later I invited her and a number of others to a six-week evangelistic Bible study in my flat. We had supper together, looked at a passage for an hour in a no-questions-barred kind of way and then stopped.

I'd invited a mature Christian woman called Sandy who was about the same age to join me in the study and once we'd done two series she started a women-only group and Jill went along to that.

At around the same time, Jill had started to go to church herself. She'd been reading Matthew's gospel and it seemed that wherever she went, and she went to several different churches, the sermon was on Matthew. After a while, it began to get to her. It was as if God had been orchestrating the sermon series of every church in the city specifically for her.

At some point in that 18 months or so, I took her through a simple gospel presentation and asked her if she wanted to receive Christ. She said 'yes'. Though the moment when she really committed herself to Christ came a little later.

What was involved? There was the witness and prayer of an individual. There was the witness of the word. There was the witness and prayers of other Christians. There was the witness of the Spirit and there was God's miraculous intervention. And there was a high level of intentional prayer and thought.

The primacy of prayer

So how then do we begin? With prayer. Ours and other people's.

Ask God to show you who in particular he might want you to pray for. Or if you are not in a workplace, ask people who are: 'Who would you like me to pray for?' It's not hard to write down a list of the people you work with and see who, as you pray, the Lord's Spirit particularly directs you towards. Nor, once you begin, is it difficult to find things to pray for people, in addition to their conversion. Issues abound: people struggling with stress or insecurity, people with teenagers who hate them, or teenagers they hate, people wrestling with debt or fighting a drink habit, people in difficult relationships or facing heart-rending decisions

> Ask God to show you who in particular he might want you to pray for.

about care for their elderly parents. People.

Involving other Christians is vital. Too often, because we go to work alone, we can try to do Christ's work there alone – without the support of our church community or the support of other Christians who are either in our workplace or who understand the workplace. Workplace evangelism, like every other form of evangelism, is a body business. We need each other.

Invite your pastor to visit you at work, if it's at all possible. It will, believe it or not, help them too, however unglamorous your context might be. Many pastors testify to the positive difference it's made to their ministries. Bishop James Jones, for example, used to visit someone at work at least once a month and instilled the same habit in many of the curates who worked for him. So, do your pastor a favour, get him to work.

Ask other people to pray for you. It could be your home group or your family or a couple of friends. You might want to produce a little sheet of paper once a month so they know what to pray. And if you want to pray for someone else, or make it easy for others to pray for you, the LICC website has a prayer slip that you can download with five questions applicable to a workplace or any other frontline:

1. What could I pray for your task?
2. What could I pray for your workplace/ frontline?
3. What could I pray for your colleagues, people you meet?
4. What could I pray for you?

Risky business?

Of course, the fact that we have so many contacts at work does not make workplace evangelism easy. Indeed, one of the challenges of workplace evangelism is precisely the reality that we do work with people for a long period of time, and so it feels much riskier than some other forms of evangelism. After all, it's one thing for an evangelist to stand in a pulpit or on a stage and preach to people they don't know and are unlikely to meet again. That has its own deep spiritual challenges. But it's quite another to tell a person with whom you spend 10, 20, 30,

40 hours a week in the same workplace how you became a Christian or how they might follow Jesus themselves. So what is the antidote to the fear of telling your story when opportunity arises?

The antidote to fear

In Acts 4, the disciples find themselves in a dangerous situation in Jerusalem. Jesus has been crucified. Peter and John have healed the paralysed man at the Gate Beautiful, have been arrested for preaching Jesus and have been thrown in jail. They are then brought before the elders who command them not to speak or teach in the name of Jesus. Peter and John refuse but are released and then return to their own people.

Will they continue to speak or not? Will they be next for the cross? The risk is considerable. This is what the disciples pray:

> 'Now, Lord, consider their threats and enable your servants to speak your word with great boldness. Stretch out your hand to heal and perform miraculous signs and wonders through the name of your holy servant Jesus.' (Acts 4:29–30, NIV)

They pray for two things:
1. For God's intervention
2. For boldness

Seven times in the book of Acts we read that the disciples pray for boldness – even though they'd spent three years being trained by Jesus himself. They don't try to pretend that there are no risks. Furthermore, their fears were legitimate. Jesus had been crucified, Stephen would be stoned to death and Saul would soon embark on a campaign of violent persecution.

Of course, there are risks today, even if, in the UK, not usually life-threatening ones. Some people are offended by the gospel because it is a stumbling block, some are hostile to Christians, some people will think you are marginally less intelligent than a plankton and marginally less cool than a trainspotter in an anorak on a Margate platform on New Year's Eve humming Barry Manilow tunes.

We do have to recognise a real risk in living christianly in a culture that is often schizophrenic about Christian engagement. On the one hand, our involvement is welcomed in so many areas of public life where secular solutions are proving bankrupt. On the other hand, suddenly people rear up on their hind legs in snorting outrage at the very notion that faith might be mentioned in the public sphere. All of us, then, are faced, like Shadrach, Meshach and Abednego in Babylon, with the reality that faithfulness to God may generate significant opposition and put our jobs in jeopardy. As my PA, Christina Winn, put it, *'Ultimately, unless our jobs, careers, reputations and popularity are surrendered to God, unless we trust him to provide for us and our families, unless we rely on him to defend and vindicate us, unless we honour him above corporate culture or disciplinary proceedings, fear will probably hinder us from being an authentic witness in the workplace. We are called to complete faith in God's ability to vindicate his word, whatever happens – "but even if he does not [rescue us], we will not bow down . . ."'*

Still, when you offer to tell someone the story of how you became a Christian, or the story of what Jesus has done for you, or your reasons for not sleeping around or refusing to do that particular deal, not many people take offence.

Prayer in context

In Acts 4, the disciples don't pray about some abstract, general context but about their particular situation. They ask God to 'consider' the threats that have been made against them. So we too bring to God the actual context we find ourselves in.

'Oh Lord, consider the atmosphere in my workplace that seems so indifferent to you.'

'Oh Lord, consider the reality that I am alone in this workplace.'

'Oh Lord, consider the reality that my colleague's wife is deeply opposed to your ways. Soften her heart as well as his.'

'Oh Lord, consider the reality that this person's parents are Muslims.'

So the disciples in Acts 4 pray for boldness and they ask God to intervene in some miraculous way – to 'stretch out his hand'. I wonder if we dare to ask for similar interventions. Might God perform miracles in your workplace?

Miracles in the workplace?

When I was working on Madison Avenue in the fourth largest advertising agency in the world, God performed at least one miracle of healing. And I have heard countless such stories. God gave sight to a teenager blind in one eye in the school hall of a comprehensive immediately after a Christian teacher gave an assembly on the healing of the man born blind in John 9. God spoke words of reassurance through a Christian to a woman who it seemed was unable to have children. 'It will be OK,' her Christian boss was convinced he should tell her, despite all that had gone before. And it was. God promised a Salford nurse who worked on Caesarian sections that no baby would ever die in the operating theatre under her care. And none has.

Might we also not pray that God would do marvellous things?

Heal a work colleague. Break an addiction. Bring peace to a fractured relationship. Bring business in to an apparently failing organisation. One man working in a business that had no orders went down on to the factory floor and laid hands on

> Boldness in communicating the truth about Jesus is not a function of personality type, it's a spiritual gift.

every idle machine and prayed that God would bring in work – in front of the factory team. Within a week the machines were humming again. Or perhaps you might simply pray for an opportunity to talk about him because none seems to arise in the busyness of the day:

'Oh Lord, the pace of work is so intense, that I just never seem to get an opportunity to talk to Mike/Sue/Rahee/Ahmed about you. Stretch out your hand to create an opportunity.'

Thirdly, the disciples pray that God would 'enable your servants to speak your word with great boldness'.

Boldness in communicating the truth about Jesus is not a function of personality type, it's a spiritual gift. It's not as if only extroverts can speak God's word, or people with the eloquence of Obama and the rapidity of response of Paul Merton. No, boldness in witness comes from God.

Great ideas

Ideas for cooperative effort abound, some obviously more applicable to larger companies or to contexts like business parks or city centres where there may be a number of organisations around but it only takes two to start a prayer group.

• Start an Alpha or Christianity Explored style course in your workplace – before work, at lunch or in the evening.

• Consider what the needs of your fellow employees might be and see how they might be met. You could find some people who could start a marriage or a parenting course. The CEO of a major company had been happily married for ten years but it was his second marriage. He wasn't a Christian but he realised that when his marriage was strong, his work was strong. And he wanted that for his team. Recently, he met a Christian and he's now actively considering running the HTB marriage course for the top 50 executives in his company.

• Similarly, one Christian group in Edinburgh discovered that one of the biggest needs of local businesses was bereavement counselling for their employees, so they found people who could go in and offer those services. After all, if you don't have a faith and you don't have a supportive community around you how do you deal with the anguish of losing someone you love? You may not be able to meet particular needs yourself but you may know someone who can.

• Create a special evangelistic event with a Christian speaker who's well known in your industry, or just well known enough to attract an audience.

• Put on a workplace carol service in a local church and collect for a local charity.

• Put together a group of singers – Christian and not – to sing carols in the car park/reception and collect for a local charity.

• Invite people who aren't Christians to get involved in a local charity with you – working together on something for other people can build really powerful relationships.

• Get involved with non-Christian co-workers in a charity that they might be involved with.

• Put on a grill-the-Christian event in a nearby pub/wine bar/breakfast cafe.

• Offer prayer. One Christian group found that, for all their meeting together they didn't seem to be having any impact on the people in the company, so they decided to let people know that they would be praying in a particular room at a particular time. They sent out an email, inviting anyone to submit prayer requests. Many did and some non-believers actually started to come to the meetings themselves. One said, *'I don't believe myself but it can't hurt.'* Prayer is elemental, and answered prayer a huge encouragement.

• Suggest your company gets a chaplain. Or if you have your own company, think about hiring one. Even for a small company. The regular, even fortnightly presence of a chaplain for a couple of hours can make a huge difference to company morale, employee retention, absenteeism and performance – as Simon Macaulay's experience at Anglo-Felt in Whitworth makes wonderfully clear (see www.licc.org.uk/macaulay).

> Get involved with non-Christian co-workers in a charity that they might be involved with.

• Throw out bait by leaving a book on your desk or a Bible. Ask God to show you what might be appropriate in your particular frontline.

• Invite a work colleague for a coffee, lend them a book that you like and that has some helpful themes in it – either on a topic they're interested in or in a type of literature they like. A Rugby fan might appreciate reading Jason Robinson's autobiography, a thriller fan might enjoy reading John Grisham's *Testament* or Andrew Young's *The Shack*. You could suggest they listen to a CD. Again it doesn't have to be Christian but might raise issues of life, death and eternal purpose.

• Ask them to a social event where they might meet some of your Christian friends, (particularly the one who shares the same unlikely passion they have for Herman's Hermits or the Arctic Monkeys or the Tropical Penguins).

• Invite them to a service that might be particularly relevant to them, or to read some Scripture with you before work, give them a mini Easter egg, with or without a card, a star at Christmas, a copy of *Why Jesus?* or *What's the Point of Christmas?* instead of a Christmas card...

Doing your bit in the big picture?

Still, quite independent of how God might lead you forward in evangelism at work, it is important to recognise that God may well be working elsewhere through other people: the neighbour who's befriended them, the Christian who talked to them on the bus yesterday, the Bible they opened in a hotel.

We do our part and leave the rest to God. In 1 Corinthians 3:5–6 Paul addresses those who try to elevate one person's evangelistic contribution over another's:

> 'What, after all, is Apollos? And what is Paul? Only servants, through whom you came to believe – as the Lord has assigned to each his task. I planted the seed, Apollos watered it, but God made it grow.' (NIV)

So, we are in this with God and with his wider church. We pray, we ask others to pray, we seek to bless our colleagues and we are intentional in seeking the salvation of others.

So may the Lord be with you in all you do.
May the Lord bless the work of your hands,
the words of your mouth
and the thoughts of your mind,
and bring forth good fruit through you to
his glory.

RESOURCES

Go to www.licc.org.uk for a fuller list of workplace resources, links to other organisations involved in workplace ministry and a new hymn about work by Graham Kendrick.

For ministry and evangelism

Change the World 9 to 5 features 50 simple, practical things which we can all do during the working day to make a difference to the world and those around us, regardless of our profession. Short, £6.99.

God at Work, Ken Costa, is a helpful introductory book tackling ethical dilemmas in business by very senior City banker and Alpha International Chairman. Covers the key issues well and is packed with real-life case studies. Continuum, £7.99.

Love Work, Live Life: Releasing God's Purpose in Work by David Oliver explores ways to bring passion and a vibrant spirituality to our workplaces. Authentic, £7.99.

Thank God it's Monday, Mark Greene, is a fun, fast, story-filled general book which includes material on theology of work, vocation, ministry, evangelism, ethical challenges and work-life integration. Scripture Union, £6.99.

For theology of work

The Jubilee Gospel, Kim Tan, is a timely and compelling exploration of Bible's teaching on Jubilee and its implications for home, business and political life. Authentic, £7.99.

So may the Lord be with you in all you do. May the Lord bless the work of your hands.

Your Work Matters to God, Sherman and Hendricks. Good exploration of the biblical view of work itself. NavPress, £8.99.

For business

Anointed for Business, Ed Silvoso. Much acclaimed exploration of how business is a means by which the kingdom of God is advanced, written by this Argentinian entrepreneur. Nova, £7.99.

For prayer

Pocket Prayers for Work, Mark Greene. A compilation of primarily contemporary prayers, mostly written by workers. Covers a range of issues in a variety of styles, including a selection of congregational prayers. CHP, £5.99

Touching the Pulse: Worship and Where We Work, Bernard Brailey (Ed). A superb anthology of over a hundred hymns, songs, poems, readings, prayers and helpful thoughts. Stainer & Bell, £8.25.

For group engagement

Alpha in the Workplace: Alpha shaped to work in shorter lunchtime or after-work formats. http://alpha.org/workplace.

Bands at Work: An innovative format for purposeful work-based groups. www.bandsatwork.co.uk.

Christianity Explored: Christianity Explored goes to work. www.christianityexplored.org.

Christian Life and Work, Mark Greene, 6-part, 2-hour, DVD. Includes a leader's guide keyed to *Thank God it's Monday*. Topics include: theology of work, evangelism, the boss, truthtelling, pressure, and work/life integration. Sessions include a creative Bible reading, teaching, exercises and commentary from workers in different contexts. Entertaining and practical. Scrioture Union, £25.

Work, Beverley Shepherd. Four studies that explore our work, the job description God has given us, and the workplace as a context for growth in skill, character, stewardship and mission. CWR, £3.25.

For pastors and church leaders

The Abolition of the Laity, R. Paul Stevens. Stimulating book with strong theological and historical material making a potent case for 'A people without laity and clergy.' Paternoster, £14.99.

The Heavenly Good of Earthly Work, Darrell Cosden. Genuinely original book which makes the case for the eternal significance of our daily work. Tightly argued, vitally important theological reflection. Paternoster, £8.99.

Supporting Christians at Work – Without Going Insane, Mark Greene. A concise guide for pastors which sets out the vision, the theological foundations and provides a host of practical ideas for everything from preaching to groups to décor that can help create a worker-friendly church without distorting the rest of the church's work. LICC, £5.

For Students/Graduates

Transition – The Christian Handbook to Life after University, Tim Vickers (Ed). Very helpful practical resource including material on work, work-life integration, money, sex power, relationships, finding a church . . . With wisdom from graduates, recent and not so recent. UCCF/LICC, £3.00.

Using the Bible for inspiration...
What would be your picture of hope?
What image would you create?

An art competition

For your school, church, art club or youth group

Images of Hope

Receive Bibles to give away as prizes!
(Available to 300 competition organisers on a first-come-first-served basis)

Advice on getting started and generating publicity
Call 01793 418222
Email contactus@biblesociety.org.uk
Visit www.biblesociety.org.uk/imagesofhope

HoPE
in our villages, towns & cities

bible society
making the bible heard

CHAPTER 18
HOPE-FILLED PRAYER

Jane Holloway, World Prayer Centre, and Liza Hoeksma, Soul Survivor

I urge, then, first of all, that requests, prayers, intercession and thanksgiving be made for everyone – for kings and all those in authority, that we may live peaceful and quiet lives in all godliness and holiness. This is good, and pleases God our Saviour, who wants all men to be saved and to come to a knowledge of the truth. 1 Timothy 2:1–4, NIV

Just as St Paul urged Timothy in his letter above, our aim was to make prayer central to all that took place in connection with HOPE. So often as Christians we want to rush into activity, without taking time to really get God's heart on what he wants and we can end up making prayer an 'add-on' to our plans. We didn't want that to be the case for HOPE so we launched it in October 2006 at the World Prayer Centre Trumpet Call V prayer event when thousands of people stood together to commit themselves to pray and work to see God's kingdom come across our nations. We dedicated 2007 as a Year of Prayer and invited individuals, churches and organisations to pray as never before for friends, neighbours, work colleagues, communities and nations.

And calling on God has stayed right at the heart of the HOPE mission. We wanted to encourage

> Calling on God has stayed right at the heart of the HOPE mission.

everyone and anyone to take up different models of prayer that suited them, get creative and get praying – and you did! In villages, towns and cities where Christians have met to pray in both small and large contexts, it has helped build unity and community. In places where prayer has traditionally been an 'in-church' or 'in-private' activity we have seen that totally change. Yes, we've been committed to praying in our churches, small groups and times alone with God but we've heard great stories of lots of you taking prayer out onto the streets to bless your communities.

Be inspired as you read what churches have been up to and see if you pick up some new ideas that you could put into practice in your community!

STARTING THE YEAR IN PRAYER

There were loads of great prayer events to kick off the year of HOPE combining time spent seeking God with blessing people who were out celebrating the New Year. Everyone agreed it would be a great way to start any year! Which kind of event would work in your community?

• **York Minster:** Andy Hawthorne spoke on the gift of hope before the gathered group spilled out onto the streets at midnight to bless the partygoers with free bottles of water!

• **Soul Survivor** hosted a night of prayer starting at 10.30pm and finishing with coffee and croissants at 6.30am! As well as praying for the HOPE high points, the night included times of worship, an opportunity for people to give testimony to what God had been doing in the previous year and space for people to rededicate themselves to God to be used in the coming year.

• **Leicester Cathedral** opened its doors from 8pm to 2.30am so people could come and chill out on bean bags with hot chocolate and have space to chat. There was a rolling programme of prayer over the night with bands, prayer graffiti walls, a prayer labyrinth and Taizé style meditation.

• **Glasgow:** Christians in Glasgow met at 8pm in the city centre to hand out bottles of water to partygoers, then went on to a Watchnight prayer and commissioning service in the cathedral at 11pm.

• **Northampton:** prayer walkers started from seven different points across the city and met in front of a church in the town centre to spend time in prayer and worship.

• **Cornwall:** on New Year's Day people from all ages and denominations gathered in Truro Cathedral to pray for the year of unified mission.

The Declaration of HOPE for 2008 prayer (see www.hope08.com) was used throughout the year in homes, churches and community prayer events – why not write one for future years that lay out some common prayer themes?

As the first year of HOPE kicked off, the prayer video by the Archbishop of Cantebury, Dr Rowan Williams, and Martyn Atkins was downloaded more than 3,100 times over the Christmas and New Year period!

Andy Hawthorne spoke on the gift of hope before the gathered group spilled out onto the streets at midnight to bless the partygoers with free bottles of water!

Healing on the Streets

Healing on the Streets is an idea developed by Causeway Coast Vineyard church in Coleraine, Northern Ireland, and for several years they have been exploring what happens when the church begins to demonstrate the kingdom of God outside its own walls. This year, all over the country, many people have been inspired by this idea and have been going out onto the streets of their villages, towns and cities, offering to pray for people for physical healing. A group of Christians from all denominations of churches in Watford told us what they've been up to.

What do you do? We go into the town centre every Saturday and set up our 3m-high banner (that says 'Healing' on it) in the same place. We hand out flyers to people who come past explaining who we are and what we're offering, we chat to people and, if they'd like us to, we pray for them. We have a couple of chairs so people can sit as they're prayed for and we have an awning in case it's raining.

Why? We didn't want to keep the church safely behind four walls – we wanted to get out into the community and ask God to heal and meet with people and provide a safe environment for people to get prayer.

Top tips

• Contact your council to explain what you're planning on doing. You need permission from them and it's good for them to understand you're not preaching but offering a free service.

• Be in the same place, at the same time each week, even if it means being out in the rain/cold/sleet, as consistency counts for a lot.

It means you get 'regulars' and can build relationships with local shops and businesses. The local grocer started off very sceptical of us but now he sends people our way for prayer even though he's not a Christian!

• Be gentle with people. You can't push prayer or conversation on anyone and if you try you may end up doing more damage than good.

• Never accept money! You'll be surprised how many people offer to pay you.

• Start by praying together as a team in the street if possible.

• To do our best to make everyone go away feeling loved, we give them a letter which explains a bit more about healing. It details how even if they didn't get healed that day, God still loves them.

Lessons learned

• Many people feel like they have nothing to offer but everyone and anyone who knows Jesus can pray for people. Encourage potential new members of the team to come along and pray with someone else to start with to build their confidence.

• We've found that many homeless people come along to chat so we now make sure we have information sheets we can give them on hostels and shelters that can help them.

• We only had a small team of six people when we first started. The more other Christians heard about the healings, the more they were intrigued and started to come along so we now have about 30–40 people on our rota. It takes time to build a solid team so don't be discouraged if you have to start small.

• Try and find somewhere to store your equipment (chairs, flyers, banner, sandbags to weigh down the banner, etc.) near where you meet. A local shopkeeper kindly looks after ours and it makes such a difference not needing to find someone to bring it with them each Saturday.

The outcomes

We've built great relationships, seen people come to Alpha after their contact with us and of course seen a number of healings – both physical and emotional. As an example one guy we handed a flyer to was actually on his way to hospital with an asthma attack. He asked for prayer and the asthma attack stopped! Many people have asked us to pray for difficult circumstances in their lives and have said they've felt filled with peace too.

Our aim is to have a church service on the street so that anyone can join in. We're taking our first steps towards this and are going to start having a band for a time of worship.

Want to get involved? How about trying to set up your own Healing on the Streets programme? Visit www.out-there.org for more information.

Healing Rooms

Or how about setting up a healing room where people in need of healing can come and encounter the healing power of God through Jesus Christ? A team of 20 people from five churches in Nottingham have set one up and they have seen God touch many people physically, emotionally and spiritually. They open every Thursday afternoon and evening and, in under a year, have prayed for over 150 people, seeing some people come back a number of times. See www.healingroomsengland.com or www.healingrooms-scotland.com for more details of how you could set one up.

Light Life are doing some great work in Scotland offering healing prayer and prophetic readings to the general public as well as training and support for Christians wanting to do something similar. See their website www.lightlife.org.uk for more details.

Prayer walking provides a wonderful way both to get to know our communities and meet new people:

In Crowthorne, Berkshire, Christians have been doing prayer walks on every Friday afternoon and the 1st Saturday of each month. Every other week an 'informed intercession' get-together has happened to ask God about specific things surrounding HOPE activities and to receive his counsel. Pete Sherman said, 'The HOPE

eden

...because transforming communities is a way of life

As the temptation to be a 'consumer Christian' increases, more and more people are questioning their faith-life and making radical decisions about authenticity and community. Over the last ten years, around 300 people from all walks of life have sensed God calling them to live this deliberately different lifestyle in a growing network of missional communities called Eden.

Eden is a ground-breaking approach to urban youthwork and community transformation. It originated in Manchester in 1997, flowing out of the innovative schools' work and music of 'The Tribe'. Eden focuses on the most challenging urban areas, sharing God's life-changing love in word and action. Eden teams choose to live long-term in these communities, sharing the joys and challenges of those growing up there and ministering to their neeeds. It's not comfy and it's not easy but it is incredibly fulfilling and rewarding.

To request an info pack including free DVD
contact eden@message.org.uk

For more info and to apply visit: www.eden-network.org

"Hope 2008 has transformed communities across the UK as the Gospel has been declared in word and deed. Youth for Christ could transform your youth group......"
Hope 2008 founder and Vice President of Youth for Christ, Roy Crowne.

yfc
Youth for Christ
taking good news relevantly to every young person in Britain

68 local Centres work with churches to ensure evangelism and youthwork is relevant to young people

300,000 young people reached every month

Sport, music, film and drama teams take the good news to young people

Marginalised youth encounter Jesus' love and realise their potential

Evangelistic and discipleship resources help churches in their youth ministry

Schools resources allow young people to discover a dynamic and vibrant Christian faith

17-25 year olds get involved in mission for 3, 6 or 11 months in the UK or overseas on YFC year-outs

Tel: 0121 502 9620
Visit **www.yfc.co.uk** to find out more

British Youth for Christ, Registered Charity 263446, SC039297 initiative has given us a marvellous excuse for our denominational boundaries to fade away, leaving a united family under one God desiring simply to ask, listen and to play a small part in his bigger story of mission for Crowthorne.'

Stephen in **Eastbourne** said, 'Every month we have been prayer walking through one particular part of the town. We asked one church in the area what we could be praying for and the vicar told of five areas of concern and difficulty. We had a powerful time of prayer about these issues and the vicar asked us to go back. When we spoke to him again a few months on, he told us that there had been a complete change in all the areas and he was seeing great blessings in the church, including people coming to faith.'

A small church in **Swindon** weren't deterred that they didn't have the physical ability to get out and work in their community. Instead they leafleted 800 homes asking for prayer requests and then held a service and prayer walk. The guided walk had prayer prompts at different stages and for those who couldn't make it round, a PowerPoint presentation was used at the church so they could do a virtual walk.

Try Praying is a resource produced by There is Hope in Hull. It's a short booklet that you can give away to encourage people who aren't Christians to try praying for a week. Those that have used the booklet are then encouraged to 'release the book into the wild' – by leaving it in a public place where someone else can pick it up and use it. Check out their website for more details www.trypraying.org.

Laying the foundations in Prayer – Manchester

The HOPE Greater Manchester team have been finding every possible opportunity to get people praying. There have been lots of activities ranging from large-scale city-wide events, weekly emails, prayer walks and prayer triplets through to supporting personal prayer. Key to the success has been to close the gap between mission and prayer –

Prayer walking provides a wonderful way both to get to know our communities and meet new people.

by linking the two together like the cutting blades of a pair of scissors.

24-7 Prayer has been a strong part of that strategy. The year before HOPE began, from midnight on January 1st to midnight on December 31st, Greater Manchester was covered in 24-7 prayer with an estimated 134 churches or groups taking part across all boroughs of Greater Manchester and Macclesfield. All mainstream denominations got involved – youth groups, elderly congregations, Churches Together groups and even a Roman Catholic convent for retired nuns!

Some churches covered a few hours, others a day or two, and some one or two weeks. Some churches kept to the 24-7 prayer room, while elderly congregations, or those in less safe areas chose to at least partially do prayer chains overnight. The Salvation Army were amazing, willing to cover Christmas and January periods, and the Black Majority Churches were brilliant at covering night periods. There was also one church with only twenty-four members who managed to cover a full week of 24-7 prayer at two weeks' notice!

Top tips to make 24-7 Prayer happen:

• The 24-7 prayer rota was kept online at www.hopemanchester.com alongside downloadable resources including a guide to co-ordinating 24-7 Prayer, a guide to setting up a prayer room, a rota people could print off and fill in names, and prayer points. All were based on the 24-7 Prayer guidelines, then tailored to Greater Manchester with the specific purpose of praying for HOPE. The prayer points were five pages long, with bullet points so every minute of the hour was covered with something to pray or meditate about. Many Christians who struggle with prayer commented on how useful they were. The prayer guide was produced monthly, mirroring the high points of HOPE.

• Prayer was emphasised as being the number one priority for all HOPE activities and the team used every avenue to share the vision and inspire people to participate. It was promoted through HOPE roadshows, weekly prayer emails, the North West leaders forum, websites, networkers and perhaps most importantly by personally phoning up church leaders. The team have been encouraged at the success of many HOPE initiatives, knowing the prayers of a unified church were foundational. All glory and honour go to God!

• 24-7 or day and night praying can take many forms, and there are different examples currently taking place around the UK. To find out how to get started on 24-7 prayer and track what is happening around the nation/world go to http://uk.24-7prayer.com and www.prayerforum.org.

A Christian presence at Spirit fairs

At the Colchester HOPE day in their town centre, the churches set up a stall using the Jesus Deck as part of the activities. The Jesus Deck is a set of playing cards that show events in Jesus' life, from his birth through to his resurrection, and members of the public were invited to pick a number of cards which then led to the team being able to discuss the event depicted and relate it to events in that person's life. The deck is a great way to have a Christian presence at Body, Mind and Spirit fairs. Others have simply gone along to psychic fairs where members of the public are charged for things like tarot readings and offered to listen to God for them for free.

For an academic look at the Christian symbolism of tarot cards try reading *Beyond Prediction: The Tarot and Your Spirituality* by John W. Drane, Ross Clifford and Philip Johnson.

Other great ideas we heard about that might inspire you . . .

• Many fun days and festivals had a prayer tent or teams of people asking those in the crowd if they would like prayer. What a great way to introduce our faith in a non-threatening environment!

• A group in Peterborough used the national HOPE prayer resource leaflet, *Friday Focus,* every week when they met together at 8am in Stilton

The Jesus Deck is a set of playing cards that show events in Jesus' life, from his birth through to his resurrection.

Church. Current resources to pray for our nation can be found on www.prayerforum.org.

• Send greetings cards at Easter or Christmas to local homes that have detachable prayer request slips. Churches in south Manchester did just that and had a great response – they then held a prayer service to pray for all the requests that came in. See Chapter 7 for more details.

• In Southampton 1,000 people were each given a piece of a jigsaw puzzle with an aerial view of their city to take away and use as a reminder to pray.

• Presence – a Christian-owned gift shop and spa in Watford, Hertfordshire, offers customers spiritual readings, prayer for healing or dream interpretation sessions free of charge. Spiritual readings are times when the team ask God to speak to them for the person, offer them words of encouragement and insight into their character, how God sees them and their future.

• For the Global Day of Prayer, Christians in Exeter gathered for a prayer picnic in the grounds of the cathedral then released 200 balloons to represent the 200 nations taking part in the prayer day. For details of the next day see www.globaldayofprayer.co.uk.

• During their week of mission Beeston churches used fliers to advertise a prayer hotline that residents could call with prayer requests.

• Project postcode: visit www.projectpostcode.org and sign up to pray for a postcode that has significance for you. It may be where you live now, an area you'd like to move to, where your children go to school, where your small group meets . . . anywhere! As you pray you may find that opportunities for service and ministry begin to emerge and that the spiritual climate begins to change (you'll find stories online of people who prayed and found just that!).

RESOURCES

Websites

· **www.crossrhythms.co.uk/prayerrooms** – add your own prayers at The Incinerator.

· Visit **www.ctbi.org.uk** to get more details of the week of Prayer for Christian Unity.

· Go to **www.globaldayofprayer.co.uk** for details of future international prayer dates and events which are attended by millions of people around the world.

· **www.gg2w.org.uk** – Getting God to Work.

· **www.healingroomsengland.com** and **www.healingrooms-scotland.com** for more details on offering prayer for healing (see the case study in this chapter for more info).

· **www.noonministries.com** – Need Of Our Nation (NOON) encourages people to pray between noon and one o'clock for our nation.

· **www.out-there.org** – Healing on the Streets information.

· **www.prayer-alert.net** weekly prayer email for current national European and world issues.

· **Pray-as-you-go** is a free daily prayer session, designed for use on portable MP3 players (or computer), to help you pray whilst travelling – **www.pray-as-you-go.org**.

· **www.prayerforum.org** – connecting ministries, organisations, churches and individuals across British Isles and Ireland: news updates, calendar of events, resources, prayer initiatives.

· **www.radiantlight.org.uk** – encouragement in the Catholic faith through paintings and meditations.

· **www.rejesus.co.uk/spirituality** – post or download a prayer, find a sacred space and learn about prayer labyrinths.

· **www.uk.24-7prayer.com** – everything you need to know about the 24-7 Prayer movement, including how to run a prayer week, boiler room and lots of stories.

Send greetings cards at Easter or Christmas to local homes that have detachable prayer request slips.

· **www.waymakers.org** – free monthly email prayer guide helping focus prayer for those not following Jesus Christ.

· **www.when2pray.net** – helping couples pray together.

· **www.worldprayer.org.uk** – mobilising prayer nationally and globally.

Books

The 24-7 Prayer Manual and CD-ROM, £9.99.

40 Day Prayer Guide (for Lent or at other times of the year) produced by There is Hope. Download for free at www.40-days.com.

Community Prayer Cells – How to be Good News Neighbours, Jane Holloway, Church Pastoral Aid Society, £5 – www.cpas.org.uk.

The Dynamics of Effective Prayer, Alistair Cole, £11.00 inc postage and packing. Available from Alistair Cole by email alistair.l.cole@btinternet.com or tel 01457 866177/866213.

The Grace Outpouring – Blessing Others Through Prayer, Roy Godwin and Dave Roberts, D. C. Cook, £7.99.

Grove Booklets Spirituality Series such as *Simple Tools for Stillness*, Wanda Nash, £2.95 – www.grovebooks.co.uk.

Seven Ways to Ignite Outrageous Prayer, Nigel James and Carl Brettle. Authentic, £7.99.

Ignition cards help you pray for three friends who aren't Christians. Order for free by emailing info@igniteme.org – www.igniteme.org.

Prayer – A Guide for Beginners, Jane Holloway, Bible Reading Fellowship, £4.99.

Prayerworks – The Manual, 24-7 Prayer and Faithworks have joined together to create this resource which will help your church run a community-focused week of prayer and also launch a community project from that week. Authentic, £6.99.

Prayer – Unwrapping the Gift, John Preston. Encouraging the local church to pray with photocopyable prayer resources, including a prayer audit. Authentic, £3.50.

Redeeming our Communities – 21st Century Miracles of Social Transformation,
Debra Green, New Wine Ministries, £ 9.99 – www.newwineministries.co.uk.

Saints at Prayer, Michael Mitton. This course is an ideal resource to teach people to pray in groups with confidence. Available from ReSource, 01235 553922 www.resource-arm.net. Leader's Manual £7, Link Workbook £4

Try Praying A short booklet (and free download via website) designed for those outside the church who are spiritually hungry to help them to pray, produced by There is Hope. Free download at www.trypraying.org.

Your Kingdom Come, J.John. Study guide for home groups on the Lord's Prayer from the Philo Trust, £3.99 – www.philotrust.com.

Get a weekly prayer update on your mobile, highlighting the main issues we face in our society each week.

Miscellaneous

Prayer DVD – testimonies, stories and practical tips from Redeeming Our Communities www.redeemingourcommunities.org.uk, £3.50.

Prayer Magazine A quarterly, inter-denominational publication to resource churches and small groups. Digital version available at www.prayermagazine.net or call 0844804 4808.

www.prayrightnow.net Text PRAY to 82088 to get a weekly prayer update on your mobile, highlighting the main issues we face in our society each week.

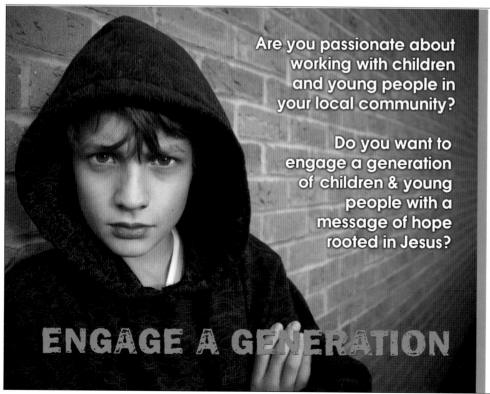

CHAPTER 19

HOPE IN SPORT

Barry Mason and Sarah Davis, Youth For Christ

'Sport has an unmatched ability to mobilise and excite people in their millions.'
Government Department for Culture, Media & Sport

Sport is undeniably a favourite British pastime; it matters to people. There are few places you will find people more passionate than when playing or watching sport. And if it matters to a large majority of the population, then it should matter to us, the church, in our efforts to bring HOPE to villages, towns and cities. In fact it provides us with an amazing opportunity to get to know people, to bless them and to have fun. Plus one of the great things about sport is the range of expressions it can take. The glamour of the Olympics may seem to be a little daunting to organise on a budget collected from a gift day (!), but taking a ball and a couple of jumpers to the local park, with a bag of oranges and a bottle of water doesn't take much time, money or effort. It might just change someone's life . . .

We heard about loads of great sporting events happening around HOPE and wanted to share this selection with you to inspire you in how you could be using sport to reach your community for Jesus.

> Sport is undeniably a favourite British pastime; it matters to people.

Football Initiative

A few passionate football players from churches in Crowthorne, Hampshire, realised that they could use their love of sport as a great way to connect with members of the community.

How did they do it? Crowthorne's HOPE football initiative incorporates two matches each month:
1) There is an 'all age' match, consisting of a bunch of football enthusiasts preparing the local recreation ground and then inviting anyone to come and join them – playing until the ref can't take any more players!
2) There is an 'end of the month' match where the more regular players host a match against different sectors of the community e.g. local dads who coach kids or other teams, local waiters, teachers from the community, police, the fire brigade and hospital patients.

The games provide a great time of healthy activity, friendly competition and a chance to meet new people. Those involved in the games themselves have been able to strike up some great conversations and connections with teammates, opponents, spectators, 'fans' and passers-by. The games always carry a positive atmosphere. The most recent game had five Christians amongst the 22 players! Part of the practice involves praying all together before the match and playing with the attitude of representing Christ on the pitch. These two combined together prove to be a great witness to those involved who do not yet know Christ for themselves.

Want to do something similar? Each village, town and city has sporting activities at various levels of ability which would benefit from a group of Christians who are willing to give up their time to get involved. How about using football, basketball, rounders, cricket, jogging or leisurely walks as a way to get out and connect with new people in your area?

Running with HOPE

Where? Brentwood, Essex.

What did it look like? Brentwood's annual 'Fun Run and Half Marathon' opened a wonderful door of opportunity for those at Sawyers Church. It was a huge event – 3,500 runners with massive crowds of support – and the church made the most of this by seeking to connect with people that flocked into the vicinity from the borough and surrounding areas. With the church being opposite the start line it seemed the obvious choice to open the building for the morning, forego the morning service, and serve free refreshments to the crowds instead. There were loads of options for the kids – bouncy castles, face painting, crafts, etc. and many cups of tea available for folks waiting for their sporty counterparts to complete their strenuous endeavours.

Prior to the day an order was placed for 75 'HOPE in Brentwood' T-shirts (not enough as it turned out!) so most of the helpers and runners had the HOPE logo and details of a local website www.hopeinbrentwood.com displayed on their person for all to see. Hundreds of people streamed through the building and took away free literature and details of the church's services. Helpers were able to engage in great conversations and prayed that hearts would be receptive to God's truth.

The outcome

The event proved a great opportunity to combine community presence with gospel impact and

Pray for opportunities to talk to friends about Christ.

it was evident God honoured the efforts. The day gave church members the chance to engage meaningfully with non-believers and share the reason for the hope that they have; new folk turned up in church the following week which was a huge encouragement!

What a simple but brilliant idea! Why not try something similar in your area?

There are so many regular sports activities happening that if setting up something of your own seems a bit daunting, you could follow Sawyers Church example and offer to serve the community at events that are already taking place. Have a think about where the local football pitches and playgrounds are in your area. Keep an eye on local papers and news programmes and see what town/city-wide promotions are happening and get involved. People will always love having somewhere to sit and chat over a cup of tea . . . especially the friends and family who've come along in support of the sports enthusiasts!

A PASSION FOR SPORT

We chatted to Mark Blythe from Molesey Community Church, Surrey, to find out how he thinks a passion for Jesus and a passion for sport can be combined with fantastic results!

In a brilliant book called Wild at Heart *by John Eldredge a key passage reads, 'Don't ask yourself what the world needs. Ask yourself what makes you come alive, and go do that, because the world needs people who have come alive.' Sport makes me come alive, I love it, I love sports people, I love Jesus and I love people seeing and hearing something of God's love for the first time. At Molesey Community Church in Surrey we have an all-year-round sports ministry programme. We believe that evangelism doesn't just last for a cricket or a football season, it is friendship all year round and for many years. Some folks come to faith early, most take years to break down the barriers of prejudice and stereotypes, but doing what you love to break down those barriers is never a chore!*

What makes you come alive? At Molesey we encourage all church members to see their hobbies as their mission field. We have a golf club that goes to the range during winter, enters the National Christian Golf Cup, holds events, plays matches against a local pub and goes away on tour for a weekend. The aim is evangelism through lifestyle witnessing, occasional gospel presentations and invitations to other church events as appropriate. Christians from any church and those not yet in church all join in.

Free football for 5–15s

Football is a big part of our local outreach. Each Saturday morning during term time we hold free kids' football for children aged 5–15 years old. The leaders come from three different churches in Molesey, co-ordinated by the Community Church. An average of 70 kids attend and are taught teamwork and skills in a non-swearing environment. The parents love it. They also love the free tea and coffee provided by the volunteer church members who come down to serve at 8.30am each week; what a witness! As part of HOPE we staged a 5-a-side tournament with the helpers wearing 'Team Molesey' T-shirts, which also had a cross on them. The thought is that we are one team, united loving Jesus, even though we worship in different ways at different churches. We had 30 teams, 200 kids, 400 spectators and after presenting the Christian message we gave a medal to every child who participated.

Eighteen years of running an adult football ministry has seen our club grow to four adult teams playing each week. We have one veterans group (over 35s) and three open age teams, which many youngsters from the kids' footy have progressed up to. We have tried all forms of outreach and structures, made every mistake possible and still seen folks come to faith. To help prevent others making the same mistakes I have written a book called Football 2, Football Ministry 3, *i.e. footy is good, but football ministry is even better! See the Resources section for more details.*

Cricket, running, triathlons, cycling, gym clubs, aerobics, walking, dance, watching motor racing; whatever the passion, we encourage folks to follow the Christians in Sport model of 'Pray, Play, Say' – Pray for opportunities to talk to friends about Christ, Play or watch your sport together, and Say something about Jesus when asked or at appropriate times.

It works, just go for it!

Nomad: Mission in a cage

Where? All over the country including Crawley, West Sussex; Ivybridge, Devon; Inverness, Scotland; Birmingham, West Midlands; Bournemouth; Lutterworth; Glasgow; Trafford, Manchester; Oswestry and many more . . .

What did they look like? Each of these events looked completely different! The Nomad team are a travelling urban sports team who have a mobile cage which can be set up in almost any location to hold sports tournaments. The team have worked in schools, cathedrals, leisure centres, town centres, recreational areas and even pub car parks!

In Trafford the team spent the whole week working in one school, and came into contact with every pupil in the town of Partington. Every day the team delivered coaching in P.E. lessons, educational awareness in R.E. lessons and built great relationships in and around the cage during break times. On the Thursday evening, Nomad also delivered its Late Night Nomad event, where the cage, games consoles and video clips all played a part in getting alongside the young people and being able to share testimonies and a gospel message with them.

Why? Trafford YFC had been working in the school throughout the school term and had seen a real need for the young people to know that they were special and that something could be done just for them. (Throughout the week, the Nomad team had some amazing conversations, just off the back of the question 'Why have you come to us?') The R.E. teacher in the school, Dan Hunt, wanted to see a fresh perspective being brought into his lessons and to meet the educational challenge to connect the content of two curriculum subjects.

How did it work? Initially the head teacher had refused permission for the Nomad team to come in to school, believing that there would be no interest from the pupils, the cage would be damaged by pupils during the break time and that the team members would be made to feel unwelcome. In timetabled lessons the initially resistant P.E. staff were completely won over by the energy of the team and the atmosphere created in and around the cage; the pupils treated the team as if they'd known them forever; everyone in the school was talking about the R.E. lessons in which they'd had to 'build their own cage out of straws before the flood came'; the cage had a queue around it every lunchtime.

The outcomes

- Those attending the Thursday evening session said they would attend every week if the church put something like that on . . . including the talk about Jesus.
- By midweek the head teacher played in the cage with his pupils and asked if this would be an annual booking!
- The cage and Nomad team even survived the week without abuse or damage! Dan Hunt, the R.E. teacher, won the Best Teacher of the Month award for his creativity around R.E. and P.E. lessons.
- The Nomad team had a great time and were encouraged by the responses of the young people they met.

Alternative deliveries: The cage concept has also been delivered as part of one-off days in schools and stand alone events in town centres and on village greens. The cage has stood in the middle of Ely Cathedral, Matlock football pitch car park, a school hall in Solihull, the ruins of Coventry Cathedral, on the Isle of Man, and on the 'rec' in Leeds housing estates. These have sometimes been delivered without publicity – the setting up of the cage is often enough to see a crowd of young people gather out of interest.

Top tips for if you'd like to do something similar:

- Check what sports teams options there are available to come and work with you – see www.yfc.co.uk/teams.
- Plan the evening event with young people in mind – i.e. relevant activities; convenient and comfortable location and time.
- Contact your local school – they may seem resistant at first, but are often glad of the

> Be uncomfortable in their territory, rather than expect them to come to you and be uncomfortable.

energetic input from outside agencies.
- Make sure the event is of a high quality – young people are not easily impressed.
- Check where young people are gathering and go to them. Be uncomfortable in their territory, rather than expect them to come to you and be uncomfortable. Consider asking the young people for permission to come on to 'their patch'.
- Carefully consider in advance when any talks may come. Enjoy building relationships with young people without pressure for delivery, and then be ready to share your faith when they are comfortable enough to ask questions.

Family Skate

Tim Funnell has been running an outdoor skate park in Clitheroe in the Ribble Valley, East Lancashire, to engage with young people and show them the love of Jesus. He organises a number of events including Family Skate over the summer holidays which is an opportunity for parents/carers and their kids to skate together, usually with the kids teaching the adults. Tim said, *'It's a great session and it is so good to see family relationships developing over the weeks.'* When a young lad (17) was kicked out of his home, the skate park team were able to meet with him and his mum and take him to the Job Centre etc. He moved back home and signed up for college . . . and started tagging along with the team to church on Sundays too!

Don't forget to make the most of all the opportunities around the 2012 Olympics! More Than Gold is a charity facilitating a coordinated response from the UK church to serving the Olympics and Paralympics – to find out more go to www.morethangold. org.uk

Thinking about using sport as a way to reach people in your community? Here are some more ideas that might work in your village, town or city:

- The HOPE Bradford group maximised on their community's love of sport by having their Alpha taster evening at Bradford City Football Club and had the club's former player-turned-coach as their guest speaker. See Chapter 9 (HOPE Explored) for more details.
- Golf days are a good way to gather the men (or women) who may not normally

be attending church services. Plan the day with 4 balls, allowing conversations on the course, and further opportunity for a talk or socialising atmosphere afterwards.

• Lisa Adams from Soul Survivor Watford set up a weekly keep-fit class on a local estate. The initial programme ran for a term and after the last week everyone wanted to do a social event as it was Christmas. Lisa invited the group along to the church Alpha taster evening and every one of the women who had been coming to the class went along and had a great time!

• You could hold a 'Night of Champions' event for young people with competitions, team building and a range of tasks from 5-a-side football to problem solving activities. This can work for groups from 20 to 200. The higher quality the content, the greater the energy around it – consider good prizes, T-shirts and quality equipment.

• Street Soccer – use football as the great bridge-building tool that it is. A quick kick around can give everyone a level playing field with regards to status and breaks down barriers very quickly. Great conversations often come out of the refreshments afterwards. This has taken off in Manchester where a group used street soccer as an outreach to homeless people in the area – check out www.barnabus-manchester.org.uk/street_soccer.

• Sports night – host the big screen viewing of major sports events like St Peter and St Paul's Parish Church in Shepton Mallet. They used the Olympics and Euro 2008 as their excuse but you could try Formula 1 racing, the Superbowl, the FA Cup Final or a match featuring your local team. Whatever it is, sports fans will fit it into their diary. Or you could initiate a gathering at the local pub to build relationships there.

• A number of churches in Shepton Mallet also worked together to organise a local sports day with silly and serious sports and family team games.

• Sports Quiz night – invite people to bring friends along to make up a team. Put real energy into the set-up of tables, decorations, etc. Make sure the quiz master is energetic and the format is creative and challenging. A fun night can help people enjoy the new friends they might make or awareness that churches are not all stuffy buildings.

• Fitness classes – health is such a major issue in today's culture. Create simple activity groups with certain ages in mind. Baby active sessions, young people's 'Energy Hour', exercise classes, group walks. Anything that will help keep people active in a safe environment which makes them feel welcome.

RESOURCES

Christians in Sport work with sports people across all age ranges and 80 sports. They have loads of great events and resources for Christians who are passionate about sport. One of their aims is to help Christians **pray** for their sporting friends, **play** sport in a way that honours Jesus and to share their faith through what they **say**. See their website www.christiansinsport.org.uk to find details of:

Events

• **Adults and professionals conference** weekends.

• **National Sports Networks** which link together Christian sportspeople who play the same sport and provide opportunities for sportspeople who are not Christians to hear something of the good news of Jesus in a relevant way. There are currently networks for hockey, rugby, ultimate Frisbee and women's football.

• **Sportsfest** is an evening or afternoon event filled with banter, barbecues and competitive team sports for adults. They're also a great chance to bring friends along to hear a bit more about the great news of Jesus.

- **Sports Plus Conferences** for upper school young people to learn more about Jesus and how to share him with their friends who are not Christians.
- **Sports Plus Camps** – intensive weeks of specialist sports coaching and Bible teaching for 11- to 17-year-olds.
- **Youth Pray, Play, Say Groups**, University Groups and Adults Groups.

Resources and downloads, including:

- **Free study guides** for adults and young people, school assembly outlines and talks to listen to.
- **'How to'** guides including how to organise a sporting dinner, a golf day, holiday club, sports tournament or quiz, and big screen event.
- *Pray, Play, Say – The Youth Way* containing 10 studies to help young Christian sports players make a difference for eternity in their world of sport, £3.

Is hockey, rugby or football your passion? If so contact Christians in Sport to obtain info of their networks of like minded people – www.christiansinsport.org.uk, tel: 01869 255 630.

Ambassadors in Sport: Do you want some qualified soccer coaches to come in and teach quality football to your group and then also give an appropriate Bible study? Contact Ambassadors in Sport on 01204 363606.

Mark Blythe is passionate about reaching the world of sport for Christ and is available to help church members and leaders set up sports ministry programmes. He helps to provide administrative support to the network of UK Sports Ministries which are available to help and resource local churches. Contact via mark@mccfc.org.uk.

Christian Adventure Centres: Do you like archery, climbing, canoeing and have some adventurous friends, a youth group or sports team? Take them away to a Christian Adventure Centre for an unforgettable experience – check out www.barnabas.org.uk.

Is hockey, rugby or football your passion? If so contact Christians in Sport.

Football 2, Football Ministry 3 by Mark Blythe is a book to help people in their new or existing sports ministry. Available from www.veriteshop.com for £10.

National Christian Cricket Festival: If you and your friends enjoy cricket, put a team into the National Christian Cricket Festival in Bristol which includes a gospel presentation to start discussions. Email mark@mccfc.org.uk for info.

National Christian Football Festival: Over 30 churches take their teams of footballers, mainly non-church guys, to the National Christian Football Festival each year, for a weekend of football, fun and deep chats. Contact Ambassadors in Sport on 01204 363606 for more details.

National Christian Golf Cup: Play Golf? Invite a non-church friend to be your partner in the National Christian Golf Cup. There are tournaments around the country with the winners playing in a grand final. Check out www.christiangolfsociety.org.uk.

Sports Missionary Organisations: Love sport and love Jesus? Then check out the many Sports Missionary Organisations and events that are listed on the website www.uksportsministries.org. Find jobs, gap year information, testimonies and lots more.

Visit **www.sportsoutreach.com** for a free download on why sport should be taken seriously by the church.

Youth For Christ: To find out more about Youth For Christ sports teams visit www.yfc.co.uk/teams.

CHAPTER 20
A SUMMER FULL OF HOPE

Pete Gilbert, Re:Act

The idyllic picture of summertime: cities baked in pavement-shimmering heat; market towns the nation over preparing their Summer Fayre; village greens echoing gentle applause as the next batsman approaches the crease. Summer is full of hope for good weather, long lazy days, balmy nights, and bargain holidays, despite what previous rainy summers have taught us!

Summer is actually full of opportunities for churches to engage with their community. The pace of life slows a little. Smiles come to faces a little more readily. The weather lends itself to outdoor activities. Holidays are less fixed than they used to be, meaning that there are always people around to be blessed by the church. Tourism brings new faces and, in some parts of the UK, an international mission field to our doorsteps. The long school summer holidays make for the ideal opportunity for releasing the energy, fun and commitment of Christian young people in evangelism, and at the same time provide the church with plenty of time and space to bless families with attention-grabbing, energy-diffusing, child-minding activities.

Here is some of what happened during the first summer of HOPE. These stories are just an example of what God did, and inspire us all to think about what we might do in partnership with him in future summers . . .

> Holidays are less fixed than they used to be, meaning that there are always people around to be blessed by the church.

HOPE comes to Burton

Where? Burton-on-Trent (a midlands town).

What? A deliberate targeted attempt to reach all aspects of the population; children, youth, the elderly and everyone else!

Why? For some years the churches in Burton have been demonstrating their unity with an emphasis on their diversity and on churches big and small. HOPE was seen as another opportunity to do this.

How? HOPE, including summer activities, launched at the churches initiated Civic Service attended by leaders of the community. The churches formed a registered charity for funding purposes and launched a steering group.

The outcome

Children between the ages of 7–11 were activated across the churches to be involved in community action projects over a total of six days in six different areas including car washing, garden clearing, free cafes, and many links were formed to the local primary schools. The youth across the churches were involved in providing concerts, visiting the elderly in their homes, action projects across gardens, graffiti and canal clearing. An ambitious project with the elderly was carried over to the following summer involving visiting two to three residential care homes for one-day events themed around Holidays at Home (where each day takes a different emphasis, such as the seaside, French holidays, Caribbean holiday, etc.). Meanwhile the general community were blessed with a Party in the Park, also attended by civic leaders including the mayor and about 5,000 of the populous. Two hundred local church volunteers delivered a cracking event with inflatables, side-shows, stage area, refreshments, and an Alpha tent which was kept busy throughout the afternoon. One local mum commented that she could never have afforded such a day for her three children unless it had all been provided free by the local churches.

Top tips

Themed T-shirts used by the youth during their community action provided a real sense of branding identity across the churches and this could be expanded. Local church leader Bill Craggs also identified the following hot tips:

- *Recognise key people* who are full of vision and commitment and ensure that they have the full support, resources and encouragement that they need.
- *Leave them to do it* – the steering group only met a few times as they delegated resources and jobs out to smaller teams.
- *Don't get discouraged* – not all churches or Christians want to get involved, just bless them and do what God has called you to do.
- *Build up good relationships with the local council and other agencies* – this has been going on for several years in Burton developing an atmosphere of trust and favour that contributed to the success of HOPE. For more on working with your local council see Chapter 22.
- *Keep prayer as the main focus* – regular prayer gatherings throughout the year keep you all focused.

Lessons learned

It was all great fun but starting earlier with greater levels of forward planning would have been helpful.

> Keep prayer as the main focus.

HOPE in Ewell

In Ewell, Stoneleigh and Cuddington (just outside Epsom in Surrey), a group of 12 churches met together out of a desire to demonstrate Christian unity, bless the community and to share their faith. They put on a family fun day with refreshments, a kids' crafts area, a quiz, a pre-school kids' toys area, a prayer tent, a bouncy castle, live music, testimonies, escapology, a primary school choir and information on parenting classes, all of which was free! Around 200 people from the local community came and an 8-year-old was heard to say, '*I don't want to leave, everyone is so happy here.*' The team said they'd love to do it again and next time would use more testimonies for an even greater impact of the gospel.

Battle of the bands

As a way to get loads of young people involved in their HOPE in the Park summer festival, Warfield churches held a 'battle of the bands' competition in the evening. A few months earlier they held preliminary rounds where eight local bands performed three songs each to a panel of judges including a local BBC music reporter. Then, after a summer's fun day, the three finalists took to the stage in front of a 1000-strong crowd. All the bands were made up of non-churched youth who of course invited their friends along to see them perform and therefore heard the gospel presentation that was given during the evening.

Totton Family Fun Day

Where? Totton, a village on the edge of the New Forest near Southampton.

Who? All the churches in Totton.

Why? '*Keep dropping pebbles in the pond to keep seeing the ripple effects taking place,*' said John Cunningham from HOPE Totton's Management Team.

What? They started with a week of social action, and followed it up with a free Family Fun Day with Army displays, police, council, youth clubs, charities, businesses plus corporate Scalextric

Racing. They completed the weekend with Church in the Park. *'We never have anything like this in our community anymore . . . it is so good to see,'* commented an elderly lady who needed a fence fixing.

The outcome

Some 6,500 people attended the fun day with 500 at the Sunday morning Church in the Park, where some gave their lives to Jesus. The next event is already planned! Comments from the fun day included: *'Wow is this all really free?', 'I need to know what this God thing is all about', 'I am so impressed that the churches can put something on so professionally'* and *'This shows that the church really does care about our community'.*

Lessons learned

The preceding week of social action helped portray a holistic gospel making local people feel welcome to come along to the fun day. The nature of such an event is catalytic and each repeat potentially builds on the last, making persistency, consistency and repetition important rather than having a one-off event.

Partnering with Extra-local Resources

Some of the stories in this chapter were 'homespun' but some also drew in partner organisations with a track record in summer evangelism. These included DNA's Gap Year Trainees, Nexus Christian Bands, YFC Social Action Programme The Net (Burton), Miracle Street's outdoor stages, On The Moves BBQ Mission expertise, Urban Saints React Family Fun Days, as well as drawing on YWAM, NGM and, in Scotland, Firestarters. All of these bring a level of training, personnel and equipment to supplement the local resources. Here's an example of how Re:Act works.

An Incredible Summer of Re:Act Fun Days

Where? Throughout England and Wales.

What? In previous summers, Re:Act have run a tour to six different locations helping local churches reach their communities by putting on fun days. For HOPE that number was increased to see hundreds of teenagers taking a massive seven

'This shows that the church really does care about our community'.

tours to a total of thirty-nine locations, with over 35,000 people attending!

The fun days were run by Urban Saints in partnership with DNA, YWAM, Nexus, Miracle Street and NGM. After a three-day training residential, the Re:Act teams were commissioned and left for their tours of six family fun days with Church Outdoors in numerous locations.

How did it work? The days involved set-up and small group discipleship for the team in the mornings, followed by the teams canvassing their local area raising awareness about the evening and afternoon events. In the afternoon the event ran from 2pm until 5pm with inflatables, a free barbecue, a cafe marquee, hair braiding, face painting, sports and much more. During this time there was also a lorry with staging running a road show with live music. After a short break, there was an open air service from 5:30pm until 7pm. This featured worship, dance, testimony and an evangelistic message with an opportunity for people to respond.

The outcome

Across the tour, over 160 people became Christians and 150 made re-commitments! Additionally people were healed after prayer – including 11 people in one place!

There have also been fantastic stories from a number of the locations visited:

'Our Re:Act event was awesome – over 2,000 people came, the weather was great and everyone had a good time! Quite a few people asked for more info on local churches as well.' (Hemel Hempstead Re:Act day)

'It really was a great fun day, surpassing what most of us were expecting . . . the Lord is so good. It's difficult to say exactly how many folk turned up but we think it was around 1,500. What a testimony of churches working together.' (Stratford-upon-Avon Re:Act day)

There are also some universal specifics that have emerged, in terms of outcome:

• Young people have discovered that they can attempt and achieve things for God that they could not have dreamt of doing before they went on Re:Act. Many have grown in their spiritual and practical development during the eleven-day mission.

• Churches and other Christian organisations were drawn to work together in partnership and vision, forging valuable relationships and trust.

• The communities where the Re:Act days happened were blessed and many churches are working together for the first time.

• A number of locations reported good take-up for Alpha courses, following on from these summer events.

• Lots of young people have come back with an increased enthusiasm for mission and serving others in their community.

The overall impact of the Re:Act programme is probably best summed up by paraphrasing the words of one local co-ordinator who said that for all the hard work, time and energy invested into making each day happen, the outcomes clearly demonstrate that it was all worthwhile. It is incredible to think that in many places this is the first time that an event of this kind has been attempted. The combination of everything and everyone together really expressed the hope that we have in Jesus – hope declared through words, hope revealed by action, hope demonstrated with service, hope experienced in relationships.

Top tips if you'd like to do something similar:

• If you involve a number of different churches, then the resources and pool of skills available to you is far greater. A united front from local churches is fundamental to the success of such a venture.

• Plan, plan, plan! Detailed, forward-planning is essential.

• Secure a great site on which to hold your event. Examine the minutiae of council regulations, e.g. many council sites do not like the use of barbecues.

• Have a wet weather option such as a nearby venue alternative or the use of marquees.

• Hold an evaluation session on the last day, or immediately afterwards, so that everyone

> A number of locations reported good take-up for Alpha courses, following on from these summer events.

involved can have a chance to reflect and feedback.

We heard about loads more great summer activities. Would any of these work where you live?

• Manchester City Centre played host to a climactic seven-hour musical extravaganza drawing crowds of hundreds and building on a week of community projects.

• Stockport ran an impacting 5-a-side football competition in the Big Match.

• Wardle near Rochdale embarked on a day's free car washing to bless their community.

• HOPE for Macclesfield utilised an eye-catching bus in the town centre linked to community action projects and a Sunday festival.

• The youth clubs of local churches in Prestwick raised £17,000 to provide a free summer weekend community fun day that included a talent show and climbing wall, with thousands impacted, blessed and hearing the gospel.

• Thames-side saw 20 local churches join together for a joint united Sunday worship service attended by hundreds building on the earlier community projects and succeeded by the fun day. The first of its kind there but already to be repeated in future summers.

• Wigan churches hired Wigan Athletic Football Stadium for an evangelistic event that came straight off the back of a late summer term schools week.

• The five churches of Chapeltown, a suburb of Sheffield, pulled together to deliver an evening concert and a next day Picnic in the Park. *'The Methodists were without a minister at the time, but the parishioners decided to just get on with it!'* said Robert Elliot, one of the organisers of HOPE in the area. In addition there was a free car wash and a craft fayre, face painting and a story-telling tent for children. Churchgoers in the town are estimated at around 400, but the Picnic attracted 1,100: *'It was so fantastic . . . there are real opportunities to overwhelm people here with grace.'*

• In Market Bosworth near Nuneaton five churches held a Summer Garden Party with cream teas and stalls with pottery painting. One local supermarket donated most of the scones *'so community and church and commerce came together in the power of HOPE,'* said local church leader Lynne Eveson, who described the event as *'a great hit'.*

• Meanwhile Bath hosted 'Bath's Biggest BBQ' in venues across the city but with centrally themed and designed publicity. These were downloadable from their HOPE website, a great idea for a local event with community access but connected to a bigger picture. Local printers were also given digital files of the publicity so that a church could also have them professionally printed if required; what a great idea!

How about trying one of these great ideas for bringing HOPE to your town, village or city?

• Children's Holiday Clubs with themed content, fancy dress characters and arts and crafts. Get a mix of Christian and not-yet-Christian helpers and have a presentation performed to parents on the final Sunday morning followed by a barbecue and/or Family Fun Day.

• Cafe drop-in in a disused shop front (peppercorn rent or free) or marquee in the local park for young mums and the elderly at different timeslots of each day.

• Youth drop-in linked to sports activities and detached youth work.

• Quality, cringe-free, fun-filled, thought-provoking streetwork particularly in pedestrianised shopping streets, precincts and arcades.

• Theatre in the Park with picnic hampers and a quality Christian production, e.g. from NGM.

• Putting summer sports activities such as cricket, football and Wimbledon on big screens in the open air at local recreation grounds and/or public facilities hosted and paid for by local churches.

• Play Station nights, FIFA Football, computer competitions with football themed prizes.

• Group visits to local sporting events.

• Rural areas are great for impromptu star-gazing evenings, late night walks, hog roasts, clay pigeon shoots, etc.

More top tips

• Plan well ahead, ideally starting in January at the latest for summer of the same year.

• Identify and build on key people with energy, time and commitment.

• Keep good channels of communication open between churches, church leaders and church activists.

• Organise prayer support for projects but also for people Christian and not-yet. Include prayer triplets to pray for named as yet unsaved friends.

• Liaise with council and police groups as appropriate (see Chapter 22 for more info).

• Ensure adequate risk assessments, health and safety, child protection policies and public liability insurance.

• Resource publicity professionally and fund it properly. Think about websites, local press, hoardings, TV and radio editorials as well as literature like flyers.

• Research your local area, the demographics of the population, the needs, and the people groups.

• Think persistent and consistent rather one-off activities if possible.

• Link gospel action (community projects) to gospel words, testimonies, preaching, etc.

• Work together across churches wherever possible.

• Avoid clashes with other major public events like the Wimbledon Final and the Grand Prix!

• Use extra-local resources including training resources wherever appropriate.

RESOURCES

Champions Challenge is a self-contained holiday club idea based on Mark's gospel. The Scripture Union website has a range of free downloadable materials for those wanting to put on a Champions Challenge including parent release slips, media release forms, work sheets and drama scripts – www.scriptureunion.org.uk.

Christians in Sport offer advice on running sports tournaments, big screen events, sports holiday clubs, etc. at www.christiansinsport. org.uk

DNA provide teams of discipled, church-based gap year trainees to both do evangelism and lead local teams in discipleship and evangelism around the UK. www.dna-uk.org.

Fusion Youth & Community offer training and support in developing strategic 3–5-year plans for the transformation of communities. Contact by email: office@fusionyac.org.uk.

KidzKlub offer a term's worth of resources for £40 including games, Bible studies, object lessons, etc. each based on a different theme (e.g. Pirates, Wild West) with five different themes to select from. www.kidzklub.biz.

Make Jesus Known is an organisation that reaches out to people in the UK with the news about Jesus through street music, fun days, roadshows and other community events. Find out more and get in contact to book a team through www.makejesusknown.com. They can also provide concert trucks with inbuilt stage and lighting, rappers, DJs and evangelists.

Christians in Sport offer advice on running sports tournaments, big screen events, sports holiday clubs.

Miracle Street – to help facilitate your summer event contact Miracle Street for mobile stages, crowd pulling attractions and evangelists – www.miraclestreet.com.

NGM provides specialised teams on a short-term basis who utilise the performing arts as a means of communicating a sense of value, esteem and worth to people, and offers mission teams to support and serve the work of local partners providing long-term, sustainable projects within needy communities – www.ngm.org.uk.

On The Move – working with churches across communities to set up free community BBQs including worship – www.onthemove.org.uk.

Re:Act Family Fun Days – an inclusive package of national recruitment training, inter-church evangelism, discipleship and Family Fun Day's with BBQ – www.urbansaints.org/react.

Youth For Christ have teams who can come and serve churches over the summer including sports and evangelists – see www.yfc.co.uk/ teams for details. **Firestarters** do the same thing with teams in Scotland, particularly in the Glasgow area. Contact: www.firestartersuk.org.

CHAPTER 21

BEING A GOOD NEIGHBOUR

Laurence Singlehurst, CELL UK

Most Christian research in how people come to faith comes back to one overriding and fundamental statistic that at least 70% have been helped along in that process by friendship with a Christian. This same research points out that most non-Christians need at least seven or eight positive interactions with Christianity before they are ready to go on an Alpha-style course or take a serious interest in the Christian message.

Jesus told us the story of the Good Samaritan which powerfully illustrates what a good neighbour is. It is one of those stories that never fails to move people because somehow it touches a chord within our hearts. Of course this story emphasises the Old Testament concept of hospitality and the theme is of the Great Commandment to 'love your neighbour as yourself'. These neighbours are, of course, not just our Christian brothers and sisters but those who live outside the sphere of our churches.

So our strategy is to love people. Ed Silvoso (founder and president of Harvest Evangelism) introduced a metaphor that I think helps us to see friendship, evangelism and being a good neighbour in a new way. He encouraged every Christian to think of themselves as a secret pastor with a congregation made up of non-Christians. I have added to that premise two further thoughts.

> Jesus told us the story of the Good Samaritan which powerfully illustrates what a good neighbour is.

Firstly, we must love people unconditionally, regardless of whether they respond or not. We are not loving people or making friends for the converting potential but because of a genuine expression of our hearts. Also, we seek their spiritual welfare. Through our authentic lifestyle, through our words, through our hanging out, through sitting in smoke-filled rooms we express our care and love and speak the words when the opportunities arise.

Secondly, being hospitable – being a good neighbour is a theme throughout the Bible from the Old to the New Testament.

So how have churches made this strategy a reality for them? There were loads of activities carried out for HOPE – take a look at these creative ways groups found to be good neighbours:

Call us if you need a hand . . .

Who? Churches Together in Polegate, Willingdon, and Jevington in Eastbourne.

What? A Contact Care scheme which is a phone line for the community to call if they need any practical help or support. The initiative had been running for a couple of years but HOPE gave the team the impetus to move the scheme on to another level. More volunteers were recruited so the project could be expanded and offer more help to more people. There was even a civic launch for HOPE, with the local council keen to take the scheme town-wide.

Why? To be Christ's hands in the community, reaching out in a physical and tangible way.

How does it work? There is a pool of volunteers from churches that offer to man the line and help people – doing errands like taking people to the doctors or providing relief for young carers. The scheme operates using a mobile phone which is passed from duty officer to duty officer Monday to Friday each week. The phone is on from 09.30 – 12.30 weekdays and has an answer phone at all other times. Clients ring in and speak to the duty officer about their needs. The duty officer looks through the volunteer records to match the need with an available volunteer. The appointment is then confirmed with the client.

What kind of help do they offer? Anything that's needed! Volunteers have been involved in transporting people to various appointments (doctors, eye tests, etc.), taking someone to visit a spouse in a care home and picking up a person's pension. They help people with their shopping or do it for them; have one person who reads a blind person's letters for her; they have changed batteries in smoke alarms and given relief to a carer by sitting with their loved one so they could go out.

Top tips
- Don't advertise too widely when you start out. You don't want to build up too many expectations so tell your churches and use word of mouth to start with.
- If you start small this also gives you a chance to build up your volunteer team.

The outcome
Helping in these simple ways has made such a difference to the people who have called the care line. For some it has taken off the financial strain of needing to get taxis to see loved ones in hospitals, for others it's given them a much needed break from their care role while a volunteer has taken over; this service has given many people a freedom

> 'God blessed us with sunshine but the biggest blessing was definitely gathering with all of our lovely neighbours.'

that wasn't previously there. The aim now is to build on what has already been achieved, to gather more volunteers and to advertise the scheme more widely within the area.

Neighbourhood BBQ

A small group of Christian families who live on one particular road in Bath decided to hold a HOPE barbecue in the summer. They invited everyone on the road and decided to split the cost between themselves. They said, *'God blessed us with sunshine but the biggest blessing was definitely gathering with all of our lovely neighbours of all beliefs to have lots of fun and laughter. We played an egg and spoon race, a dress up relay race and, of course, the good old three-legged race. Everyone who came said how great it was to meet together for fun and food. It was such a special time that we have all decided to hold one every year from now on!'*

Getting to know the neighbours

The Banko family felt called from the USA some little while back as 'tentmaker' missionaries to Britain. In early 2008 Anthony Delaney, who was then part of St Mary's COE in Leatherhead met up with Dave (a regional HOPE co-ordinator), his wife Renay and some of their friends to celebrate Dave's birthday. Anthony said, *'There was a mix of people from our church and theirs (Engage), but I ended up sitting with a few people who I didn't recognise. It turns out they all knew each other though – they were all living on Dave and Renay's street, a small cul-de-sac in Leatherhead. There were three couples and two single men (one German, the other Persian). They had nothing to unite them – except the Bankos! Independently and with no prompting these neighbours described to me through the course of the evening meal how they hadn't known anyone else or each other, until the Bankos arrived and started having barbecues and Thanksgiving parties and generally finding excuses to get the street together. "Of course not everyone came to start with, but now we all do!" one of them said. One lady even told me, "I would never want to live anywhere else now."*

'They all wanted to know more about the kind of church someone like Dave would go to; they were excited that we had a laugh and were normal – expecting a bunch of miseries. One of the most enlightening times was my talk with the Persian guy – a bright go-getter from an Islamic background. As I spoke further with him he told me that some years before he had accepted an invitation to a church in Oxford, and had gone – he was amazed at how happy the people were there, and that they prayed for the sick and expected to see results! He asked if I knew of any churches like that in the area and I said we were one!'

In July 2008 Dave attended a meeting where he felt he received an anointing for healing and he asked himself *'What am I going to do with this?'* Dave said, *'My Muslim friend [his Persian neighbour] had just broken his hand, so I went over to his house and asked if I could pray for him. He said sure, so I put my hand on his broken hand and prayed a simple prayer to release healing. He looked up in shock – he felt something and the pain went away! He started pushing it and didn't feel any pain. I told him to take the brace off and move it which he did without pain. He told everyone at our neighbourhood picnic the following day how I came over to pray for his hand and it was healed! A short time after I was able to talk to him about Jesus being the one who healed him and he was so grateful that he invited Jesus into his heart! Since then he has been attending church regularly and is growing in his faith in Jesus Christ. Other neighbours, too, have since started coming to church including the German man and his family.'*

Anthony said, *'Dave and Renay are amazing examples to me of what the HOPE initiative is really all about; just loving people like Jesus does. On the street where God had called them to live they were being the gospel and bringing hope, in word and deed – with amazing results!'*

Turning a garage into a lifeline

When a church in Aldbrough, a small village on the coast in East Yorkshire wanted to reach out to their neighbours they decided to open up their double garage as a charity shop, under the HOPE banner, selling second-hand clothes and small items every Wednesday. They serve free teas,

'We are often told by people in the village who come in, that it really is a lifeline for them.'

coffees and home baking, with all money from sold items going to local good causes. Martin and Margaret Senior said, *'It took off immediately with new people coming in every week and more stock coming in than we could handle! We soon decided to open on a Saturday as well to give people opportunity to come in who work during the week. In just over a year we have given away over £4,000, but more importantly one lady called Val has given her life to Jesus. Three others have either been to church or expressed a wish to do so. We are often told by people in the village who come in, that it really is a lifeline for them, a place to come for much needed company.'*

Prayer Point
To find out more about Project Postcode, a great prayer initiative, see chapter 18.

Water and lollipops

Network Churches in Hertforshire got permission from the management of a local nightclub to set up a table outside the venue from 01.00 to 04.00 every other Friday night. They hand out free bottles of water to rehydrate young people as they leave and lollipops to bring up their sugar levels and reduce tension. The team are also looking into bringing blankets in cold weather to keep people warm and flip flops to protect the feet of those who aren't wearing any shoes.

The young people greet them like long lost friends and look forward to their free water and lollipops. For many young people they have seen for the first time that Christianity has something to offer as these Christians seek to be good neighbours.

A holiday at home

Kingswood Salvation Army in Bristol ran an initiative called 'Holiday at Home' for lonely and isolated people in their community. They invited them to come to their local Methodist church for two days to take part in different activities such as painting, card making and a talk about Douglas Motorcycles. They then enjoyed a healthy lunch before being entertained by a local musician and then ending the day with a 'thought for the day'. As a result of this day they have seen at least six people regularly attend one of their weekday clubs for over sixties. Four churches in Thrapston, Northamptonshire, ran similar events with a daily keep-fit session, quizzes, a beetle drive, craft and old movies.

Help for flood victims

Many areas of Hull suffered from severe flooding over the summer so much of the HOPE work in the following months went into helping and supporting the victims. They came up with a number of ideas:

• A 'Great Plant Give-away' where all the churches in the market town of Driffield got together to grow plants to re-stock flooded gardens. Two local nurseries also got involved. A link was made to New Life Church in Hull city centre which turned itself into a garden centre for the day and invited people whose gardens had been destroyed by the floods to come and take up to 20 plants each. It was an amazing time!

• The same church also provided Christmas hampers for a very large number of families whose homes had been flooded, they put on entertainment evenings (e.g. songs from big shows sung by their own choir), provided pamper days for stressed mothers and a free photo session for families who had lost their family photographs in the flood. Brilliant! In rough terms, the church believes it made contact with around 5,000 people, of whom 500 came to events in the church building and of whom some 50 have developed an ongoing link.

For many young people they have seen for the first time that Christianity has something to offer as these Christians seek to be good neighbours.

• In another village the churches linked up with the local council to provide a voucher for flood victims to have a drink and refreshments in one of the local cafes and the opportunity to request any support that they might like to help them cope with their situation. Many were either moved away from their homes altogether or had to live in caravans on the drive – sometimes for up to a year. Requests they were able to respond to included help with caring for a large dog that found life in a caravan challenging. One person needed help understanding what the 'quotes' were the insurance companies were asking for. They also helped an elderly lady who had become disconnected from the community when she was moved to a different town for most of the year while her home was being repaired.

How could you be a good neighbour? Check out these ideas that have happened around the country for more inspiration:

• Four churches in Thrapston, Northamptonshire, held a 'meet the neighbours' cheese and wine lunch for people who had moved on to a new housing estate where they gave out information about the local area. They also left welcome cards with the local estate agents to be given to newcomers to the town including church details.

• On the day of the Pakistan elections (in 2008) St Augustine Church in Bradford decided to support their neighbours – 75% of whom are Muslim, mostly with Pakistan heritage, by holding a half-night of prayer.

• Kilmington Baptist Church and St Giles, Kilmington in Devon, worked closely with the council on a Parish Survey to help them understand community needs and found that there was a keen interest in the environment. They decided to bless their neighbours by delivering low energy light bulbs and reusable shopping bags free of charge to their homes.

• St Luke's Church in Watford leafleted homes in the area offering to pick up items for recycling such as old mobile phones, ink cartridges and batteries. The money they received for some of the recycled items was donated to a local project for homeless people. They also planted bulbs to flower in spring in the local park (with the agreement of the council!).

• Children in Sunday school in Stortford, Hertfordshire, made posies and then gave them out round the streets.

• Young people from Cottingham Road Baptist Church in Hull took flowers from their church to a local care home where recipients were amazed and very appreciative. The young people (who were accompanied by an adult) said it made them realise a little action could make a big difference to someone else.

• A church in Shropshire held a 'Bring a friend and share' lunch to kick off a week of hospitality. Over 80 people came, two-thirds of whom were guests – two of whom said they were thinking of coming back to church.

• A number of churches have started Street Pastors in their area for HOPE – an interdenominational response to urban problems where teams go out onto the streets to engage with marginalised groups. See Chapter 16 to find out what happened when a church in Bath started Street Pastors in their area.

• Two churches in Weston-super-Mare joined together to deliver fridge magnets to each of the 3,500 homes in their area. Each magnet was a tropical scene that said 'Love each other as I have loved you' (from John 15:17) and was attached to a piece of white card stating the magnet was a free gift and giving details of the two churches.

• Sevenoaks Vineyard in Kent used annual events like Shrove Tuesday and Bonfire Night to have social events that got their church members mixing with their neighbours.

• Young people from Kingswood Methodist Church in Bristol spent two days weeding in their local park.

Young people from Kingswood Methodist Church in Bristol spent two days weeding in their local park.

• The Church of the Good Shepherd in Four Marks, Hampshire, got their elderly members of the congregation to donate pot plants which were then given to local neighbours.

• A church in Allesley, Coventry, got together with Age Concern to tackle the problem of older people in the community feeling isolated. The team of volunteers befriend, make tea and offer lifts, and the church uses its hall to host the over 50s for a monthly morning of friendship, chat, refreshments and entertainment.

AOK days

Every Friday, Soul Action encourages people to commit 'Acts of Kindness' to try and make someone else's day. Previous acts have included texting people to tell them why you think they're great, baking a cake for a neighbour and swapping places with someone who is behind you in a queue. The acts may be small but they're all about letting someone know you care and they really spark people's imagination. Stephanie in London and Jan from the Isle of Wight got their whole school year groups involved so that everyone could join in the fun! For a new AOK idea each week and to read stories people have sent in go to www.soulaction.org/aokday.

There are loads of other ways you could be a great neighbour! Have a look at the following and see what might work in your area.

Neighbourhood Watch: This is a fantastic scheme that obviously helps to make our neighbourhoods much safer and, as Christians, we can either join in as an active member of an existing group or indeed start one. www.neighbourhoodwatch.net.

The Name Challenge: Do you know the Christian name and surname of the six dwellings immediately around you? People feel so valued when you greet them by name.

Prayer Walks: More of this in Chapter 18 but most of us walk up and down our street fairly regularly so why not informally pray for the houses as we wander by on the way to the shop or other activities?

Christmas!: Christmas is a great time to invite your new friends and neighbours to events at church like carol services.

Clean the Street: The streets of England are sadly marred by plastic bags, drink cans and rubbish, and if you just make an effort to pick up those bits and pieces sooner or later your good works will be seen and you will be noted as a good neighbour.

Campaign groups and neighbourhood based activities: Every now and again your street and/or your neighbourhood will have something that affects it, such as new housing or an airport expansion and you can be sure a group will be formed to campaign for or against, whichever is appropriate. These are great opportunities for you to get to know other people and show your commitment to the neighbourhood.

Improve the area: Sometimes there are projects in our neighbourhood that we can do together with other churches or mobilise our own church to do something a little bigger. For example, St Mary's Church Luton noticed a broken down playground within their community. They mobilised resources, got permission and spent a day cleaning, painting and making safe a disused and dangerous area. This act of being a good neighbour was seen by hundreds and now the children can play in safety.

Spreading the word: If you're a church leader why not think about preaching on being a good neighbour, perhaps from the very parable that Jesus himself told us about? Then, as a church, let's encourage our members both individually and together to be good neighbours and to come up with new and creative ways to bless those around us.

Do you know the Christian name and surname of the six dwellings immediately around you?

RESOURCES

Angels on Your Doorstep by Paddy Beresford explores the different aspects of hospitality, to non–Christians, our neighbours, people at work and those we meet outside our homes explaining that hospitality is a biblical way of evangelism. Kingsway, £6.99.

Change the World for a Fiver by We Are What We Do is a great book with 50 ideas that you and your friends/family can put into practice to make the world a better place. Short Books, £5.

Community Prayer Cells by Jane Holloway – a workbook (£5) and video (£8.50) that provides eight sessions of training for leaders and members to help your small group pray for its community. CPAS.

The Good Neighbours Pack from Tearfund offers you loads of great ideas for getting to know your neighbours. The material is designed to be run as one or more sessions for churches or small groups and invites discussion so that everyone can learn from each other. Call 0845 355 8355 to get a copy.

Sowing, Reaping, Keeping by Laurence Singlehurst – this book helps the reader explore what it means to love people, to sow seeds of faith, to reap the harvest at the right time and to nurture growing faith. IVP, £6.99.

Teach Your Granny to Text – is the children's sequel to *Change the World for a Fiver* with 30 small actions that can make a big difference. Short, £5.50.

Every year the **UK Neighbourhood Watch Trust** runs a 'Good Neighbour' day to encourage people to think about their neighbours and how they can be a good one. They also provide information on protecting yourself and your neighbours from crime. See www. neighbourhoodwatch.net for more details.

Who is My Neighbour?: World Faiths and Christian Witness by Martin Goldsmith and Rosemary Harley. The Christian is called to love his neighbour. If we love someone surely we want to understand them. What is his background? What does he believe? What are his problems and how can we help? This book tackles these questions clearly and practically, as we are challenged to witness to people of all backgrounds and religious faiths through our actions and attitudes. Authentic, £8.99.

CHAPTER 22

WORKING WITH LOCAL POLICE, GOVERNMENT AND MEDIA

Matt Bird, Make It Happen, with contributions from Ian Chisnall, HOPE Co-ordinator

Working in partnership with local police and government can lend credibility to your projects.

GOVERNMENT AND POLICE

As groups of people who are passionate about seeing change in our communities and are willing to commit time, energy and resources to see it happen, we know we have a significant contribution to make to community life. Police and local councils share many of our desires and we can be a fantastic resource and blessing to one another as we work in partnership to see that change happen.

In the past there has often been uncertainty on both sides about the compatibility of the groups working together. The perception others have had of us as Christians may have been that we're only looking to serve people if they will come to church and to faith. Of course we long for people to have relationships with God, but we want to demonstrate the love of God to those around us regardless of what they believe. We know that God wants us to take care of people and a key way to explain this to external groups is that we are a 'faith-based but not faith-biased' group of people who are looking to serve and be a blessing to the whole community.

For our part, we may have been fearful of getting tangled up in police and council red tape or worried that they might try and water down the faith element of our activities. But, the truth is, we share many common objectives and can achieve so much more when we work together as evidenced by some of the great projects we heard about through HOPE!

There are significant benefits to working with police and government:

- It's a great opportunity to contribute to how the powers-that-be tackle issues in our communities.
- Police and government generally know a lot about local communities, and about how to work within them. They are always keen to share this knowledge.
- Working in partnership with local police and government can lend credibility to your projects – helping the wider community, including the media, to take you seriously.

• Although this is all about partnership, police and government can sometimes also offer financial resources to local groups. If you're helping them meet their targets, they may be able to help you meet your costs.

There have been some fantastic partnerships happening through churches that are committed to HOPE and their local police and government. New initiatives have been started and old ones have been strengthened and blessed. Read these stories and see just what an opportunity awaits us, as we work with the police and local councils, led by the same desire to see our communities functioning at their very best.

Igniting HOPE in Cardiff

Loads of young people got stuck into practical projects as part of the HOPE on the Streets and Hours of Kindness initiatives run in May (see Chapter 8 for more details). In Wales, the organisation Ignite set up 'Ignite HOPE' which brought together hundreds of young people in Cardiff for four days of social action projects, along with worship and street mission. Nathan Davies from Ignite said, *'There were 24 different project areas right across South Wales, consisting of teams from 10–40 people doing nearly five hours each of social action each day over the long weekend. They painted railings and walls, did gardening, land clearance and litter picking as well as helping out with sports fun days, dance workshops, face painting, family fun days and BBQs all totalling around 6,500 hours of community kindness. In the evenings we had worship and evangelism times back in central Cardiff where nearly 800 people came each night. We saw many people come to faith! We worked closely with local councils and the police to ensure they were fully on board with the project and they loved the work we did.*

'One of the most exciting things to come out of working with the police was an Ignite HOPE "night team" which was sent out onto Cardiff's city streets between 11pm and 3am, to give out water and generally show pastoral care. We have just heard from the police that on those nights there was a huge reduction in crime which the police have no answer for other than the impact of Ignite HOPE!'

'One of our key projects is run on Friday and Saturday nights where volunteers go out in the Community Police van and chat to young people.'

Frome Police Involvement

Frome Police have been involved in HOPE projects since the start of the year. William Phillimore of the local HOPE committee said that *'one of our key projects is run on Friday and Saturday nights where volunteers go out in the Community Police van and chat to young people'*. Two of the Community Police attended a meeting to plan future events and asked for litter picking projects to be launched in certain areas of Frome. William said that *'overall we have been greatly encouraged by all that has been done this year, including establishing links with the police. We believe it is an answer to prayer for Frome.'*

Burton-on-Trent Civic DVD

When the churches in Burton-on-Trent held a free family fun day in the summer they asked the local mayor to open the event that was attended by over 5,000 local people. As part of their annual civic service, the fun day organisers also made a DVD profiling how successful the fun day had been which was shown to all the councillors who were in attendance, as well as heads of police, health and education. Bill Craggs is one of the key organisers of HOPE projects in Burton, and he says the response to the DVD was very encouraging. *'The Town Hall was packed,'* he says, *'and the DVD and talk by Roy Crowne went down a storm. We had a good number of civic leaders there including the leader of the local council.'*

Street Pastors all over the country

Loads of groups have started Street Pastors in order to look after young people who are out late at the weekends and keep them safe. Local councils and police are very supportive of the initiatives – see Chapter 16 to find out more about the scheme.

Getting the mayor involved in Frome

In Frome the previous year's mayor and mayoress launched HOPE and therefore stayed interested in how everything was going. Organisers also got the current mayor involved in HOPE activities. By all accounts she was keen to play her part – including playing air guitar on stage!

Flavours of Hereford festival

Churches in Herefordshire worked closely with the council who put on the Flavours of Hereford festival – the churches had a large marquee where they put on a variety of events including a performance by The Hereford Police Choir.

Other great ideas

• A team from a church in Crowthorne played football against a team from the local police to help build relationships.

• When King's Church Quantocks hosted a HOPE Community Fair for the villages and hamlets in the Quantock Valley, Somerset, they invited the police to come along with their Community Bus as well as getting the fire brigade and St John's Ambulance along too.

• You can find out and contact local police officers who are Christians via the Christian Police Association – see www.cpauk.net.

• When local police had concerns about incidents and accidents around the neighbourhood, a group of HOPE bikers in Crowthorne, Berkshire, got together to build an 'adult peer' team, driven by the Christian community (but open to all) to focus on delivering aspects of safety, training and mechanics to local young people.

• In Wimbledon around 30 church leaders worked with local police and their MP's representative to address the issue of young people hanging around at a shopping centre after school. These young people were sometimes perceived as being intimidating by other people but were also vulnerable to being victims of crime themselves. Together the local churches and police pooled financial resources with the support of the MP to engage the services of professional detached youth workers to befriend the young people and signpost them towards positive youth activity programmes.

• New Life Church in Woking worked with their Borough Council and other organisations to put on a Christmas Day dinner for anyone in Woking who would otherwise be on their own

Joint projects that were run included back to work programmes, fun days and hundreds of hours of kindness.

on that day. A present and Christmas card conveying the significance of Christmas were given to the 70 guests, as well as to the 30 who could not come but received 'Meals-on-Wheels'. The mayor and mayoress of Woking attended the event, shared in the splendid Christmas dinner and joined in the carol singing and entertainment.

• The HOPE team in Preston have been working hard to develop relationships with the local police and government. Joint projects that were run included back to work programmes, fun days and hundreds of hours of kindness.

• Young people from Kingswood Methodist Church in Bristol spent two days weeding in their local park in conjunction with their local council.

• A group from Hull used HOPE as the impetus to develop more effective links with their local authority's 'Crime reduction neighbourhood action group'. As a result they worked jointly with the council and the police Community Support Officers to undertake 'tidy-up' days in and around their village.

Prayer Points

Praying for your MP: Join the network of prayer groups that are committed to praying for their constituency MP at www.christiansinparliament.org.uk.

Another area in which we have seen the favour of God during the first year of HOPE has been in connection with initiatives working with and for the police force.

Redeeming our Communities, which aims to foster working partnerships between the police and local churches, is now active in a number of towns and cities across the UK. There are many stories of how this prayer and action is seeing crime reduction take place. For example, at a meeting in Barnstaple in North Devon in November 2008, those gathered heard some encouraging answers to prayer. Two hundred people joined the 'Moving Forward Together' united prayer meeting inspired by HOPE in the region. In April, Inspector Roger Bartlett shared how there was a concern in Barnstaple over the detection rate for crime which was low – meaning that those responsible for crime were not facing justice. By November he was able to report that since then those rates had improved so much so that Barnstaple had the second best detection rate in the whole force area.

He also shared that in April he asked for prayer about the number of thefts from vehicles, as in the year finishing in April 08, there had been a 32% increase in this type of crime. He reported that since praying for that, in the seven months since then, thefts from vehicles had dropped by – quite incredibly . . . 32%!

Local Strategic Partnerships and Local Area Agreements

Most Local Authorities have a Local Strategic Partnership (LSP) whose membership includes services providers such as government, police and health. These partnerships are intended to help coordinate services and avoid duplicated effort and ultimately improve the quality of life for all residents. They are responsible for identifying the community's joint strategic priorities. These partnerships usually also include business and voluntary sector representatives and the original guidance (Local Government Act 2000) suggested that faith communities should be included.

Many of the LSPs in 'upper tier' Local Authorities are responsible for developing an agreement with Central Government called a Local Area Agreement (LAA). These set a number of priorities which the Local Authority with its partners (including the voluntary sector) agrees to deliver, and which commits Central Government to provide increased resources and flexibilities. A copy of the LAA can be obtained from your local authority's website, and could be very helpful in identifying areas of shared concern between local authorities and churches.

The police are often responsible to the LAA on a theme known as Safer and Stronger Communities, such as crime prevention and community cohesion. In these areas there is often a cross over – where the church agenda meets that of the LAA. A church that wants to help young people avoid crime and access education, for example, is often working to achieve similar outcomes as the local police.

Over the last decade, although there has been an overall fall in crime levels, many people across the country have become more fearful of crime. The Neighbourhood Policing Programme is a response to these concerns, creating a more visible presence of police on the streets so as to reassure people, but also seeking to work with partner agencies to share responsibility for making our communities secure.

Neighbourhood policing requires that police officers get to know all those who make up the local community. The church is a community group that is present in most areas so the police have a responsibility to work in partnership with the local church, as well as the many other community stakeholders. The Christian community can therefore approach the police with confidence that they will be welcomed, and that there will be a willingness to work together.

RESOURCES

Redeeming Our Communities is a ministry of City Links, promoting partnerships between churches, the police and local authorities, to address the causes of crime and bring hope to local communities throughout the UK and abroad. See www.redeemingourcommunities. org.uk for more details.

Redeeming Our Communities: 21st Century Miracles of Social Transformation is a book by Debra Green featuring practical stories about the difference that the people of God have made through intelligent, united prayer expressed sacrificially in society. New Wine Press, £8.99.

WORKING WITH THE MEDIA

Working with the media provides a great opportunity for the church to raise awareness about all the things it's up to. The more people know about the projects on offer – and the heart behind them – the more people may want to get involved in your activity and/or come to church! In the past, churches have often been wary of the media, worrying that they will twist things we say and that they have a hidden agenda to make us look bad. The truth is that most local journalists are just looking for a good story that will interest their readers – something that no doubt all your activities in the church can provide!

Many churches used their HOPE activities to contact their local press for the first time – with great results! Read these stories and top tips to help you think about whether you could work with the media on any of your upcoming projects.

Getting the message out via the media

Alan Saunders works for the Message Trust in Manchester, and managed to get lots of HOPE stories into his local newspapers. One of the most exciting stories that he got featured was that of a young resident, Amy Bladen's, visit to Number 10.

Prime Minister Gordon Brown invited HOPE volunteers to join him for a Christmas celebration

> Working with the media provides a great opportunity for the Church to raise awareness about all the things it's up to.

at the end of 2008. The HOPE national office selected Amy as one of the delegates to attend because of how much work she'd put in to HOPE in her home town of Prestwich.

Alan immediately recognised the significance of this story, and put together a piece that would grab some attention. He says, '*Firstly I tracked down a photo. I wanted one of Amy with the PM but as there wasn't one available I got a nice shot of her with the HOPE group outside Number 10.*'

Next, Alan checked with Amy that he had permission to write the article, getting a few good quotes from her about the day in London. He then wrote the article, taking care to include all the main points i.e. the national scope of HOPE, Amy's involvement locally and what the PM said in his speech. He then rang the local reporter – having found contact details from the Internet. He made sure to ask for the News Desk when he rang.

'*I then enthusiastically explained what had occurred and asked if they would be interested in covering the story with an article.*' Alan offered to send more information and a photo, and they ran the story!

Alan is passionate about churches telling their story saying that, '*it gives us credibility in our communities, and confidence to share our faith. We should let our light shine – and we shouldn't be afraid to include an evangelistic quote or two from someone like a vicar!*'

Top tips

But what if you've never worked with your local press? How should you go about telling them what your church is up to? Here are our top tips:

- Local and regional media are always interested in reporting **good local interest stories**. This is not free advertising however (if you want to control exactly what gets said then think about paying for some advertising space) – a story must have an angle that will catch people's attention.
- So how do you create a local interest story that may appeal to your local news editor? Often, the projects you are already doing are fantastic but they need some kind of 'event' to be considered news worthy. For example, you could have a project opening ceremony, a special finale, an

awards ceremony or simply a visit from a special guest to draw attention to the work you're doing. The special guest could be a local MP, or maybe a local celebrity – as long as they provide extra interest for the media.

• If an event offers good **photo opportunities**, then the media will be more interested. Things that have worked before include inviting people to build and live in a makeshift shelter to highlight the needs of the homeless or walking four miles to collect water to raise awareness about poverty in developing countries.

• It's a good idea to look at local press to get an idea of what they cover to help you decide what your story might be. You can pick up copies of the local paper/s in your newsagents, and collect the copies of the free press that come through the door. It's also helpful to tune in to local and regional radio stations.

• The Newspaper Society provides an excellent website database providing contact information on daily, weekly and monthly publications at http://www.newspapersoc.org.uk/ISBA-maps/weekly-maps.htm and the BBC provides a list of its regional radio services http://www.bbc.co.uk/england/radindex.shtml.

• From this research you will be able to build up a list of local and regional media contacts – particularly email addresses. Email is the quickest and easiest way to get your stories where they need to go but it is also very important to have telephone numbers, as picking up the phone to a news editor will help your story to be run.

• It is best to draft a press release prior to the event, and then you can simply tweak the details after the event. In this way you can ensure that the press release gets in the hands of the media as soon as possible after the event. Please see the box on 'How to write a press release' for more details.

• Once you have sent your press release through to your local and regional media, give it a day and then pick up the phone to the news editor to confirm they have received it. The more you

It's a good idea to look at local press to get an idea of what they cover to help you decide what your story might be.

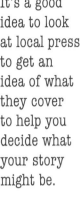

can build a positive rapport with the newspaper or radio station, the more likely they are to look favourably at your stories.

• It may be that you would like to invite local and regional media to attend your event. This can be advantageous as they may send a photographer who will take a professional shot. However, news editors are always on tight deadlines and things can crop up at the last minute so don't build your hopes on this too much. If they don't make it to the event, a press release after the event will do the job!

Other great ideas

• New Life Church, Woking, launched South Woking News, a quarterly 8-page Community Newspaper in co-operation with their local Residents Association and other Woking churches. As well as news about various local organisations, the police, etc., it carries a Christian message and reports on the various HOPE projects happening in the community.

• A group in Coventry used a short-term radio licence to run broadcasts ahead of HOPE and this has led to joining with Cross Rhythms to get a full licence for community broadcasts which will go live in 2010.

• Matthew Hulbert offered his professional journalist skills to his local HOPE team and became a 'Roving Reporter' for HOPE events, visiting initiatives around the country and reporting back for the local HOPE website. During a week-long event in Leicester called 'nCounter' he posted a daily blog and included interviews he'd recorded with those involved – highlights of which were then played on the local hospital radio.

• Oasis Christian Fellowship in Benfleet, Essex, are launching a website telling people what God is doing on the streets in their borough including recent testimonies.

• Churches in Nottingham found that interviews and press releases regarding their HOPE weekend celebrations resulted in more articles about their week of social action projects too.

HOW TO WRITE A PRESS RELEASE

Format – Use a single A4 page, double space the lines and use size 11 or 12 font. If, when you have written the Press Release, it is longer than you thought cut it back to one page by using 1.5 spacing for the lines and editing the text (don't be tempted to simply reduce the text size to fit it all in).

Date – State the date clearly at the top of the page.

Heading – At the top of the page write a VERY short and punchy heading for the story. The heading should be underlined in bold and in UPPER CASE.

First paragraph – An introduction clearly and concisely describing the 'who, what, where, when and why' of the story.

Further paragraphs – You may include up to three or four further paragraphs, depending on length, which can quote someone involved, describe facts, tell a brief story and/or quote a leader.

Words – Use language that is used in our culture avoiding jargon words that you might only hear in the church community.

Contact – At the bottom of the page include the name, telephone number and email of a nominated media spokesperson and a web address for the relevant organisations if available.

Photograph – For press contacts do provide a quality digital photograph which can be attached to the press release email.

Some ideas

· **Make your story about local people** – Demonstrate the benefit your project brings for a particular group of local people, such as young people, the elderly or single parents.

· **Celebrities** – Involve a local celebrity or public figure such as a Member of Parliament in your project or programme's event, as this will provide the media with another point of interest in your story.

· **KISS** – 'Keep It Simple Stupid', decide what your simple key message or messages to the media are and stick to your script.

· **Photocalls** – Set up a photograph opportunity for the local media that involves an interesting group of people, in an interesting place, doing something interesting.

· **Statistics** – Link in your story to any local or regional statistics that demonstrate the community need you are addressing, such as the fact that youth crime rates are high as kids are bored in the holidays so you're running a youth initiative for them.

· **Community Questionnaire** – You could run a very simple community questionnaire in order to gain some figures on what people think about particular issues or situations. For example 77% of local people are concerned about the lack of activities for young people.

· **Research Local Media** – Use the Internet to find a wide range of media opportunities including using resources such as The Newspaper Society http://www.newspapersoc. org.uk/ISBA-maps/weekly-maps.htm and the BBC http://www.bbc.co.uk/england/radindex. shtml.

RESOURCES

The Bible Society have developed a Bible Style Guide to assist the media in understanding matters of faith. This 80-page handbook includes an A–Z glossary of hot topics to help broadcasters and reporters get up to speed with issues as varied as intelligent design and when Jesus was really born. The document can be downloaded for free from www.biblesociety.org.uk/pressreleases or hard copies are available to newsrooms by calling 01793 418222.

The Churches Advertising Network run national advertising campaigns and provide resources for churches to develop the campaign in their area. Find out more and get in touch at www.churchads.org.uk.

The Evangelical Alliance has developed a series of resources to help you make the best use of the media. On their website http://www.eauk.org/media/resources/index.cfm you'll find a collection of links that will help you use the media effectively, contact your local media, compose a letter to an editor and give you tips for being interviewed. They also provide examples of press releases and tips for building a church website so that it can be an effective outreach tool and a way to reach out to your community.

How to be Heard in a Noisy World by Phil Creighton is a guide to help bring all aspects of your church's publicity and communication into the 21st century. Whether it's improving the noticeboard or sending the right information to your local paper, Phil Creighton has the answers. Packed with cost-effective tips and advice, this covers every aspect of church communication and will help you move forward with confidence. Authentic, £8.99.

CHAPTER 23

HOPE IN YOUR SMALL GROUP

Laurence Singlehurst, CELL UK

Many churches have come to the conclusion that church works best in the big and the small, in the corporate and the community and those holistic small groups, sometimes called cell groups, can become the real building block of church.

Churches have historically relied on the energy coming from their corporate leadership, celebrations and church meetings but it seems, as in the book of Acts, in the story of John Wesley and Methodism and in many other places through history, churches have discovered this secondary and powerful energy source. It is an energy source because these groups decide that they are not only places to understand God's word, or places to look after one another, but they also become places that empower one another to be missional and to bring hope.

Scientists have told us how healthy cells multiply. In the human body healthy cells have two strands of DNA but to multiply they must create a little bit of space and let a third strand emerge, and it is three strand DNA that multiplies. So to look at it as in the Great Commandment in Mark 12:30–31 we can see these three strands. The first strand is to love God, the second strand is that we should love one another as Christians, but the third strand is to love a lost world. So we could think about it in the following way. If you have one strand of DNA

> Many churches have come to the conclusion that church works best in the big and the small.

in your group loving God, this is a Bible study, fantastic but maybe God wants more. If we add to that the second strand that we love one another and have community then we are a home group. This, too, is fantastic but God wants more. If we add the third strand of being missional, of reaching out and loving people we become a holistic group, sometimes referred to as cells. It is these groups that will cause multiplication.

So has this been happening in small groups during HOPE? Here are some examples of stories we heard from small groups around the country.

Fundraising for a local school

A homegroup from Holy Trinity Boston in Lincolnshire took up the HOPE challenge from their vicar to find ways to contribute to their community. An article in a local paper about the need for a sensory room at John Fielding Special School inspired them and they decided to hold a fundraising coffee morning outside one of the group member's homes. Being on the school run route for four schools meant it was an ideal location. One group member made a large banner to advertise the date and time of the event, another produced leaflets that were then dropped through local doors. Everyone got involved by baking cakes and scones, blowing up balloons and running a 'Guess the name of the Teddy' competition. The coffee morning was very well supported and the homegroup's efforts raised £250 for the school!

The homegroup enjoyed the activity so much that they went on to do a Christmas Cheer event with mulled wine, mince pies and carols. A local coffee shop donated a basket of goodies to be raffled and overall the group raised another £500 for the school! Through the great relationship built with the school, the homegroup leader, Lynda, is now volunteering there one afternoon a week and, as she said, *'Sometimes it just takes a little nudge to get something going. We all have it in us to do something, however small. Great oak trees from little acorns grow!'*

Graffiti Grant

A youth house-group from Oadby Baptist Church successfully applied for a £2,400 grant from their local authority to set up a graffiti art project. The church then got graffiti artists to run eight sessions over three months, firstly creating graffiti boards and then using a wall that the council had agreed was suitable inside the local park. Other members of the church went along each week bringing donuts and chatting to the young people involved. Over the eight weeks, 14 people took part, 13 of whom had no previous connection with the church!

'We're there to let the light of Jesus shine through us, in love and not judgement.'

HOPE in the massage parlours of South Manchester

A small group from St James' and Emmanuel in Didsbury, Manchester, felt challenged to find the massage parlours in their area and take a Valentine's card to each of the women working there. Firstly they did a prayer walk around the area and then, as advised by the police, the female members of the group went to the massage parlours during daylight hours, in pairs, whilst the rest of the group stayed outside and continued to pray. They decided to take simple gifts of flowers and cards for each woman with a scripture and a warm invitation to come to church. They found that, on the whole, their visits were treated with smiles and a gracious welcome. Not wanting to leave it there, the group went back at Easter with chocolates, in August with fruit and in December with Christmas treats. By now the women in the parlours remembered the visitors and warm conversations were had. As one of the small group members said, *'We're there to let the light of Jesus shine through us, in love and not judgement . . .'* and the whole group said they felt blessed beyond their expectations

Sowing, reaping, keeping

A Harpenden-based church used *Sowing, Reaping, Keeping* as their study book for their small groups. Each week they looked at different chapters of the book with the view that the material would inspire and encourage church members to be missional.

The money secret

A cell/small group within the Network church in St Albans were looking for a project they could do to take them beyond their existing relationships. They had within the group a man who was extremely wise when it came to money and a cell leader who was very good with people. They got hold of *The Money Secret* book and resources written by Rob Parsons and advertised in the local newspapers for people who might be having money difficulties, told their friends and hired a hall so they could run a course. Eleven visitors came, many of whom were helped considerably by the material which included 'How to look after your money' and 'How to get out of debt'. At the end of the five weeks the eleven guests were keen to learn more as many of them had realised during the course that one of the reasons their money was out of control was due to the fact that they spent to gain identity. This prompted a further three weeks covering subjects such as 'Who are we?' The outcome of this was that this cell group had impacted eleven people who had lived outside the normal sphere of church.

> *'The harvest is plentiful, but the workers are few. Ask the Lord of the harvest, therefore, to send out workers.'*

Prayer Point

One small group decided to choose a person each week who they would pray for. In Luke 10:2 (NIV) it says: 'The harvest is plentiful, but the workers are few. Ask the Lord of the harvest, therefore, to send out workers.' So they decided to pray for the workers, i.e. the small group members, one each week in two ways. Firstly, they thought about their salt and light witness in the workplace and asked them what pressures they faced at work and prayed for them that they could live out their faith in the context of how they did their work and treated people. Secondly, they asked what missional activities they were involved in. Were they a secret pastor, a good neighbour or involved in a HOPE project? Then they prayed for them as the worker in that context.

Gifts of HOPE

A Community Bible Study (CBS) group in Letchworth hit upon the idea of giving gifts to their local shopkeepers so they went around their town centre distributing flowers for free to encourage, comfort or inspire those they met. People were very surprised to get something for nothing and one group member, Karen, said, *'Some people told us that we'd turned up just when they were struggling and really needed some*

kindness.' A few months later the group decided to take flowers to local businesses – including a care home where the manager enthusiastically invited them to come back regularly. Many of the residents at this care home suffer from Alzheimer's, so instead of a standard Bible study they sing Christian songs to the residents, as well as reciting prayers that would be remembered from childhood.

The CBS group also got involved in donating hours of kindness to their local hospice, helping to shift 40 tonnes of manure! They're planning to give flowers out again each Easter as *'most shops in our area are independent so have been hit hard this year,'* says Karen. She will be taking prayer requests and inviting shopkeepers to an informal prayer meeting. She said, *'This idea is great because it doesn't take much organisation or any special skills – we're just Christians who believe that God can make a difference.'*

Small groups across the country contributed to the 'hours of kindness' in amazing ways. Take a look at these for inspiration of how your small group could get stuck into the community:

- Southampton – 2 hours donated by a group cleaning graffiti off a local wall.
- Peterborough – another small group spent 5 hours baking cakes to raise money for refugees in the area, 8 hours decorating the hall of a refugee's home and one of the small group members hosted a ladies' breakfast at her home.
- Shoreham – 24 hours were donated by a group making drinks for, and sitting with, a chair-bound lady in their community.
- North Walsham – 340 hours of schools work. Projects undertaken include listening to children read, helping with an art open day, and volunteering as exam invigilators. This group also washed toys for the local mother and toddler group, as well as making cakes for people and visiting retirement homes.

• Various locations – 560 hours of chatting to people at GT3 championships, and offering support to the Christians in Motorsport groups at the events.

• Halkyn, North Wales – 77 hours of doing odd jobs for pensioners in the village.

• Peterborough – one small group donated 103 hours by creating a 'HOPE garden' for a pre-school nursery.

• Worthing – a group from across a few different churches formed to donate 40 hours of kindness by entertaining elderly people at residential homes.

• Peterborough – 15 hours making afternoon tea for people in sheltered accommodation and another 20 hours making dinner for those attending a local art class.

• Durham – 30 hours given in gardening for an elderly couple.

• Crewe – 32 hours given in painting local cemetery gates.

More great ideas for your small groups

• Wash the cars in the neighbourhood where you meet.

• Go on a prayer walk of your local neighbourhood together.

• Put on a meal for your neighbours or hold a street party.

• Encourage each other to get involved in AOK days to commit random Acts of Kindness. See www.soulaction.org/aokday for more details.

• Offer practical help to the friends of your cell group, e.g. if they are moving house or decorating.

• Join together to sponsor a child through a charity like Compassion who give hope to children around the world by giving them the skills, resources and support they need to break free from poverty. See www.compassionuk.org.

• Have a barbecue and watch a big sporting event in the summer, try pizza and a film in the winter or take over a local curry house for the night and invite your friends to join you.

> Offer practical help to the friends of your cell group, e.g. if they are moving house or decorating.

RESOURCES

Breaking News by J.John. A practical book that a group can go through together, designed to help you get switched on to sharing your faith. Authentic, £4.99.

CELL UK produce a magazine three times a year with inspiring articles and practical ideas for cell leaders. Available from www.celluk.org.uk, tel: 01583 463232.

Christian Life and Work by Mark Greene, 6-part, 2-hour DVD. Includes a leader's guide keyed to *Thank God it's Monday*. Topics include: theology of work, evangelism, the boss, truthtelling, pressure, and work/life integration. SU, £25.

Evangelism Through Cells, a booklet by Liz West and Laurence Singlehurst, available from CELL UK for £4.00 – www.celluk.org.uk.

Just Walk Across the Room, Bill Hybels. In this four-session small group DVD, Bill Hybels signals the next era in personal evangelism with *Just Walk Across the Room*. Drawing on fresh perspectives from the author's own experiences, as well as time-tested and practical illustrations, this curriculum encourages and equips people to develop friendships, discover stories, and discern next steps with those who don't know Christ. Zondervan, £15.50.

May I Call You Friend? a resource from the Inter Faith Relations and Evangelism Strategy Groups of the Methodist Church. This book addresses the vital questions about how we, as Christians, can share our faith with those of other religions. What is the relationship between dialogue and evangelism? How can people of different faiths work together to serve their communities? It contains guidance for discussion about six key subjects: conversion; community action; presence; sharing stories; prayer; worship and listening, and talking about God using case studies to provoke vigorous discussion. Order for £3.50 from Methodist Publishing House at www.mph.org.uk.

Sowing, Reaping, Keeping by Laurence Singlehurst. This book helps the reader explore what it means to love people, to sow seeds of faith, to reap the harvest at the right time and to nurture faith. IVP, £6.99. There is also a workbook available for small groups. £3 from www.celluk.org.uk.

Square Mile – Building 4D Churches: Square Mile is a means for the church to take up the challenge of integral mission and this fantastic resource helps equip small group members in the areas of mercy, influence, life discipleship and evangelism. Each session of the DVD-based course features a look at scriptures with the likes of Bishop Tom Wright and Tim Keller, inspiring footage of projects around the UK, and discussion from well-known practitioners such as Shane Claibourne, Jim Wallis, Mark Greene and J.John to motivate the individuals and group to action. The DVDs are accompanied by a journal that small group members can complete in-between meeting together. See www.eauk.org/squaremile for more details. DVD and guide RRP £15, journals £3.99.

CHAPTER 24

ACKNOWLEDGEMENTS

Board of Reference

Matt Baggott QPM, CBE
Chief Constable Leicestershire & Association of Chief Police Officers

Fran Beckett OBE

Revd David Coffey OBE
President of the Baptist World Alliance

Revd Joel Edwards
Micah Challenge

Revd Nicky Gumbel
HTB & Alpha

Commissioner Elizabeth Matear
Moderator of Free Church Council

His Eminence Cardinal Cormac Murphy O'Connor
Archbishop of Westminster

Caroline Spelman MP
Shadow Communities and Local Government

Lord John Stevens
Former Commissioner of Metropolitan Police Service

Rt Hon Stephen Timms MP
Financial Secretary to HM Treasury

Steve Webb MP
Health Spokesman

Advocacy & Advisory Board

Revd Dr Martyn Atkins
Methodist Church

Mr Don Axcell
CPA

Mgr Keith Barltrop
Catholic Agency to Support Evangelisation

Mr Stuart Bell
Ground Level

Mr Jonathan Bellamy
Cross Rhythms

Mrs Mary Bishop
Livability

Revd Lyndon Bowring
CARE

Mr James Catford
Bible Society

Revd Steve Chalke MBE
Oasis Trust

Mr Keith Civval
Scripture Union

Mr Gerald Coates
Pioneer Trust

Revd Dr David Cornick
Churches Together in England

Revd John Dunnett
CPAS

Revd Jonathan Edwards
Baptist Union

Mr Roger Ellis
Revelation

Mr Matthew Frost
Tearfund

Mr Andy Frost
Share Jesus International

Revd John Glass
Elim

Mr & Mrs Ray & Nancy Goudie
NGM

Mrs Debra Green
Redeeming Our Communities

Mr Ian Hamilton
Compassion UK

Mr David Heron
Premier Media Group

Mr Paul Hopkins
Youth With A Mission

Miss Katei Kirby
Afro-Caribbean Evangelical Alliance

Commissioner John Matear
Salvation Army

Mr Simon Matthews
Plumbline International

Mr Tim Morfin
The Lighthouse Group

Revd Nims Obunge
The Peace Alliance

Mr John Paculabo
Kingsway Communications

Mr Rob Parsons
Care for the Family

Mr Patrick Regan
XLP

Revd Bill Slack
BU of Scotland

Mr Matt Summerfield
Urban Saints

Mr Steve Thomas
Salt & Light

Revd Paul Weaver
AOG

Associate Groups

13th Floor
24-7 Prayer
73rd Trust
ACEA (African and Caribbean Evangelical Alliance)
ALOVE UK
Alpha
Arise Ministries
Assemblies of God
Associated Bus Ministries
Audacious
Authentic Media
Awesome Praise
Back to Church Sunday
Baptist Union
Barnabas in Churches
Bible Society
Big Blue Box
BIG Ministries
Blowing Your Cover
Book of Hope
Boys' Brigade
BRF (Bible Reading Fellowship)
Business Mens Fellowship (UK)
Care
Care for the Family
Case
CELL UK
Christian Enquiry Agency
Christian Life Resources
Christian Music Ministries
Christian Solidarity Worldwide
Christian Vision for Men
Christian Workplace Forum
Christians Against Poverty
Christians in Entertainment
Church Action on Poverty
Church Army
Church of England
Church of Scotland
Churches Criminal Justice Forum
City Links
Compassion UK
Congregational Federation
CORD
Coventry Cathedral

Crime to Christ
Cross Rhythms
CrossTeach Trust
CWR
Cytun
DNA
ECG
Elim Church
Evangelical Alliance
Evangelical Alliance – Northern Ireland
Evangelical Alliance – Scotland
Evangelical Alliance – Wales
Every Home for Christ UK
Extreme Hope
Faithworks
Farm Crisis Network
Find a Church
Fresh Expressions
Fusion
GEAR (Grp for Evangelism And Renewal in URC)
Girls' Brigade, England and Wales
Gobaith i Cymru
God TV
Gospel Ministries Trust
Ground Level
Gweini
Hope UK
Hope37 Youth Trust
Ichthus
Ignite
Innervation
Jubilee Trust
Kingdom Coffee
Kingdom Faith
Kingsway Communications
Lambeth Palace
Livability
Love Cardiff
Luis Palau Association
Mainstream
Makeway Music
MEMO
Message Trust
Methodist Church
Micah Challenge
Miracle Street

N:VISION
Nationwide Christian Trust
NE1
New Generation Ministries
New Life Publishing
New Wine
NXT Ministries
Oasis
On The Move
Open Doors
Operation Mobilisation (UK)
Outlook-Trust (Reaching Seniors for Christ)
Pais Project
Parish Pump
Philo Trust
Pilgrim Hearts Trust
Pioneer
Premier Radio
Proclaim Trust
Psalm Ministries
Purpose Driven UK Ltd
Raw Theatre Company
Reachout Trust
Reality Leicester
Redeeming Our Communities
ReSource
Rhema Theatre Company
Riding Lights Theatre Company
RUN
Salt & Light
Saltmine
Salvation Army (Scotland)
Salvation Army (UK & Ireland)
Samaritans Purse
Schools Prayer Network
Scripture Union
Selah
Send The Light – Wesley Owen
Serious 4 God
Share Jesus
Soul In The City (London)
Soul Survivor
South West Youth Ministries
Speaking Volumes
Spring Harvest
Springs Dance Company

Stewardship
Student Christian Movement
Tearfund
The Fellowship of Churches of Christ in GB & Ireland
The Net
Through Faith Missions
Through the roof
Together for the Harvest
Together in Mission
Torch Trust for the Blind
Transfusion
UCCF
UK Gospel Music
United Christian Broadcasters
United Reformed Church
Urban Saints
Vineyard
Vision 2025
Viz-A-Viz Ministries
World Prayer Centre
Worth Unlimited
YES
Youth For Christ
Youth With A Mission

Board/Leadership Team

Paul Bayes
Church of England

Matt Bird
Make It Happen

Ian Chisnall
HOPE

Steve Clifford
Evangelical Alliance

Eustace Constance
Street Pastors

Rob Cotton
Bible Society

Roy Crowne
YFC

Sarah Davis
YFC

Clive Dudbridge
Oasis Global

Andy Hawthorne
Message Trust

Jane Holloway
World Prayer Centre

Richard Jago
HOPE

Martin Kavanagh
The Grand

Ali Martin
Soul Survivor

Mike Pilavachi
Soul Survivor

Laurence Singlehurst
CELL UK

Fritha Washington
HOPE

Contributors

Many thanks to

All the writers in this publication:
Paul Bayes, Sarah Bingham, Matt Bird, Pod Bhogal, Mark Blythe, Gavin Calver, Ian Chisnall, Steve Clifford, Rob Cotton, Roy Crowne, Sarah Davis, Dan Etheridge, Pete Gilbert, Mark Greene, Andy Hawthorne, Jane Holloway, Liza Hoeksma, Barry Mason, Dave Newton, Rob Parsons, Mike Pilavachi, Laurence Singlehurst, Ro Willoughby, Rich Wilson, Jill Worth.

A special thanks to Fritha Washington for collecting stories and untold amounts of behind the scenes work.

To the photographers who provided us with images:
Howard Barlow, Jon Bullock, Martin Butcher, Ann Clifford, Cornerstone, Andy Espin, Becks Heyhoe, HTB/Alpha, Andrew Philip, Mike Thorpe.

The Board and Leadership team of HOPE wish to express their gratitude to the Management Team at Authentic Media and Wesley Owen. It has been thanks to their sacrificial support that this publication has been possible. Particular thanks to Keith Danby, Malcolm Down and Liz Williams.

A huge thanks to everyone who is on board with HOPE, including every one of you who has bought this publication. This initiative belongs to all the churches, organisations and individuals across the UK who are making HOPE happen.

Design
Many thanks to ABA design for the HOPE logo and to Mike Thorpe at The Design Chapel for designing this publication.

Contact us
You can contact HOPE through the YFC offices:
Business Park East, Unit D2, Coombswood Way, Halesowen, West Midlands, B62 8BH
Tel: 0121 502 9620,
Fax: 0121 561 4035
Email: yfc@yfc.co.uk